*Praise for*

## The **Politically Incorrect Guide** to

# AMERICAN HISTORY

"Knowing our past is essential if we are to preserve our freedoms. Professor Woods's work heroically rescues real history from the politically correct memory hole. Every American should read this book."

> —**The Honorable Ron Paul, M.D.**, U.S. House of Representatives

"An important work that refutes the misinterpretations of American history that have misinformed generations about their country, its origins, purposes, successes and failures. Riveting, highly readable."

> —**Paul Craig Roberts**, former assistant secretary of the U.S. Treasury

"Solidly based in the best and most recent scholarship and written in an agreeable, flowing style, *The Politically Incorrect Guide to American History* is a gem. It will be treasured by history buffs and by anyone who suspects that high school and college textbooks might not have told the whole story."

> —**Ralph Raico**, professor of history, Buffalo State College

"The history of America as taught in high school and college textbooks is often as distorted as the histories imposed on the hapless people of the former Soviet Union. Professor Woods's book should be required reading for college students. If it were, we might hope to recover something of the decentralized polity of the Founders."

> —**Donald W. Livingston**, professor of philosophy, Emory University

"Not long ago American historians considered it their pleasure and duty to engage in lively and stimulating debate about the big issues of our history—the meaning of the Constitution, the causes of the Civil War, the good and bad of capitalism, the responsibility for World War I and the Cold War, and so on. But since the descent of the Iron Curtain of political correctness, what has come from the pens of our historians has frequently had more to do with theory than with evidence, with enforcing predetermined orthodoxy rather than with debate. In this book, Thomas Woods has taken on some of the big historical issues with a fresh and definitely non-PC approach. His take on American history is bold, brilliant, thought-provoking, and what is even better, entertaining. Woods has almost restored my hope for the future of historical discourse."

> —**Clyde N. Wilson**, professor of history, University of South Carolina

★ ★ ★ ★ ★ ★ ★ ★ ★ ★ ★ ★ ★ ★

# The Politically Incorrect Guide to
# American History

Thomas E. Woods Jr., Ph.D.

*Since 1947*
**REGNERY**
**PUBLISHING, INC.**
*An Eagle Publishing Company • Washington, DC*

Library of Congress Cataloging-in-Publication Data

Woods, Thomas E.

The politically incorrect guide to American history / Thomas E. Woods. p. cm.

Includes bibliographical references and index.

ISBN 0-89526-047-6 (alk. paper)

1. United States--History--Miscellanea.
2. Political correctness--United States. I. Title.

E179.W83 2004
973--dc22

2004023736

Published in the United States by
Regnery Publishing, Inc.
An Eagle Publishing Company
One Massachusetts Avenue, NW
Washington, DC 20001

Visit us at www.regnery.com

Distributed to the trade by
National Book Network
4720-A Boston Way
Lanham, MD 20706

Printed on acid-free paper

Manufactured in the United States of America

10 9 8 7 6 5 4 3 2 1

Books are available in quantity for promotional or premium use. Write to Director of Special Sales, Regnery Publishing, Inc., One Massachusetts Avenue, NW, Washington, DC 20001, for information on discounts and terms or call (202) 216-0600.

★ ★ ★ ★

To my mother

# CONTENTS

Contents

Contents

★★★★★★★★★

# PREFACE

**W**ill Rogers once said that the problem in America isn't so much what people don't know; the problem is what people think they know that just ain't so.

Nowhere is the great humorist's observation more apt than in the field of American history. The story of American history that most students have encountered for at least the past several decades amounts to a series of drearily predictable clichés: the Civil War was all about slavery, antitrust law saved us from wicked big business, Franklin Roosevelt got us out of the New Deal, and so on. From the colonial settlements through the presidency of Bill Clinton, this book, in its brief compass, aims to set the record straight.

A word on what this book is not. It is not, and is not intended to be, a complete overview of American history. Readers interested in studying a given issue in greater detail may wish to consult the selected bibliography, which I have included both in order to acknowledge my intellectual debts as well as to provide a list of sources on which the reader looking for the truth about American history can safely rely. (Needless to say, I do not necessarily endorse every contention made in all the books listed there; if a book appears in the bibliography I simply mean to acknowledge that I benefited from it in some way and that I believe others will, too.) Some of the books listed are unfortunately out of print, virtually all of them are potentially available to the interested reader, thanks to electronic clearinghouses of used books like bookfinder.com.

Instead of a systematic narrative, therefore, this book is intended to be an introduction to some of the more controversial aspects of American history, and is aimed in particular at those who find the standard narrative or the typical textbook unpersuasive or ideologically biased. Some readers may find that an issue in which they have a particular interest is treated only in brief or perhaps not at all, but some kind of discrimination has been necessary for a project of this length. I am hopeful that readers will find what I *have* written here to be interesting, challenging, and a refreshing alternative to the stale and predictable platitudes of mainstream texts.

I wish to thank the Foundation for Economic Education in Irvington-on-Hudson, New York, for granting permission to use portions of articles I wrote for *Ideas on Liberty* (recently renamed *The Freeman* once again); they include "Why Wages Used to Be So Low," "The Colonial Origins of American Liberty," "The Economics of Infantilism," "Race, Inequality and the Market," and "Nullification: The Jeffersonian Brake on Government."

Over the course of writing the book I received useful suggestions from Thomas DiLorenzo, Ralph Raico, and Marcus Epstein, and I am especially indebted to Professor Clyde Wilson, editor of the *Papers of John C. Calhoun* and professor of history at the University of South Carolina, for vetting chapter five of the manuscript. Thanks are due also to the always helpful (and never complaining) Doreen Munna, Marilyn Ventiere, and Dolores Perillo of my college's interlibrary loan department. I also wish to thank my fine editors at Regnery—Rowena Itchon, with whom I worked most closely, and Paula Decker—for their hard work and helpful suggestions.

Other debts are more personal. I am particularly grateful to Regnery's executive editor, Harry Crocker III, for approaching me with the idea for the project. Finally, I wish as always to thank Heather, my wife, to whom I am indebted more than words can express.

**Thomas E. Woods, Jr.**
Coram, New York
October 2004

## Chapter 1

# THE COLONIAL ORIGINS
# OF AMERICAN LIBERTY

irst basic fact: the colonists were *not* paragons of "diversity." They came from one part of Europe. They spoke a common language. They worshiped the same God.

From 1629 to 1775 there were four waves of migration from four geographical regions of England. Here's the timeline:

**c. 1629 to 1640**   The Puritans settled in Massachusetts Bay

**c. 1642 to 1675**   A few aristocrats and a large number of indentured servants from the south of England settled in Virginia

**c. 1675 to 1725**   English from the North Midlands and Wales settled in the Delaware Valley

**c. 1718 to 1775**   Immigrants from the borders of Yorkshire, Scotland, and Northern Ireland moved inland to the Appalachian backcountry

## Suspicion + Dislike = Liberty
## A formula for freedom

Nevertheless, the cultural differences among the peoples who comprised the United States were real, significant, and enduring. Here's a sample of what the early colonists thought of one another:

### Guess what?

★ The thirteen colonies were anything but a Perfect Union.

★ The Puritans didn't steal their lands from the Indians.

★ Christianity was the most important factor shaping the colonists.

A Puritan on Virginians:

"The farthest from conscience and moral honesty of any such number together in the world."

Virginian William Byrd II on the Puritans:

"A watchful eye must be kept on these foul traders."

Puritans and Virginians on Quakers:

"[They] pray *for* their fellow men one day a week, and *on* them the other six."

Quakers on New Englanders:

"The flock of Cain."

Religion was fundamental to the colonists; and though they worshipped the same God, there was plenty of bickering. Indeed, the Religious Society of Friends, or Quakers, raised the ire of many colonists. The Puritans, who thought they had purged their worship of the Church of England's ritual and "superstition," were still too formalistic for the Quakers. Decades before William Penn settled Pennsylvania in the 1680s, Quakers living in Rhode Island traveled to Massachusetts to rouse its benighted inhabitants from their dogmatic slumber and awaken them to the aridity of their faith. Quakers disrupted Puritan church services, heckled ministers, and even walked naked up and down the church aisles. The Friends were banned repeatedly from Massachusetts.

This mutual antagonism contributed in a peculiar way to the development of American liberty: *Each denomination and colony was vigilant against interference in its internal affairs by others.* The differences among the colonies created the presumption that each should mind its own business, and so should any potential central government.

## Love thy neighbor?
## Colonial quarrels give birth to religious freedom

The First Amendment to the Constitution reflected this attitude: The federal government was prohibited from meddling in the religious affairs of the states. The First Amendment's declaration that "Congress shall make no law respecting an establishment of religion, or prohibiting the free exercise thereof," was intended, according to historian David Hackett Fischer, to preserve religious freedom in Virginia and Pennsylvania *and* to guarantee that the religious establishments that existed in Massachusetts and elsewhere would be safe from outside interference.

### *The godly community of Massachusetts Bay*

It's technically incorrect to describe the original Massachusetts settlements as theocracies because ministers themselves did not hold political power, but these settlements certainly did have a theocratic aspect. In Massachusetts Bay, for example, which was founded in 1629, the law was expected to reflect biblical precept as precisely as possible. The franchise was restricted to church members who, before becoming members, had to undergo a process not unlike interrogation. The "pillars of the church" would determine whether a prospective member belonged to the elect (had been eternally predestined to heaven)—or to the damned.

The latter group, although excluded from the franchise and from reception of the Lord's Supper, were nevertheless required to go to church. Steeped as they were in covenant theology, the Puritans believed that if they succeeded in establishing a truly godly community, God would look upon them with favor; if they failed, they would be subject to His wrath.

They wished to live among like-minded folk in order to better live a shared ideal. In the Dedham Covenant drawn up in Massachusetts during the 1630s, it was resolved "that we shall by all means labor to keep off from us all such as are contrary minded, and receive only such unto us as may probably be of one heart with us."

The community aspect of early New England has been so often emphasized that the Puritans' commitment to traditional English liberties has often been overlooked. John Winthrop, a key figure in the Puritan migration and a longtime governor of Massachusetts Bay, favored as little written law as possible so that he and his judges would have the discretionary authority to rule in accordance with the Bible. His fellow colonists, however, wanted less discretion and an explicit guarantee of individual rights.

In 1641, with Winthrop temporarily voted out of office on these very grounds, the colonists established the Massachusetts Body of Liberties. The document contained more than one hundred provisions, including items familiar to Americans: the principle of no taxation without representation, the right to a jury trial, and the guarantee that no person would be deprived of life, liberty, or property without due process of law. (It also contains a provision that prohibited wife beating, excepting when the husband was acting in self-defense.) Nearly a century and a half before the drafting of the U.S. Constitution, we already find a document whose purpose is to limit and define the powers of government. It was one of many drafted by the American colonists.

Over time some of the restrictions of Puritan life gradually dissolved. For example, a growing population forced people to settle farther from the town center, making

## PC Today

**When federal courts** strike down religious expression in the states, they are willfully perverting the policy of what the Framers of the First Amendment intended: *complete federal nonintervention in religious issues.*

them less easily observed and controlled by government and religious authority. In addition, theological liberalism proved increasingly attractive to many colonists. What originated as a group enterprise placed increasing emphasis on individual liberty.

### Meanwhile, in wild and woolly Jamestown...

The development of Jamestown, Virginia, took the opposite path. It *began* as a distinctly individualistic colony, and only later acquired group cohesion. The early settlement of Virginia was dominated by young, single men. A host of factors, prominent among them Virginia's (not entirely undeserved) reputation as a disease-ridden deathtrap, served to discourage the kind of family migration that had characterized the Puritan experience. But as the mortality rate declined and the colony's prosperity became widely known, it became more sensible for entire families to make their homes in the Chesapeake.

As Virginia became more established, it also became more aristocratic. The aristocracy was attached to the principle of self-government, and these men took their responsibilities seriously. It was a strict requirement that every member be present for the opening session of the House of Burgesses, and that any absence had to be excused. (Poor James Bray: In 1691, the House of Burgesses was so offended by his explanation for his absence that the Speaker actually issued a warrant for his arrest, and held him in custody until he made an apology.) This elite was composed of an extraordinarily talented group of men who, when the crisis with the British came, were able to articulate precisely where and how American rights and liberties were being threatened.

Ultimately, the colonies succeeded in providing the individual liberty that makes civilized life possible while cultivating a community sentiment that led them to resist centralization. That community sentiment translated into an attachment to one's own colony, a kind of local patriotism.

Historians have noted the extent to which the Virginians were devoted to their plot of earth. This was true of all the colonies; as late as 1787, Marylanders still referred to their state as "the nation."

## PC Myth: The Puritans were racists

The colonists also had to devise some kind of policy toward the American Indians they encountered, and some were more successful, and more just, than others. Few would deny that the American Indians have been the victims of injustice and maltreatment over the course of American history. But those injustices have led many Americans to believe that the colonists had nothing but contempt for the American Indian, and sought merely to expel him or "steal" his land. But by its second decade Harvard College welcomed Indian students. Colonists could and did receive the death penalty for murdering Indians. Indian converts to Christianity living in the "praying towns" of New England enjoyed considerable autonomy.

Today the Puritans' desire to win the natives to Christianity is often met with impatience and smirks. But consider the greatest of the Puritan missionaries, John Eliot, who lived from 1604 to 1690. What Eliot did in order to spread the Christian faith among the Indians almost defies belief. The Algonquins had no written language. So Eliot learned the spoken language of the Massachusetts Algonquins, developed a written version of their language for them, and then translated the Bible into that language. If Eliot and the Puritans had simply wanted to oppress the natives, they could have come up with an easier way.

It is *not* true that the Puritans possessed a sense of racial superiority over the Indians. They certainly did consider themselves *culturally* superior, though it is not clear what else they were supposed to think when they met peoples who did not use the wheel, possessed no written language, and were, in effect, living in the Stone Age. But *race* did not enter into the question. Roger Williams, who founded Providence, Rhode Island, believed that the Indians were born white, a view that was generally shared by the Puritans; the effects of stains and the sun were said to have darkened their skins.

Scholars in recent decades have softened their earlier judgments about the harshness of Puritan treatment of the natives. But the research of specialists typically takes a long time to make it to the texts written by generalists. For instance, some overviews of European history still portray the Middle Ages as backward and barbaric, when medieval scholars know full well the contributions of the Middle Ages to European civilization, particularly in the origins of modern science, the development of the university system, and the fruitfulness of medieval intellectual life. The same is true of scholarship on the Puritans and the Indians: the generalists continue to speak badly of the Puritans, while specialists often conclude that the Puritans' record is considerably better than people have been led to believe. This is true also in studies of the Puritan-Indian wars. "In generalists' eyes," explains historian Alden Vaughan, "the Puritans provoked every clash and intended—indeed sometimes accomplished—genocide. Specialists, whether of military history or of related topics, viewed the causes of the English-Indian wars as less simple, less unilateral, and the outcomes, though appallingly lethal, never genocidal."

★ ★ ★ ★ ★ ★ ★ ★ ★ ★

## PC Today

**It is not true,** as most people believe, that the Indians had no conception of land ownership and did not understand what they were doing when they sold their land to the Puritans. No evidence has ever been found of any New England tribe that thought of all land as common property.

## No, the Puritans didn't steal Indian lands

The Puritans are widely reputed to have stolen Indian land, defrauded the Indians, or committed genocide against them in the Pequot Wars.

This myth, believed to this day by the vast majority of Americans, is evidently impossible to overturn despite all the scholarship that refutes it. The Pequots, who were never a large tribe to begin with, continued to be listed as a distinct group living in Connecticut through the 1960s. Moreover, while the king had issued colonial land grants, the Puritan consensus, evident in their words and their actions, was that the king's charter conferred *political* and not *property rights* to the land, which Puritan settlers sought by means of voluntary cession from the Indians.

The colonial governments actually punished individuals who made unauthorized acquisitions of Indian lands. As for initial settlement, Roger Williams obtained title from the Indians before settling in Providence; Plymouth obtained title after settlement. Even this distinction is minor enough, since Indian consent to the Plymouth settlement was immediate. Connecticut and New Haven followed the pattern established by Williams in Providence. English settlement in the Connecticut Valley was positively *encouraged* by some tribes in the 1630s, who hoped the English might prove a useful obstacle to the ambitions of the Pequots, a hated tribe that had begun to force its way into the area. Once settled, these New England colonies went on to purchase whatever additional land they desired.

Each colony negotiated with the Indians, who were all too happy to sell land—a commodity that they enjoyed in great abundance, particularly considering the sparseness of the North American population at the time. "In return," writes legal scholar James Warren Springer, "the white man offered metal knives, hoes, and other implements of rare value to a neolithic society; in lieu of these the Indian might ask for cloth, clothing, jewelry, and other luxuries to brighten his life. The native often took the initiative in such transactions, for he coveted the white man's goods as keenly as the settler yearned for more land."

The Puritans recognized Indian hunting and fishing rights *on lands that the Indians had sold to them.* In fact it would have been foolish for the Puritans *not* to allow hunting rights to the Indians, since they themselves were not hunters, and recognition of Indian hunting rights on Puritan lands meant that the Indians could acquire the beaver skins that the Puritans were so anxious to have. And although disputes occasionally arose, New England courts frequently ruled in favor of

> ## A Book You're Not Supposed to Read
>
> *New England Frontier: Puritans and Indians, 1620—1675* by Alden Vaughan; Norman, Oklahoma: University of Oklahoma Press, 1995.

Indian litigants who alleged that agreed-upon boundaries were not being observed. The colonists did believe that deserted or desolate land could be occupied by whoever discovered it, but this idea was never used to dispossess Indians of their lands; such land was even returned to Indian owners who later presented themselves.

## Self-government is non-negotiable

The colonists were wary of joining intercolonial confederations, unless for practical purposes, and if the unions were limited and did not infringe on each colony's self-government. In 1643, the Confederation of New England was formed in case of conflict with the Indians. Even so, Massachusetts established the principle that each colony held a veto over the actions of the Confederation.

The robust and zealous nature of community life in Puritan New England and its habit of self-rule were dramatically apparent toward the end of the seventeenth century, when the Crown attempted to establish its authority more firmly throughout the northeast. King James II established the Dominion of New England, which combined Massachusetts, Maine, and New Hampshire into a single government under a royal governor. James II annexed Rhode Island, Connecticut, New York, and the Jerseys to the Dominion, and had his sights on Pennsylvania at the time he was ousted. The most memorable figure associated with the Dominion was *the hated Sir Edmund Andros, who took power in late 1686. Andros enraged the colonists by imposing taxes and jailing those who protested.*

### Ousting a tyrant

On April 4, 1689, word reached Boston that William and Mary had deposed King James and "all magistrates who have been unjustly turned out" should resume "their former employment." Colonists threw Andros and his councillors into jail, the eminent Puritan divine Cotton Mather drew up the "Declaration of the Gentlemen, Merchants, and Inhabitants"; the confederate "Dominion" was abolished; and self-rule was restored.

The same spirit led the colonists to reject Benjamin Franklin's proposed Albany Plan of Union in 1754, which called on the colonies to yield authority to a new intercolonial government to help coordinate defense against the Indians. Not a single colonial assembly ratified the plan.

### The legacy of colonial America

The colonists loved liberty and were wary of confederations, which is why three states—Virginia, New York, and Rhode Island—explicitly reserved during the ratification of the Constitution the right to withdraw from the Union should it become oppressive. They were exercising the libertarian principles that were America's first principles.

★★★★★★★★★★

# AMERICA'S CONSERVATIVE REVOLUTION

When most people think of the causes that led to the American War for Independence, they think of the phrase "no taxation without representation." This principle played a role, but it was only part of a much larger constitutional struggle in favor of limited government. The Americans who protested against British encroachments on colonial liberties wanted to preserve their traditional rights. They were not revolutionaries seeking the radical restructuring of society.

## Colonial tradition or British innovation?

Colonial spokesmen possessed a breathtaking command of British history and law. They used the word "innovation" pejoratively, as in John Adams's Braintree Instructions of 1765 that held that Parliament's new taxes were an unconstitutional innovation. They were well aware of the celebrated British documents to which they could appeal in their defense, particularly the Magna Carta (1215), the Petition of Right (1628), and the Bill of Rights (1689).

The controversy surrounding the Stamp Act of 1765 is instructive. Designed as a revenue measure for the British government, the Act required that a wide variety of paper products in the colonies—from

### Guess what?

★ The American Revolution was not a "revolution" at all.

★ The colonists were conservatives—they wanted to maintain the rights they enjoyed from tradition and custom.

★ The American Revolution was *not* like the French Revolution.

## What the Founders Said

**John Adams,** among others, condemned the Stamp Act as unconstitutional. In support of his position he referred to the "grand and fundamental principle of the constitution, that no freeman should be subject to any tax to which he has not given his own consent, in person or by proxy."

legal deeds to newspapers, from tavern licenses to wills—bear revenue stamps, indicating in each case that this new tax had been paid. From the American point of view, such taxation without consent was an intolerable novelty.

Among the great heroes of the Stamp Act crisis was Virginia's Patrick Henry. Henry proposed to the colony's legislature the Virginia Resolves, a list of seven resolutions outlining the colonial position on the Stamp Act.

The first two were tame enough, insisting that the colonists possessed all the rights of Englishmen. The third proclaimed the principle of colonial self-taxation as essential to the British constitution. The fourth contended that the colony had the right, in its internal matters, to be governed solely by laws passed by its own legislature and approved by the royal governor. The fifth was a more confrontational way of wording the third, stating that the "General Assembly of this colony have the only and sole exclusive right and power to lay taxes and impositions upon the inhabitants of this colony," and that any attempt to repose such power elsewhere must undermine both colonial and British freedom. The sixth simply drew the logical conclusion of the fourth, arguing that the colonies were not required to obey laws that had not been approved by their own legislature; the Stamp Act was one such law. The seventh ended the resolves on a dramatic note: anyone who denied the principle that the colonies were subject only to legislation passed by their own legislatures was a traitor to Virginia.

Cautious legislators decided to approve only the first five of Henry's Resolves and eventually rescinded their approval of the fifth. But given the primitive communications of the eighteenth century, the northern colonies got the story wrong. In Rhode Island, for example, it was reported that the Virginia legislature had approved all seven resolves. Not wanting to be outdone, the legislature of Rhode Island promptly approved all seven Virginia Resolves.

A Stamp Act Congress, held in New York in late 1765, summoned representatives from the various colonies to approve a joint statement of grievances to be issued to the British government. They protested that their *ancient chartered rights* were being violated. The only ones who could legitimately tax them, they contended, were their own colonial legislatures.

## Fact: The American Revolution was not like the French Revolution

The Americans defended their traditional rights. The French revolutionaries despised French traditions and sought to make everything anew: new governing structures, new provincial boundaries, a new "religion," a new calendar—and the guillotine awaited those who objected. The British statesman Edmund Burke, the father of modern conservatism and a man who *did* understand the

### A Book You're Not Supposed to Read

*The Best of Burke: Selected Writings and Speeches of Edmund Burke* edited by Peter J. Stanlis; Washington, D.C.: Regnery Publishing, 1999.

★★★★★★★★★★★

### PC Today

When modern-day liberals justify extremely broad readings of the Constitution on the grounds that we need a "living, breathing Constitution" that "changes with the times," they are actually recommending the very system the colonists sought to escape. The British constitution was very flexible indeed—too flexible for the colonists, who were *in*flexibly committed to upholding their traditional rights. The "living, breathing" British constitution was no safeguard of American liberties.

issues at stake in both events, considered himself perfectly consistent in his sympathy for the Americans of the 1770s and his condemnation of

★ ★ ★ ★

Thomas Jefferson advised in the 1790s that "our peculiar security is in possession of a written constitution," and warned Americans not to "make it a blank paper by construction." Today's calls for a "flexible Constitution" betray the principles for which many early Americans gave their lives.

★ ★ ★ ★

## What the Founders Said

"Is life so dear or peace so sweet as to be purchased at the price of chains and slavery? Forbid it, Almighty God. I know not what course others may take, but as for me, give me liberty or give me death!"

**Patrick Henry**

the French revolutionaries of 1789.

In a certain sense, there was no American Revolution at all. There was, instead, an American War for Independence in which Americans threw off British authority in order to retain their liberties and self-government. In the 1760s, the colonies had, for the most part, been left alone in their internal affairs. Because the colonists had enjoyed the practice of self-government for so long, they believed it was their right under the British constitution. The British constitution was "unwritten"—it was a flexible collection of documents and traditions—but by an American conservative's reading, the British government had acted unconstitutionally in its restrictive acts and taxation.

While Americans sought the self-government to which they believed they were constitutionally entitled, the colonists did not seek the total transformation of society that we associate with other revolutions, such as the Industrial Revolution, the French Revolution, or the Russian Revolution. They simply wished to go on enjoying self-rule when it came to their internal matters and living as they always had for so many decades before British encroachments began. The American "revolutionaries" were *conservative*, in the very best sense of that word.

## What the Colonists Said

In 1842, Judge Mellen Chamberlain interviewed ninety-one-year-old **Captain Preston**, a veteran of the Battle of Concord in 1775, to understand why Preston fought against the British.

Judge Chamberlain: Did you take up arms against intolerable oppressions?

Captain Preston replied that he had never felt any oppressions.

Judge Chamberlain: Was it the Stamp Act?

Captain Preston: No, I never saw one of those stamps.

Judge Chamberlain: Was it the tea tax?

Captain Preston said no again.

Judge Chamberlain: Were you reading John Locke and other theorists of liberty?

Captain Preston: Never heard of 'em. We read only the Bible, the Catechism, Watts' Psalms and Hymns, and the Almanac.

Judge Chamberlain: Why, then, did you fight?

Captain Preston: Young man, what we meant in going for those redcoats was this: *We always had governed ourselves, and we always meant to. They didn't mean we should.*

## Chapter 3

★ ★ ★ ★ ★ ★ ★ ★ ★ ★

# THE CONSTITUTION

In the summer of 1787, delegates from every state except Rhode Island gathered in Philadelphia to discuss revisions to the Articles of Confederation, which had been drafted and ratified during the War for Independence. The states believed that the government had become weak and ineffective, and needed an injection of vigor and strength. When the delegates met, they decided instead to create a new document, albeit one that drew from passages of the Articles.

The new Constitution gave the federal government the power to tax, which it lacked under the Articles. It established three distinct branches of government—executive, legislative, and judicial—and provided "checks and balances" by which each branch could resist the encroachments of another. It provided for a two-house legislature, with representation determined on the basis of population in the House of Representatives and on equality among the states in the Senate.

## Constitution is okay, say states, but we get to bolt just in case...

While the convention delegates sought to strengthen the power of the central government, they wanted to prevent the new government from encroaching upon the states' rights of self-government. James Madison

## Guess what?

★ The Framers never said that a black person was just three-fifths of a white person.

★ The First Amendment allowed states to manage religious affairs.

★ In recent decades, Congress has abdicated its authority to declare war.

★★★★★★★★★★

## PC Today

**The typical college** freshman has been told that the "three-fifths clause" of the Constitution meant that the Framers claimed that blacks were just three-fifths of a person. This silly rendition obscures the Framers' true intent. In determining the number of representatives Southern states should have in the House, Southern states argued that slaves should be fully counted. Northerners did not think the slaves should be counted at all. The compromise was that slaves should be *counted* as three-fifths of a free person when determining representation. This compromise on a very contentious issue was not a statement about black people as "three-fifths of a person" in any metaphysical or biological sense. Those who call the Constitution "racist" miss the point. Ironically, if slaves had been counted as five-fifths of a free person, then the slave states would have had *more* power in the federal government.

suggested that the new federal government be given the power to veto state legislation. This proposal was overwhelmingly defeated, and no wonder—it would have repudiated everything the colonists had fought for in their struggle against the British. That the federal judiciary today routinely strikes down state laws is an unfortunate reminder of how far our present system has strayed from the Framers' original intent.

So concerned were Virginians about the possibility that the new Union would infringe upon their rights of self-government that upon ratification of the Constitution, Virginia declared that it reserved the right to secede from the Union. Some scholars have tried to argue that Virginia was simply setting forth the right to start a revolution, which no one disputed, rather than a right to withdraw from the Union. But this interpretation is untenable, since evidence from Virginia's ratifying convention makes clear that the delegates believed they were entering a voluntary compact among states rather than yielding their sovereignty to an all-powerful national government. New York and Rhode Island would include similar clauses in their own acts of ratification.

The new Constitution was set to take effect as soon as nine states ratified it. By 1788, nine states had. But supporters of the

Constitution were concerned that New York, a large and important state, had not. Among those concerned were James Madison, Alexander Hamilton, and John Jay. Under the pseudonym Publius, these men wrote a series of articles known collectively as *The Federalist*, first published one at a time in New York newspapers. (Although perhaps better known as *The Federalist Papers* ever since Clinton Rossiter published an edition of them under that name, they were originally called simply *The Federalist*.)

To persuade opponents of the Constitution—the Antifederalists—to change their minds, the authors of *The Federalist* wanted to reassure them that the proposed federal government would not compromise the states' rights of self-government. In *Federalist* #45, Madison explained that the powers delegated to the federal government under the Constitution were "few and defined," while those remaining with the states were "numerous and indefinite." Federal activity would be confined almost exclusively to foreign affairs. The powers reserved to the states, on the other hand, "will extend to all the objects which in the ordinary course of affairs concern the lives, liberties and properties of the people; and the internal order, improvement, and prosperity of the State."

## Antifederalist objections

As fine a document as the Constitution is, the Antifederalists, who were not frivolous men, raised some prescient criticisms. Patrick Henry was concerned that the "general welfare" clause would someday be interpreted to authorize practically any federal power that might be imagined. Others feared that the taxing power would prove an instrument of tyranny in the hands of the new government. Still others feared the power of the judicial branch, whose pronouncements on the meaning of the Constitution may well run counter to the common understanding of the Framers but against whom the people would have little recourse. That the Antifederalists may have been on to something should be evident from a casual glance at the federal government today, which is not exactly the modest institution scrupulously confining itself to its enumerated powers that the Framers intended.

Some Antifederalists dropped their objections to the Constitution when they were promised that a Bill of Rights would be added. In 1791 that Bill of Rights was ratified, in the form of the first ten amendments to the Constitution. The amendments that have provoked the most controversy in recent history are the First, Second, Ninth, and Tenth.

## Feds must leave states alone

### First Amendment

*Congress shall make no law respecting an establishment of religion, or prohibiting the free exercise thereof; or abridging the freedom of speech, or of the press; or the right of the people peaceably to assemble, and to petition the Government for a redress of grievances.*

The First Amendment was a *restriction* on the power of the federal government, not a *grant* of power. It prevented the federal government from establishing a national religion, but *it did not grant power to that government to interfere in the church-state relations decided upon by the states.* The amendment clearly says that "*Congress* shall make no law" pertaining to religion, not that Massachusetts, Georgia, or Pennsylvania shall make no law. When the states authorized the use of public funds to support various churches, no one in the early republic considered it a violation of the First Amendment, which was universally understood not to apply to the states.

The First Amendment also did not allow federal interference in state questions involving speech and press. The good sense of the people of the states and their right to self-government had to be respected. As Jefferson wrote to Abigail Adams in 1804, "While we deny that Congress has a right to control the freedom of the press, we have ever asserted the right of the States, and their exclusive right to do so."

Even with the added complication of the Fourteenth Amendment in 1868, which gave the federal government more power over the states, the Jeffersonian edifice still stood, if in somewhat attenuated form. In the early twentieth century, issues of church-state relations arose in the supreme courts of Georgia, Illinois, Minnesota, North and South Dakota, and Texas, and in each case, when the court mentioned the federal Constitution at all it was to deny that the federal government had any role to play in church-state issues at the state level.

In the late 1870s, Congressman James G. Blaine introduced what became known as the Blaine Amendment, by which the First Amendment's restrictions on the federal government would be extended to the states. Introduced again and again in subsequent sessions of Congress, it never garnered enough votes. But the very fact that it was introduced tells us something important. If the Fourteenth Amendment had really been intended to apply First Amendment restrictions to the states, why would the Blaine Amendment, which sought to do the very same thing, have been introduced in the first place?

But less than a century later, the Supreme Court would declare in *Engel v. Vitale* (1962) that local school boards were prohibited from approving even nonsectarian prayers for use in schools. Americans have been raised to believe this decision to be an expression of such sublime wisdom that they would be surprised to learn that it runs exactly contrary to the Framers' intent. Not only Jefferson but the

## A Book You're Not Supposed to Read

*The Theme Is Freedom: Religion, Politics, and the American Tradition* by M. Stanton Evans; Washington, D.C.: Regnery, 1994. (This book debunks myths about religion and government, and discusses both the original understanding of the First Amendment and the salutary role of Christianity in Western civilization.)

## What the Founders Said

"Certainly no power over religious discipline has been delegated to the general government," **Thomas Jefferson** once wrote. "It must thus rest with the states as far as it can be in any human authority." Jefferson the civil libertarian had no appetite for liberties established at the point of a federal gun.

entire founding generation as well would have considered such a ruling to be a stupefying departure from traditional American principles and an intolerable encroachment on communities' rights to self-government.

If the Framers of the First Amendment considered it legitimate for Massachusetts and other states to use tax money to support churches, it would be difficult to argue that it was meant to prohibit school prayer or the hanging of the Ten Commandments. But this is what television commentators routinely claim, and hardly anyone ever contradicts them.

## It's okay to own a gun

### Second Amendment

*A well-regulated militia, being necessary to the security of a free state, the right of the people to keep and bear arms, shall not be infringed.*

The Second Amendment continues to be a source of controversy even though its drafters knew what they meant by it and historians themselves have begun to admit that supporters of gun rights have the better of the constitutional argument. Those opposed to private gun ownership have been responsible for some of the most dishonest constitutional scholarship in American history. They claim that the Second Amendment involves not the individual right to own a firearm but only the states' rights to maintain an armed militia. According to the American Civil Liberties Union, for example, "The original intent of the Second Amendment was to protect the right of states to maintain militias." That is a rather strange interpretation of the amendment for a number of reasons, including the fact that the Constitution had already provided for the existence and arming of a militia in Article I, Section 8. Today the Left frequently claims that with state militias no longer in existence, the amendment now refers to the National Guard. But they insist that it has nothing to do with an individual's right to own a firearm.

Commentators at the time had a rather different view. According to Representative Fisher Ames of Massachusetts, "The rights of conscience, of bearing arms, of changing the government, are declared to be inherent in the people." Tench Coxe wrote probably the most systematic early overview of the Bill of Rights in the form of his "Remarks on the First Part of the Amendments to the Federal Constitution," which appeared in the Philadelphia *Federal Gazette* in June 1789. He wrote, in part, that "the people are confirmed by the next article in their right to keep and bear their private arms." Madison later wrote to tell Coxe that the ratification of the amendments would be "indebted to the co-operation of your pen."

If the framers of the Second Amendment had intended it to apply to the right of a state to maintain a militia, they would have used the word "state" instead of "people." The rest

## A Book You're Not Supposed to Read

*That Every Man Be Armed: The Evolution of a Constitutional Right* by Stephen P. Halbrook; Oakland, CA: Independent Institute, 1994.

★★★★★★★★★★

## PC Today

**Judge Roy Moore**, chief justice of the Alabama Supreme Court, was suspended in 2003 following his refusal to obey a federal court order to take down the Ten Commandments. Their presence, said the court, amounted to an establishment of religion and therefore violated the First Amendment. A lengthy debate ensued over whether the Framers had been religious men, and what they would have thought of the Ten Commandments hanging in a state supreme court building. It was irrelevant. The Framers would have been unanimous in holding that the question was up to the citizens of Alabama and that First Amendment restrictions did not apply.

## What the Early Courts Said

"The right of a citizen to keep and bear arms has justly been considered the palladium of the liberties of the republic, since it offers a strong moral check against the usurpation and arbitrary power of rulers, and will generally, even if these are successful in the first instance, enable the people to resist and triumph over them."

**Joseph Story,** 1833
U.S. Supreme Court
Justice

of the Bill of Rights is very precise in using the word "people" when referring to individuals and "state" when referring to the states. There is no good reason to believe that the Second Amendment would be the sole exception.

The text of Madison's original draft of the Second Amendment is also revealing. It read: "The right of the people to keep and bear arms shall not be infringed; a well armed and well regulated militia being the best security of a free country." In order to have a well-armed and well-regulated militia, it is necessary to recognize the people's right to gun ownership. Madison emphasizes the people's right to keep and bear arms, and only secondarily speaks of the militia. (The term "well-regulated" does not refer to government regulation. Hamilton sheds light on the term in *Federalist* #29, where he writes that a militia acquired "the degree of perfection which would entitle them to the character of a well-regulated militia" by going "through military exercises and evolutions, as often as might be necessary.")

## Just because it's not in the Bill of Rights doesn't mean it's not a right

### Ninth Amendment

*The enumeration of the Constitution, of certain rights, shall not be construed to deny or disparage others retained by the people.*

The constitutional right of private gun ownership stands even without the Second Amendment. Suppose, against all evidence, that its drafters really did mean state governments instead of individuals when they wrote that "the right of *the people*" to keep and bear arms shall not be infringed." In that case, the right to gun ownership would still be protected, but under the Ninth Amendment. That amendment was drafted to address the concerns of those who feared that if certain rights were singled out for protection in the Bill of Rights, all other rights not singled out would be insecure. This amendment made clear that the enumeration of certain rights in the Bill of Rights was not exhaustive, and was not meant to imply that they were the only rights that the people enjoyed.

The connection to the right to bear arms is clear: Since a common-law right to bear arms for self-protection and hunting was part of the British inheritance that Americans brought with them to these shores, it would have been protected by the Ninth Amendment. The reason for mentioning the importance of the militia in the Second Amendment was probably to justify the Framers' decision to make explicit mention of the right to

## What the Founders Said

"What is the militia? It is the whole people. To disarm the people is the best and most effectual way to enslave them."

**George Mason,** father of the Bill of Rights

"Laws that forbid the carrying of arms…disarm only those who are neither inclined nor determined to commit crimes.…Such laws make things worse for the assaulted and better for the assailants; they serve rather to encourage than to prevent homicides, for an unarmed man may be attacked with greater confidence than an armed man."

**Thomas Jefferson's** commonplace book, 1774–1776, quoting from *On Crimes and Punishment* (1764) by criminologist Cesare Beccaria bear arms rather than to leave it as an unenumerated right protected by the Ninth Amendment.

## Whatever the states didn't let the Feds do was left to the states

**Tenth Amendment**

*The powers not delegated to the United States by the Constitution, nor prohibited by it to the States, are reserved to the States respectively, or to the people.*

The Tenth Amendment guaranteed the states' rights to self-government. If the states had not delegated a particular power to the federal government, and if the Constitution had not forbidden the power to the states, then it remained as reserved to the states or the people. For Thomas Jefferson this was the cornerstone of the entire Constitution. Its presence in the Bill of Rights serves to remind us of the importance of self-government in the minds of Americans of the early republic.

Since the states existed prior to the federal government, they were the source of whatever power the federal government had. Thomas Jefferson determined the constitutionality of proposed legislation on this basis: If he did not find the power spelled out in Article I, Section 8, then it remained reserved to the states. It would be unconstitutional for the federal government to exercise the proposed power. If the Tenth Amendment were still taken seriously, most of the federal government's present activities would not exist. That's why no one in Washington ever mentions it.

## War powers: Congress wimps out on its responsibility

We frequently hear that the president has the right to send men into battle on his own authority by virtue of Article II, Section 2, which deems the president the commander in chief of the armed forces of the United States. The Framers had a very specific idea in mind when they drafted and approved this provision of the Constitution, and it did not include the power to declare war, a power that is reserved to Congress. This is why Woodrow Wilson went to Congress for a declaration of war before plunging the United States into World War I. Even Franklin Roosevelt, after the surprise attack by the Japanese at Pearl Harbor, went to Congress for a declaration of war, and did not simply send American troops into battle against the Japanese on his own authority. He knew perfectly well that the Constitution gave him no such authority.

Ever since the Korean War, however, Article II, Section 2 has been interpreted to mean that the president may act with an essentially free hand in foreign affairs, or at the very least that he may send men into battle without consulting Congress. But what the Framers

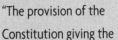

## What a President Said

"The provision of the Constitution giving the war-making power to Congress, was dictated, as I understand it, by the following reasons. Kings had always been involving and impoverishing their people in wars, pretending generally, if not always, that the good of the people was the object. This, our Convention understood to be the most oppressive of all Kingly oppressions; and they resolved to so frame the Constitution that no one man should hold the power of bringing this oppression upon us. But your view destroys the whole matter, and places our President where kings have always stood."

**Abraham Lincoln,** 1848

meant by that clause was that *once war has been declared*, it was the president's responsibility as commander in chief to direct the war. Hamilton spoke in such terms when he said that the president, although lacking the power to declare war, would have "the direction of war when authorized or begun." The president acting alone was authorized only to repel sudden attacks (hence the decision to withhold from him only the power to "declare" war, not to "make" war, which was thought to be a necessary emergency power in case of foreign attack). Overwhelming legal precedent, dating from the earliest years of the republic, supports this interpretation.

The Framers of the Constitution were abundantly clear in assigning to Congress what one scholar has called "senior status in a partnership with the president for the purpose of conducting foreign policy." Consider what the Constitution has to say about foreign affairs. Congress possesses the power "to regulate Commerce with foreign Nations," "to raise and support Armies," to "grant Letters of Marque and Reprisal," to "provide for the common Defense," and even "to declare War." Congress shares with the president the power to make treaties and to appoint ambassadors. As for the president himself, he is assigned only two powers relating to foreign affairs: He is commander in chief of the armed forces, and he has the power to receive ambassadors.

At the Constitutional Convention, the delegates disclaimed any intention to model the American executive after the British monarchy. James Wilson, for example, remarked that the powers of the British king did not constitute "a proper guide in defining the executive powers. Some of these prerogatives were of a Legislative nature. Among others that of war & peace." Edmund Randolph likewise contended that the delegates had "no motive to be governed by the British Government as our prototype."

To repose such foreign-policy authority in the legislative rather than the

★ ★ ★ ★ ★ ★ ★ ★ ★ ★

## PC Today

**D**espite its involvement in many conflicts since World War II, the United States has not officially declared war once since then, including the cases of the Korean and Vietnam Wars. Sometimes the president has simply sent men into battle without consulting Congress at all. Other times we have had cowardly and unconstitutional congressional resolutions authorizing the president to use military force if and how he deems necessary. Congress has no power under the Constitution to delegate its war-making power to the president, which is precisely what it is doing when it authorizes him to take whatever action he thinks necessary, including the use of force abroad.

executive branch of government was *a deliberate and dramatic break* with the British model and that of other nations. The Framers of the Constitution believed that history amply testified to the executive's penchant for war. As James Madison wrote to Thomas Jefferson, "The constitution supposes, what the History of all Governments demonstrates, that the Executive is the branch of power most interested in war, and most prone to it. It has accordingly with studied care vested the question of war in the Legislature."

These are a few important aspects of the U.S. Constitution of which all Americans should be aware. If the Constitution were to be preserved, Thomas Jefferson explained, the people would have to keep vigilant watch over the federal government and be alert to its encroachments upon the rights of the states and of the people. As Jefferson said, "In questions of power, then, let no more be heard of confidence in man, but bind him down by the chains of the Constitution."

## Chapter 4

★★★★★★★★★★

# AMERICAN GOVERNMENT AND THE "PRINCIPLES OF '98"

The 1790s were a contentious decade. Washington's Treasury secretary, Alexander Hamilton, came to his post armed with an economic program that could be enacted only if the Constitution were interpreted broadly rather than in the more restrictive sense that secretary of state Thomas Jefferson and his allies preferred. Hamilton was concerned that the states would render the federal government feeble and impotent.

## Providing for the "general welfare": The roots of big government

The first major constitutional controversy in American history involved the issue of a national bank, a key part of the Treasury secretary's program. Hamilton believed that a national bank was critical to the new nation's economic well-being and could be constitutionally justified on the basis of the "necessary and proper" clause and other grounds. Jefferson believed both that a bank was not necessary and that the states had never provided the federal government the constitutional power to establish one.

Jefferson joined James Madison, then a member of Congress, in his constitutional objection to the bank. Madison later gave in on the bank.

### Guess what?

★ Providing for the "general welfare" doesn't mean that the federal government gets to spend money on whatever it wants.

★ An early draft of the Constitution opened with the words "We, the States."

★ Granting individual states the power to nullify unconstitutional federal laws was a debate the Founders took seriously.

31

But on the eve of his departure as president in 1817, Madison vetoed the "bonus bill," which authorized federal expenditures for constructing roads and canals. In his veto message, Madison wrote that the use of federal funds for road and canal building was a good idea, but he insisted that the Constitution would have to be amended first to make it possible. As matters stood, the federal government had no constitutional authority to do such things.

Madison dismissed the claim that the proposed legislation could be justified by the Constitution's clause authorizing the federal government "to provide for common defense and general welfare." To the extent that politicians today even bother to justify federal legislation on constitutional grounds, they appeal to this clause. But to argue this way, Madison said, would render "the special and careful enumeration of powers which follow the clause nugatory and improper. Such a view of the Constitution would have the effect of giving to Congress a general power of legislation instead of the defined and limited one hitherto understood to belong to them." If the "general welfare" clause of the Constitution authorized the Congress to do *anything* that tended toward the general well-being of the country, then why had the Framers bothered to *specifically list* the powers of Congress in Article I, Section 8? This very fact logically precluded the possibility that the general welfare clause constituted a broad, open-ended grant of power.

Madison continued to promote this view in the years that followed. In 1792 he argued:

> If Congress can employ money indefinitely to the general welfare, and are the sole and supreme judges of the general welfare, they may take the care of religion into their own hands; they may appoint teachers in every state, county, and parish, and pay them out of their public treasury; they may take into their own hands the education of children establishing in like

manner schools throughout the Union; they may assume the provision for the poor; they may undertake the regulation of all roads other than post-roads; in short, everything, from the highest object of state legislation down to the most minute object of police, would be thrown under the power of Congress.

What Madison warned about is precisely what has come to pass today. So far has Washington drifted from constitutional government that the question of the constitutionality of legislation, which was so central to eighteenth- and nineteenth-century congressional debates, is no longer raised.

### Checks and balances: The fox guarding the chicken coop

The Framers of the Constitution were well aware of the tendency for power to concentrate and expand. Jefferson spoke of the calamity that would result if all power were to be concentrated in the federal government. Checks and balances among the executive, legislative, and judicial branches, a prominent feature of the Constitution, offer little guarantee of

★ ★ ★ ★ ★ ★ ★ ★ ★ ★

## PC Today

**Many historians often portray** states' rights as merely code words for slavery. But as historian Eugene Genovese reminds us, of the five Virginians who made the greatest intellectual contributions to the strict constructionist interpretation of the Constitution—George Mason, Thomas Jefferson, John Randolph of Roanoke, St. George Tucker, and John Taylor of Caroline—only Taylor could be described as pro-slavery, and "even he regarded it as an inherited misfortune to be tolerated, rather than celebrated."

limited government, since these three branches could unite against the states and the people. That is precisely what Jefferson warned William Branch Giles about in 1825: "It is but too evident, that the three ruling branches of [the national government] are in combination to strip their colleagues, the State authorities, of all powers reserved by them, and to exercise themselves all functions foreign and domestic."

Since the states were the constituent parts of the Union and had enjoyed an independent existence long before the Constitution was established, early American statesmen wanted the states to have some protection against the federal government. The federal government could not be permitted to have the exclusive authority to interpret the Constitution. It would consistently hand down rulings in favor of itself, and over time, consolidate power.

## The Republicans versus the Federalists
### Round One: The Alien and Sedition Acts of 1798

Amid the naval skirmishes and diplomatic tension in America's quasi-war with France, the Federalists managed to enact legislation that would become notorious: the Alien and Sedition Acts. The Federalists, a political party to which Hamilton belonged, generally favored a strong central government and a broad construction of the Constitution—the very opposite of Jefferson's Republicans, who were anxious to defend the rights of the states and insisted upon a strict construction of the Constitution. The alien legislation, which authorized the president to deport resident aliens who had "treasonable" leanings, was a source of concern to Jefferson and other Republicans; Jefferson believed the legislation was aimed at Albert Gallatin, the important Pennsylvania Republican who had been born in Geneva. (He later became Jefferson's own Treasury secretary.)

But it was the prohibition of seditious libel that they found most objectionable. For Jefferson, the problem wasn't simply that this prohibition would be enforced in a partisan way—though of course it was, with numerous Republican newspapers and spokesmen targeted for harassment, fines, and even jail time. (Correspondence between Jefferson and Madison at the time includes concerns that their mail was being tampered with.) And it wasn't that seditious libel could be arbitrarily or loosely defined—although, again, in practice it was: One poor soul, who expressed the fond wish that the presidential saluting cannon would "hit [President John] Adams in the ass," was fined $100.

The primary issue was the acts' dubious constitutionality. Jefferson based part of his objection on their violation of the First Amendment, though the point was arguable. He added that the acts violated the Tenth Amendment, to him the foundation on which the entire Constitution was based. Nowhere had the states delegated any authority to the federal government to pass legislation on the freedom of speech or press. In enacting such legislation, then, the federal government had encroached on a state prerogative. For Jefferson, who spoke of binding men by the chains of the Constitution, immediate action was necessary lest such federal usurpations begin to multiply.

### Round Two: The Kentucky Resolutions of 1798

Was there a constitutional remedy—a solution short of secession or violent revolution—to oppose such laws as the Alien and Sedition Acts? Figures like Massachusetts senator Daniel Webster and Supreme Court justice Joseph Story (and later Abraham Lincoln) didn't think so. Since they subscribed to a nationalist theory of the Union—whose core belief was that the Constitution was not a compact among sovereign states but had been adopted by the American people in the aggregate—this appeared to them as an unlawful revolt by an arbitrary portion of the people rather than as an exercise of authority by a sovereign body.

Webster lent weight to his argument in his famous 1833 speech "The Constitution Not a Compact Between Sovereign States." He pointed to the

## What the Founders Said

**Alexander Hamilton**, while an advocate of a strong central government, nevertheless envisioned a role for the states in restraining the federal government, arguing in *Federalist* #28 that "the State governments will, in all possible contingencies, afford complete security against invasions of the public liberty by the national authority."

words of the Constitution: Did it not say *We, the People*, and not *We, the States*, do ordain and establish this Constitution? But Webster's exegesis of the Constitution's preamble is faulty. In fact, the Constitution as originally drafted did say "We, the States." This wording was removed for practical reasons by the committee on style. Since no one could know in advance which states would ratify the Constitution and which would not, it made little sense to list all the states by name before each had made its decision. The substitute phrase "We, the People of the united States" referred not to a single American people taken in the aggregate, but to the people of Massachusetts, the people of Virginia, the people of Georgia— in other words, *the people of the several states.*

The fact that this textual change was unanimously accepted proves it could not have been intended to alter the nature of the Union. Had the new text really meant what Webster later claimed it did, vocal and lengthy debate would have ensued. It certainly would not have been unanimously approved.

To Jefferson, the only way a state could remain in the Union and retain its liberties in the face of an unconstitutional act by the federal government was for the state to declare that a federal action was null and void and would not be enforced within the state. But this action should be taken by the state only in dire circumstances.

There is, obviously, no provision in the Constitution that explicitly authorizes nullification. That was not Jefferson's point. Jefferson, and later John C. Calhoun, suggested that no one side in a compact could have the exclusive right of interpreting its terms. This was especially true in the case of the federal compact, since it was Calhoun's contention that the federal government *was not a party to the compact*, since it was itself established by the joint action of the states.

Jefferson (who was vice president at the time) anonymously penned what became known as the Kentucky Resolutions of 1798. They spelled out the objectionable aspects of the Alien and Sedition Acts as well as the states' rightful response: nullification. (No state actually nullified these acts; the crisis with France came to an end, and the acts were slated to expire in early 1801.) James Madison penned similar resolutions that were approved by the Virginia legislature.

The following year the Kentucky legislature passed another resolution, this time including the word "nullification":

> Resolved . . . That, if those who administer the General Government be permitted to transgress the limits fixed by that compact, by a total disregard to the special delegations of power therein contained. . . . That the several States who formed that instrument being sovereign and independent, have the unquestionable right to judge of the infraction; and *that a Nullification by those sovereignties, of all unauthorized acts done under color of that instrument is the rightful remedy.* . . .

Madison penned his own Virginia Resolutions, which likewise warned of federal encroachments and reminded the population that the state governments had the responsibility to protect them from unconstitutional measures at the federal level.

## South Carolina nullifies tariffs

Perhaps the most important nullification theorist was John C. Calhoun, one of the most brilliant and creative political thinkers in American history. The Liberty Press edition of Calhoun's writings, *Union and Liberty*, is indispensable for anyone interested in this subject—especially his Fort

Hill address, a concise and elegant case for nullification. Calhoun proposed that an aggrieved state would hold a special nullification convention, much like the ratifying conventions held by the states to ratify the Constitution, and there decide whether to nullify the law in question. This is how it was practiced in the great standoff between South Carolina and Andrew Jackson. When South Carolina nullified a protective tariff in 1832–33 (its argument being that the Constitution authorized the tariff power for the purpose of revenue only, not to encourage manufactures or to profit one section of the country at the expense of another—a violation of the general welfare clause) it held just such a nullification convention.

In Calhoun's conception, when a state officially nullified a federal law on the grounds of its dubious constitutionality, the law must be regarded as suspended. Thus could the "concurrent majority" of a state be protected by the unconstitutional actions of a numerical majority of the entire country. But there were limits to what the concurrent majority could do. Should three-fourths of the states, by means of the amendment process, choose to grant the federal government the disputed power, then the nullifying state would have to decide whether it could live with the decision of its fellow states or whether it would prefer to secede from the Union.

That Madison indicated in 1830 that he had never meant to propose nullification or secession either in his work on the Constitution or in his Virginia Resolutions of 1798 is frequently taken as the last word on the sub-

## What the Founders Said

"Resolved...That the Government created by this compact was not made the exclusive or final judge of the extent of the powers delegated to itself, since that would have made its discretion, and not the Constitution, the measure of its powers; but that as in all other cases of compact among parties having no common Judge, each party has an equal right to judge of itself, as well of infractions as of the mode and measure of redress...."

**Thomas Jefferson,**
Kentucky Resolutions of 1798

ject. But Madison's frequent change of position has been documented by countless scholars. One modern study on the subject is called "How Many Madisons Will We Find?" "The truth seems to be, that Mr. Madison was more solicitous to preserve the integrity of the Union, than the coherency of his own thoughts," writes Albert Taylor Bledsoe.

It is true that at the time, Virginia and Kentucky found little support among the other states for their resolutions (though since some of those states were strongly Federalist, they supported the anti-sedition legislation), and that South Carolina was practically alone in 1832 and 1833 (not quite "all alone," as historians typically claim: Virginia sent an official mediator to meet with South Carolina legislators to attempt to work out a solution, and prominent Virginians said they would stand by South Carolina against the federal government if it came to that). But actions speak louder than words, and if the Northern states sharply criticized South Carolina's nullification of the Tariffs of 1828 and 1832, on the other hand they used the unmistakable language of the Virginia and Kentucky Resolutions of 1798 when nullifying the fugitive slave laws. This 1859 statement of the Wisconsin legislature is striking:

> Resolved, That the government formed by the Constitution of the United States was not the exclusive or final judge of the extent of the powers delegated to itself; but that, as in all other cases of compact among parties having no common judge, each party has an equal right to judge for itself, as well of infractions as of the mode and measure of redress.

> Resolved, that the principle and construction contended for by the party which now rules in the councils of the nation, that the general government is the exclusive judge of the extent of the powers delegated to it, stop nothing short of despotism, since the *discretion* of those who administer the government, and not the *Constitution*, would be the measure of their powers; that the

several states which formed that instrument, being sovereign and independent, have the unquestionable right to judge of its infractions; and that a positive defiance of those sovereignties, of all unauthorized acts done or attempted to be done under color of that instrument, is the rightful remedy.

Does that sound familiar? These ideas, laid out by Jefferson and Madison, elaborated upon by others, and echoed above by the legislature of Wisconsin, became known as the "principles of '98," recalling the Virginia and Kentucky Resolutions of that year.

## Why nullification isn't as crazy as it sounds

Responding to the claim that the federal judiciary and not the states had the final word on the constitutionality of federal measures, James Madison's Report of 1800 argued that "dangerous powers, not delegated, may not only be usurped and executed by the other departments, but...the judicial department may also exercise or sanction dangerous powers, beyond the grant of the Constitution....However true, therefore, it may be, that the judicial department, is, in all questions submitted to it by the forms of the Constitution, to decide in the last resort, this resort must necessarily be deemed the last *in relation to the other departments of the government*; not in relation to the rights of the parties to the constitutional compact, from which the judicial as well as the other departments hold their delegated trusts" (emphasis added). Thus the Supreme Court's decisions could not be considered absolutely final in constitutional questions touching upon the powers of the states.

The most common argument among the early statesmen against nullification is that it would produce chaos: a bewildering number of states nullifying a bewildering array of federal laws. (Given the character of the vast majority of federal legislation, a good answer to this objection is: Who cares?) Abel Upshur, a Virginian legal thinker who would serve brief terms as secretary of the Navy and secretary of state in the early 1840s, undertook to put the fears of opponents of nullification to rest:

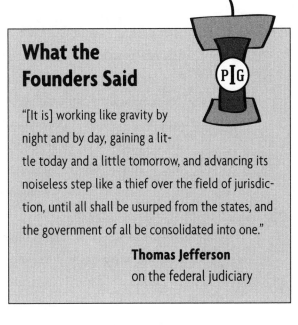

## What the Founders Said

"[It is] working like gravity by night and by day, gaining a little today and a little tomorrow, and advancing its noiseless step like a thief over the field of jurisdiction, until all shall be usurped from the states, and the government of all be consolidated into one."

**Thomas Jefferson**
on the federal judiciary

> If the States may abuse their reserved rights in the manner contemplated by the President, the Federal government, on the other hand, may abuse its delegated rights. There is danger from *both* sides, and as we are compelled to confide in the one or the other, we have only to inquire, which is most worthy of our confidence.

> It is much more probable that the Federal government will abuse its power than that the States will abuse theirs. And if we suppose a case of actual abuse on either hand, it will not be difficult to decide which is the greater evil.

> If a state should abuse its right of interposition by arresting the operation of a constitutional law, the worst that could come of it would be to suspend the operation of the law, for a time, as to that State, while it would have all its effects within the other States. This would certainly be unjust, but in most cases, would be attended with very little practical evil.

> Besides, according to the doctrine for which I am contending, this evil would be temporary only; it must cease in some way or other, as soon as the other States act upon the subject. I acknowledge, however, that it is at best an evil, but it is an evil inseparable from our system, and one which cannot be avoided except by submitting to a greater evil.

It is hard to find fault with Upshur's reasoning. Opponents of the idea always seem to fall back on some case that allegedly renders nullification impracticable, even dangerous. If the doctrine of nullification did not degenerate into confusion in peacetime, what should happen if a state or group of states should invoke it during war, potentially threatening the nation's security? Most proponents of nullification have correctly noted that it is precisely in such situations that we would expect the interests of the states to be most consonant and their allegiance to the federal government most secure. More to the point, one might well wonder what a group of states is doing in the same union in the first place if a portion of them actually desired to sabotage a just war.

The main point that nullification addresses is that a government allowed to determine the scope of its own powers cannot remain limited for long. One of the casualties of the abysmal state of American education today is that so few Americans know their own constitutional history that hardly anyone realizes the constitutional challenge that states could pose to the routine dictation they endure at the hands of the federal government. Learning our history won't change the situation, but it'd be a start.

**Chapter 5**

★ ★ ★ ★ ★ ★ ★ ★ ★ ★

# THE NORTH–SOUTH DIVISION

**T**his chapter reviews some of the most significant episodes of the antebellum period: the four decades prior to the American War Between the States. There's ample evidence in the events that took place during this period that the debate over slavery was at root a debate over geographical equality and superiority in the Union. Why, for example, were the two sides arguing over whether slavery should be allowed in the deserts of New Mexico, where no one in his right mind would *want* to bring slaves in order to start a plantation?

## You get Missouri, we get Maine

The debate that began in 1818 over the admission of Missouri, a slave state, was a critical juncture in the young nation's formation. At the time, there were equal numbers of slave and free states—eleven each—resulting in a kind of balance of power in the Senate. But the admission of Missouri would have given the South an edge in the Senate. The stalemate was finally broken in 1820 by the Missouri Compromise: Missouri was admitted as a slave state and Maine a free state.

Of much greater significance was a provision of the Compromise that pertained to the status of slavery in the Louisiana Territory. With the exception of Missouri, any territory north of 36°30' (the southern border

## Guess what?

★ The American War Between the States was as much about which region, North or South, would dominate, as it was about slavery.

★ The North's position to keep slavery out of the territories was not altogether altruistic—they wanted to save the territory for whites.

★ A *Southern district court* freed Dred Scott; it was the U.S. Supreme Court that kept him a slave.

## The Many Forms of Opposition

**Emancipation societies**—groups that attempted to persuade slaveholders to liberate their slaves voluntarily.

**Compensated emancipation**—slaveholders would be financially compensated for freeing slaves.

**Prevent expansion**—advocates wanted to confine slavery to where it already existed but prevent its expansion to additional territory; this would supposedly mean slavery's ultimate extinction, since slaveholders whose soil had been exhausted would be unable to move with their slaves to virgin territory.

**Abolition**—those who favored an immediate end to slavery everywhere, with no compensation for slaveholders (the most radical position).

of Missouri) would be forever closed to slavery, while in any territory south slavery would be permitted. Awkward as it was, the compromise prevented similar crises in the future, and remained in effect for more than three decades.

## More rhetorical blows

Among the abolitionist movement's most prominent spokesmen was the Massachusetts activist and publisher William Lloyd Garrison, who started the newspaper *The Liberator* in 1831. Garrison had nothing but contempt for gradual emancipation, a policy he called "pernicious," and would brook no compromise on the issue. His newspaper was widely influential, since larger papers reprinted its articles. Some Southerners believed it was no coincidence that the Nat Turner rebellion, a famous slave insurrection in which fifty-five whites perished, took place the same year that Garrison began his paper.

There was no evidence that Turner had heard of Garrison or *The Liberator*. But the connection did not need to be that direct. Many Southerners were shocked at the tone of abolitionist literature, which seethed with loathing for the entire South and at times seemed to urge violent resistance to slavery. Such rhetorical assaults on an entire region only served to discredit local anti-slavery activity in the South. As of 1827, there were more than four times as many anti-slavery societies in the South as in the North. The abolitionist movement, in peppering their message with belligerent and vitriolic anti-Southern rhetoric, made it all but impossible for Southern anti-slavery activists not to be viewed with suspicion. Massachusetts senator Daniel Webster, no friend of slavery, blamed the abolitionists of the North for having contributed in no small measure to Southern obstinacy.

Sectional conflict was further aggravated by the Wilmot Proviso, which was introduced in Congress in 1846 by Congressman David Wilmot, a Democrat from Pennsylvania. The proviso was attached to an appropriations bill authorizing funds for the Mexican War, then under way. Its premise was simple: Slavery would be prohibited in any territory acquired from Mexico in the war. Wilmot was outlining a point of view that became known in American history as the "free-soil" position, according to which slavery would remain undisturbed in the states in which it already existed but would be prevented from expanding into new territories, such as those that might be added to the American domain as a result of the war with Mexico. Although it never became law (it passed the House numerous times but failed in the Senate), the proviso contributed greatly to the tension between North and South.

## Keep slavery out of the territories! (to reserve them for whites)

Wilmot introduced the proviso not out of humanitarian concern for the slave, but to keep blacks out of the territories to preserve those lands for free white labor. He disclaimed any "morbid sympathy for the slave," insisting instead that he was acting on behalf of "the cause and the rights of white freemen." He went on to explain: "I would preserve to free white labor a fair country, a rich inheritance, where the sons of toil, of my own race and color, can live without the disgrace which association with Negro slavery brings upon free labor."

As it turned out, the United States did acquire considerable territory in the southwest as a result of the war. The Treaty of Guadalupe Hidalgo, in addition to deciding the border dispute between Texas and Mexico in the United States' favor, gave the United States territories that would later become the states of California, New Mexico, and Utah, and portions of Nevada, Arizona, Colorado, and Wyoming. These lands became known collectively as the Mexican Cession. In return, the United States paid Mexico $15 million and promised to assume any financial claims that its new citizens might have against that country.

**How Do We Handle
the Territories?**

Here were the proposed
solutions:

**The free-soil tradition—**
slavery would be
prohibited in the
new territories.

**The Missouri
Compromise—**the
line established in the
agreement would be
extended to the Pacific.

**Slavery permitted—**
slavery allowed in all
the territories.

**Popular sovereignty—**
leaves the decision
to the residents of a
territory.

## States fight over plantations in…Arizona?

The prohibition of slavery in the territories advocated by the Wilmot Proviso raised Southern ire, but it would be wrong to conclude that the South was riled for this reason alone. Both North and South knew that unfavorable climate made the introduction of plantation agriculture unlikely in the new territories. Southerners believed that the proviso was an attack on Southern honor and Southern equality in the Union. According to Professor Michael Holt of the University of Virginia:

> The North was not totally wedded to the [Wilmot] Proviso, that is, to congressional prohibition in the territories. Its main concern was that slavery not expand and that the political power of the South not grow. Most Southerners, on the other hand, did *not* demand that slavery actually expand. Instead, they insisted that their equal rights be protected, that they not be forced to submit to Northern dictation and to the inferiority such submission entailed. If the territorial issue could be shifted away from naked congressional prohibition, a complete and final rupture between the sections could be avoided.

The Democrats and the Whigs were national parties with substantial followings in both North and South. What responsible Americans hoped to avoid was a political realignment in which the parties would become purely sectional, attempting to seize the federal system to pursue its own narrow interests. Not surprisingly, the presidential candidates of the two major parties in the months leading up to the 1848 election were less than straightforward about their positions on the contentious issue of the territories. (The only candidate whose position was crystal clear was Martin van Buren, the candidate of the short-lived Free Soil Party, who sought to exclude slavery from the territories.)

## Politicians dance around the issues

Whig candidate Zachary Taylor, for example, took no public position on the Wilmot Proviso. As a result, his supporters North and South could each claim him as the logical choice for their section. Southerners could point to the fact that Taylor was a Southerner. Northern supporters could point to rumors that Taylor supported the Wilmot Proviso.

Michigan's Lewis Cass, who received the Democratic nomination, was also portrayed differently in the North and in the South. In the South, Cass was pitched as the logical choice for Southerners because as an advocate of "popular sovereignty" he would give them a fair shot in the territories. Cass also pledged to veto the Wilmot Proviso. In the North, Cass supporters pointed to the arid climate of the southwest, noting that even with popular sovereignty it was very unlikely that slavery would ever develop in its inhospitable climate. Cass was said to be the logical choice for Northerners because allowing the people of the territories to vote on slavery *would almost surely have a free-soil outcome*, but without unnecessarily alienating the South—as would happen if slavery were prohibited by the legislative fiat of Congress. Simply shutting slavery out of the territories would strike Southerners as an intolerable blow to their honor and another example of the North's refusal to grant them equality in

★★★★★★★★★★

# The Second Party System

The first American party system originated in the 1790s, pitting the small-government, states' rights Republicans against the centralizing Federalists. That party system was destroyed in the years following the War of 1812, when Federalist behavior during that war, including New England's implied threat of secession, was viewed as treasonous and reprehensible. By 1820 the Federalists were not even fielding a candidate for president, and thus Republican James Monroe ran unopposed. The second party system, which originated in response to divided opinion over the presidency of Andrew Jackson, came to resemble the first party system, with the Whigs carrying on the Federalist legacy and the Democrats, more or less, carrying on the tradition of the Republicans.

the Union. Cass could thus accomplish the free-soil objective without sowing discord between the sections.

## It's about slavery, but it's not about slavery

The issue of slavery in the territories, along with several outstanding issues between the sections, would ultimately be addressed in the Compromise of 1850. It eased tension between the sections, and talk of Southern secession withered away.

The controversy over the southwestern territories, temporarily resolved by the compromise, suggests that the slavery debate masked the real issue: the struggle for power and domination. That does not mean that slavery was irrelevant or insignificant, but without understanding the sectional power relationships at stake we can be led to overstate its importance. According to the 1860 census, there were a grand total of twenty-nine slaves in Utah, and none at all in New Mexico. It makes sense to suspect that the vigorous debates over slavery in the Mexican Cession must have involved an issue more significant than whether Southerners would be allowed to bring twenty-nine slaves into the new territories. Even Republicans acknowledged that political power was at the root of debates over slavery. As one Indiana congressman put it, speaking to Southerners, "It is not room that you are anxious to obtain, but *power—political power.*"

**A Book You're Not Supposed to Read**

*The Coming of the Civil War* by Avery O. Craven; Chicago: University of Chicago Press, 1957.

The slavery issue returned again in the Nebraska Territory in 1854. It should not have, since the territory was north of the Missouri Compromise line and should therefore have been closed to slavery. But there was increasing support for a transcontinental railroad that would stretch from coast to coast, and Illinois senator Stephen Douglas was determined that the new railroad's eastern terminus would be located in Chicago. (Since railroad lines already existed in the East, a transcontinental railroad amounted to building a road from the West Coast and joining it to the existing roads in the East.)

Douglas's proposal appears harmless, but the railroad would have to pass through the unorganized Nebraska Territory. In order to secure the line from bandits or from Indian attacks, a territorial government would have to be established. To win Southern support for a Chicago terminus, Douglas proposed that the territory be split in two—Kansas and Nebraska—and that the issue of slavery be decided by popular sovereignty. The legislation would repeal the Missouri Compromise. By theoretically opening these territories to slavery, Douglas appealed to Southerners who considered prohibitions on slavery an insult to Southern honor and a blow to Southern equality in the Union. The resulting legislation, known as the Kansas-Nebraska Act, became law in 1854.

Why was the territorial issue so contentious? Some territories passed through the territorial stage quickly and rapidly became states. Others took longer. All the while, the population of the would-be state would be increasing. If slavery were prohibited during the territorial stage, slaveholders would likely stay away. When the territory became a state and the time came to decide on the issue, the absence of slaveholders practically guaranteed that the new state would decide against slavery. Had slavery been permitted during the territorial stage, slaveholders would likely have settled in the territory, and increased the possibility that it would become a slave state. This was why the legal issue of slavery *in the territories* was so important and divisive.

## The Kansas "bloodbath"

It was fairly clear that slavery would not take root in Nebraska, but the outcome in Kansas was not so certain. Supporters and opponents of slavery

★ ★ ★ ★

### The Compromise of 1850

★ Admits California as a free state

★ Organizes the Mexican Cession into the territories of New Mexico and Utah, where the status of slavery would be decided by popular sovereignty

★ Resolves a border dispute between New Mexico and Texas

★ Abolishes the slave trade in the District of Columbia

★ Establishes a tougher fugitive slave law

★ ★ ★ ★

**What the Press Said**

"[It was] merely an incident of the real controversy… [for] possession of the Federal Government is what both North and South are striving for."

The *New York Times* in its description of slavery, 1854

flocked to Kansas to influence the vote. The typical textbook describes Kansas as the scene of ceaseless slavery-related violence. Recent scholarship, however, casts doubt on this perception. Eyewitness accounts and newspaper reports appear to have been unreliable, even wildly exaggerated. In their own propaganda, both sides tended to inflate the number of killings either to call attention to their own plight or to impress readers with the number of casualties they managed to inflict on their opponents. "Political killings," writes researcher Dale Watts, "account for about one-third of the total violent deaths. They were not common. The streets and byways did not run red with blood as some writers have imagined."

A recent study concluded that of the 157 violent deaths that occurred during Kansas's territorial period, fifty-six appear to have had some connection to the political situation or to the slavery issue. According to Watts:

> The antislavery party was not the innocent victim of violence that its propagandists, both contemporary and subsequent, tried to portray. Both sides employed violent tactics and both were adept at focusing blame on their opponents, habitually claiming self-defense in any killings committed by their own men. However, the antislavery party, as the ultimate victor in the contest, was in a position to write the history of the period from its point of view.... The data, however, indicate that the two sides were nearly equally involved in killing their political opponents.

Some, apparently, recognized and even lampooned contemporary exaggerations of violence in Kansas. The editor of the *Kansas Chief*, amused at the press's hysteria, wrote in 1858:

The late civil war in Kansas did not last but a day and a half. A Kansas correspondent thus sums up the result:

| | |
|---:|---|
| **Killed** | 0 |
| **Wounded, contusion of the nose** | 2 |
| **Missing** | 0 |
| **Captured** | 350 |
| **Frightened** | 5,718 |

To have read the frightful accounts of the late war, as reported in the *St. Louis Democrat* and some of the Kansas papers, one would have supposed that at least as many as the number of the frightened above were actually killed, and had "gone the way of all flesh."

Still, difficulties in Kansas were real enough. After pro-slavery men from neighboring Missouri voted illegally in the 1855 election for the Kansas territorial legislature, it was clear that the political future of Kansas would be one of contention. Two territorial governments, one in favor of slavery and one against, operated in uneasy coexistence. Interestingly and revealingly, the anti-slavery Kansas government proposed a state constitution that would have forbidden even free blacks from entering the state.

## The rise of the Republicans

The controversy over the Kansas-Nebraska Act proved too much for the ramshackle Whig Party, which was torn apart by sectional antagonism. Filling the political vacuum left by the self-destruction of the Whig Party was the Republican Party, created in 1854 as a sectional party—just what so many American statesmen had tried to avoid. The Republicans attracted a variety of supporters with their free-soil position and their support for high protective tariffs.

As free-soilers, they opposed slavery in the territories, though the racialist motivation of such exclusion of slavery is clear from the party's 1856 platform, which read, in part, that "all unoccupied territory of the United States, and such as they may hereafter acquire, shall be reserved for the white Caucasian race—a thing that cannot be except by the exclusion of slavery." Their economic program, of which the protective tariff formed an important plank, could not have been better devised to attract Southern antipathy. Abraham Lincoln, who would be elected in 1860 as the first Republican president, had been a supporter of the protective tariff for several decades by the time he reached the White House.

### Power over what?

For the more radical Republicans, the free-soil position was only the opening salvo in what they hoped would be the ultimate extinction of slavery. Conservative Republicans, no friends of slavery either, recognized that what was going on between the sections was a struggle for power, plain and simple. According to historian Eric Foner:

> The idea of combating Southern political power and its economic consequences was the key to conservative support for the Republican party. Such measures as a Pacific railroad, a homestead act, a protective tariff, and government aid to internal improvements had been blocked time and again by the Democratic party, at the dictation, it seemed, of the South. The conservatives hoped to use the Republican party to wrest control of the federal government away from the slaveholders, and they viewed the sectional struggle as primarily a contest for political power.

The protective tariff was perhaps the most controversial economic issue of the antebellum period. High tariffs, intended to protect Northern industry from foreign competition, were a terrible burden to the agricultural South, which had little industry to protect. To Southerners, the tariffs meant higher prices for manufactured goods because they bought them abroad and paid the tariff or because they bought them from Northerners at the inflated prices that tariff protection made possible. Although certain sectors of the Southern economy, like Louisiana sugar growers, favored protective tariffs, in general the South opposed the tariff. (Tariff protection would have done little good for Southern products, since the South sold most of its goods on a world market.)

Likewise, federal land policy divided the sections. Northerners favored land giveaways by the federal government, while Southerners believed the federal lands should be sold. Southerners feared that without the revenue the federal government took in from land sales, there would be added pressure to raise the tariff to make up the loss. They also believed that a policy of free land, by increasing the overall amount of agricultural land in use, would tend to lower Southern land values. These were some of the economic issues that divided the sections, and they, as Foner observes, were never far from the surface in the debates of the 1840s and 1850s.

## Fact: Local Southern judge freed Dred Scott

Among the decade's most controversial and divisive events was the notorious *Dred Scott* decision of 1857. That case involved a Missouri slave, Dred Scott, who had been taken by his master, an army surgeon, to both the free state of Illinois and the free territory of Wisconsin. Scott later sued for his freedom on the grounds that his time in those places, where slavery was not recognized in law, had made him a free man.

The case was enormously complicated. In 1836, the Boston Female Anti-Slavery Society brought before the Massachusetts Supreme Court the case of a six-year-old slave girl who had been brought to the state by her mistress for a visit. According to the Society, since this slave girl was in a free state, the slave relation was dissolved and she was now free. (Since the girl was not a runaway, the case had nothing to do with the fugitive slave clause of the Constitution.) Arguing on behalf of the girl, Rufus Choate declared: "Comity is only policy and courtesy—and is never to be indulged, at the expense of what the State, by its public law, declared to be justice." That is, the understanding whereby states honored one another's laws was a matter of courtesy and convenience, not of unbending principle, and thus Massachusetts was not bound by another state's laws on slavery.

The rule of comity thus could not be used to challenge Massachusetts's ability to declare free those non-fugitive slaves who reached its borders. The Court, concurring with Choate, declared that "an owner of a slave in another State where slavery is warranted by law, voluntarily bringing such slave into this State, has no authority to retain him against his will, or carry him out of the State against his consent, for the purpose of being held in slavery."

Scott's case was not entirely similar to that of this six-year-old girl, since the Massachusetts Supreme Court was deciding a case in which the slave had not yet been removed from Massachusetts. Scott, on the other hand, had already been back in Missouri for years by the time he pursued his case. The Massachusetts example, however, shows that entering the jurisdiction of a free state could make a slave free.

### Why Dred Scott should have been freed

Still more pertinent is the precedent established in *Sommersett's Case* (1772), an episode in British jurisprudence that made its way into the American legal consciousness. That famous case involved a slave from Jamaica, James Sommersett, who escaped when his master brought him along on a business trip to England. After he was recaptured, Sommersett was placed in chains aboard a ship that was to take him to Jamaica to be sold. While still aboard the ship, however, Sommersett was brought by *habeas corpus* before the Court of King's Bench.

In his ruling, Chief Justice Lord Mansfield declared that slavery was an institution so "odious" and so contrary to natural law that it could exist only by statute. Unless a law established the slave relation, slavery had to be assumed not to exist. In the absence of such a statute in England, the slave relation had to be considered of no effect in that country, and therefore Sommersett should be released.

## What the Judges Said

"In this State, it has been recognized from the beginning of the government as a correct position in law that a master who takes his slave [to] reside in a State or territory where slavery is prohibited, thereby emancipates his slave."

**Hamilton Gamble,**
Missouri Chief Justice
*Dred Scott* dissenting
opinion

It was on this principle that a Missouri circuit court granted Dred Scott and his family their freedom in 1850. That freedom was granted on the basis of this well-established line of legal argument that had grown within Southern jurisprudence and which owed its inspiration to *Sommersett's Case*. As constitutional scholar John Remington Graham explains, the circuit court's decision could hardly have been surprising given the statements of the Missouri Supreme Court, and those of other Southern states, for nearly three decades. But the Missouri Supreme Court, hearing the case on appeal, reversed the decision of the circuit court and declared Scott and his family still enslaved. According to that court, the relevant law was that prevailing in Missouri, not in Illinois or the Wisconsin Territory.

The case eventually made its way to the U.S. Supreme Court, where in a 7–2 decision the Court ruled against Scott. Chief Justice Roger Taney argued that due to Scott's lack of American citizenship, he was not entitled to bring suit in the Supreme Court, and so the most recent court decision against him stood.

### The real significance of Dred Scott: Territories open to slavery

What made the Court's decision so explosive was that even though Taney acknowledged that he had no jurisdiction in the case, he nevertheless went on to make some controversial pronouncements on issues related to Scott's case. The reason he claimed to have no jurisdiction was that he contended that Scott, a black man, was not a U.S. citizen and thus could not bring suit in the U.S. Supreme Court. Taney argued that the various disabilities placed upon blacks throughout the Union, in Northern states as well as Southern, showed they were not considered part of the polity, and that citizenship rights had not been intended to be extended to them.

American history textbooks are particularly fond of quoting Taney as saying that Africans were "so far inferior, that they had no rights which the white man was bound to respect." To my knowledge, no textbook author has bothered to point out that Taney was *not* claiming this as his position. As the context makes clear, Taney was saying that by the time of the Declaration of Independence, the general opinion among whites for a century had been that blacks belonged to an inferior race, and that the idea of civil equality with whites was scarcely to be raised anywhere. Taney's point was that since this was certainly the case, then it was highly unlikely that blacks, so universally despised by the white majority, could have been intended to be citizens. Taney did not see it as his role as a justice, whose task it was to interpret existing law, to raise people to citizenship. Should people wish to extend citizenship to the Africans living in their midst, he said, they should do so by means of the normal legislative process.

What upset Northerners about the decision was primarily *not* the individual fate of Dred Scott, even if this is the only aspect of the case that modern undergraduates seem able to remember on exams. (In fact, Scott and his family were emancipated by their owner not long after the case was concluded.) The issue was Taney's comments with regard to *slavery in the territories.* Taney argued that Scott's temporary residence in the Wisconsin Territory, a free territory, did not entitle him to his freedom because the prohibition of slavery in the territories had been unconstitutional in the first place. By Taney's reasoning, the Missouri Compromise had always been unconstitutional. The territories were the common property of the United States, Taney argued, and thus they should be equally accessible to all. To prohibit slavery in the territories was tantamount to emancipating any slaves who might be brought there, and such action amounted to an unlawful confiscation of property in violation of the Fifth Amendment's due process guarantee. Thus the territories had to be open to slavery.

Given that the Missouri Compromise had already been set aside three years earlier by the Kansas-Nebraska Act, Taney's statement was of little *practical* effect. But symbolism was at least as significant as substance in the years leading up to the outbreak of the War Between the States, and Taney's dismissal of the Missouri Compromise, which some Americans had treated with the utmost reverence, was too much for some to accept. For those with active imaginations, it seemed to be further evidence of the existence of a Slave Power conspiracy aimed at Southern

## ★★★★★★★★★★

### PC Today

❝The bitter truth," writes historian John Remington Graham, "is that Taney and those concurring with him had managed in one destructive thrust to wreck a consistent and large body of jurisprudence going back at least three centuries....Great was the injustice to Dred Scott and his family, yet they were at least liberated in the end, and their innocence was made known to the world. Even greater was the injustice done to the South, for the region had fostered a large body of jurisprudence under which Scott and his family were entitled to their freedom. And a Southern judge, acting upon this jurisprudence, did grant Scott and his family their freedom. But the South suffered the infamy for this hideous decision."

aggrandizement. Republicans were especially displeased. The Republican Party had as one of its major planks the prohibition of slavery in the territories. Now, with the *Dred Scott* decision, the Republicans were being told that even if they did achieve electoral success they would not be allowed to put their program into effect. A major plank in their platform, they had just been told, was unconstitutional.

## Lunatic on the loose: Murderer John Brown returns to the scene

It is difficult to exaggerate the significance of John Brown's raid on the federal arsenal at Harpers Ferry, Virginia (now West Virginia), in 1859. Brown, who was almost certainly insane, believed himself to be on a divine mission to destroy the institution of slavery. Four years earlier, he had carried out the bloody Pottawatomie Creek Massacre in Kansas, where mutual antagonism had existed between pro- and anti-slavery factions ever since the highly irregular elections for the territorial legislature in 1855.

Brown and his companions targeted five families—none of whom owned any slaves—who in Brown's view were loyal to the wrong Kansas faction. His methods were terrifying: In each case, he and his followers dragged the man of the house from his bed and butchered him as his family screamed in horror. Following this gruesome episode Brown became a fugitive, only resurfacing in 1859 when he planned a strike against slavery that he hoped would be far more systematic and effective than the murders he had perpetrated in Kansas.

In October 1859, Brown and nineteen followers seized the federal arsenal at Harpers Ferry to foment and equip a massive slave insurrection throughout the South. It was a spectacular failure: Brown and his sup-

### A Book You're Not Supposed to Read

*The Secret Six: John Brown and the Abolitionist Movement* by Otto Scott; New York: Times Books, 1979.

porters found themselves surrounded by hostile local citizens, militiamen, and even U.S. troops commanded by Robert E. Lee. Brown surrendered after ten of his followers had been killed. He and six followers were sentenced to death and hanged.

Not surprisingly, Southerners at this point grew concerned about their safety in the Union. Virginia secessionist Edmund Ruffin, for example, distributed throughout the Southern states some cast-iron pikes that Brown had brought with him, along with a label that read, "Sample of the favors designed for us by our Northern brethren." Despite Lincoln's protestations to the contrary, and a statement in the Republican Party's platform condemning Brown's raid, many Southerners suspected Republican sympathy for Brown.

Historian Stephen Channing showed in his book *Crisis of Fear* (1974) how fears and suspicions regarding Northern intentions and behavior in the wake of John Brown's raid contributed to South Carolina's decision to secede from the Union in 1860. When it was learned that prominent Northerners (the "secret six"), who had to have known of Brown's character, had bankrolled his expedition, some Southerners understandably concluded that they were so hated by the North that the section would hardly regret, and might even welcome, their departure from the Union.

That assumption would soon be put to the test.

## What the Literati Said about John Brown:

"A saint...whose martyrdom...will make the gallows as glorious as the cross."

**Ralph Waldo Emerson**

"Some eighteen hundred years ago Christ was crucified; this morning, perchance, Captain Brown was hung. These are the two ends of a chain which is not without its links. He is not Old Brown any longer; he is an angel of light."

**Henry David Thoreau**

"St. John the Just."

**Louisa May Alcott,** author of *Little Women*

*The exception:*

"Nobody was ever more justly hanged."

**Nathaniel Hawthorne**

## Chapter 6

# THE WAR BETWEEN THE STATES

**B**y the time Abraham Lincoln, the first Republican president, took office in March 1861, seven Southern states had already seceded: South Carolina, Texas, Louisiana, Mississippi, Alabama, Georgia, and Florida. In April, Lincoln sent a ship to reprovision Fort Sumter, a federal fort in Charleston harbor. If South Carolina's secession meant anything, that state could not permit the federal government to maintain a military fort on its soil. So in an act of resistance, Southerners fired the first shot of the war on Fort Sumter. There were no casualties, but Lincoln now proclaimed a rebellion and called on 75,000 militiamen to quash the "rebel" states.

Lincoln's decision to use military force provoked the secession of four more Southern states: Tennessee, Virginia, North Carolina, and Arkansas. The use of force against American states, they believed, was a mad project utterly at variance with traditional American principles. Thus began the "Civil War."

## Was there an American civil war?

Strictly speaking, there never was an American Civil War. A civil war is a conflict in which two or more factions fight for control of a nation's government. The English Civil War of the 1640s and the Spanish Civil War

## Guess what?

★ States had the right to secede.

★ The War Between the States was not launched to free the slaves.

★ Lincoln believed that whites were superior, and favored the deportation of freed slaves.

★ The South was for free trade; the North wanted protectionism.

★ With the exception of the United States, every nation in the Western hemisphere where slavery existed in the nineteenth century abolished it peacefully.

61

## What the Founders Said

"[We should be] determined...to sever ourselves from the union we so much value rather than give up the rights of self-government...in which alone we see liberty, safety and happiness."

**Thomas Jefferson**
to James Madison

of the 1930s are two classic examples; in both cases, two factions sought to control the government. That was not the case in the United States between 1861 and 1865. The seceding Southern states were not trying to take over the United States government; they wanted to declare themselves independent.

What is sometimes suggested in place of Civil War is "War Between the States," the term used in this book. This term, too, is not quite accurate, since the conflict was not really fought between the states—i.e., Florida was not at war with New Hampshire, nor Rhode Island with Mississippi—but between the United States government and the eleven Southern states that formed the Confederate States of America in 1861. Other, more ideologically charged (but nevertheless much more accurate) names for the conflict include the War for Southern Independence and even the War of Northern Aggression.

## The states had the right to secede

The question that no textbook bothers to raise is whether the Southern states possessed the legal right to secede. They did. Jefferson Davis, president of the new Confederate States of America, argued that the legal basis for secession could be found in the Tenth Amendment to the Constitution. That amendment had said that any power not delegated to the federal government by the states, and not prohibited to the states by the Constitution, remained a right of the states or the people. The Constitution is silent on the question of secession. And the states never delegated to the federal government any power to suppress secession. Therefore, secession remained a reserved right of the states. This was partly why James Buchanan, Lincoln's predecessor in the White House, had allowed the first seven Southern states to leave in peace. Although he did not believe they possessed a right of secession, he also did not believe that the federal government had the right to coerce a seceding state.

Another argument in support of the right of secession involves the states of Virginia, New York, and Rhode Island. Readers may recall that those states included in a clause in their ratifications of the Constitution that permitted them to withdraw from the Union if the new government should become oppressive. It was on this basis that they acceded to the Union. Virginia cited this provision of its ratification when seceding in 1861. But since the Constitution is also based on the principle of co-equality—all the states are equal in dignity and rights, and no state can have more rights than another—the right of secession cited by these three states must extend equally to all the states.

William Lloyd Garrison, the most prominent abolitionist in America, actually passed a resolution through his American Anti-Slavery Society insisting that it was the duty of each member to work to dissolve the American Union. (It read, "*Resolved*, That the Abolitionists of this country

## What a President Said

"Any people anywhere, being inclined and having the power, have the right to rise up, and shake off the existing government, and form a new one that suits them better. This is a most valuable, a most sacred right—a right which we hope and believe is to liberate the world. Nor is this right confined to cases in which the whole people of an existing government, may choose to exercise it. Any portion of such people that can, may revolutionize, and make their own, of so much territory as they inhabit."

**Abraham Lincoln,** 1848

should make it one of the primary objects of this agitation to dissolve the American Union.") He held this view in part because the North, once separated from the South, would no longer be morally tainted by its association with slavery ("No Union with slaveholders!" he declared), but also because he believed Northern secession would undermine Southern slavery. If the Northern states were a separate country, the North would be under no constitutional obligation to return runaway slaves to their masters. The Northern states would then become a haven for runaway slaves. The enforcement cost of Southern slavery would become prohibitive, and the institution would collapse.

William Rawle, a Philadelphia lawyer of Federalist sympathy and no friend of slavery, conceded in *A View of the Constitution* (1825) that under certain conditions it would be perfectly legal for a state to withdraw from the Union. Rawle's text was used to teach constitutional law at West Point from 1825 through 1840.

## What a Prominent Statesman Said

"The indissoluble link of union between the people of the several states of this confederated nation is, after all, not in the *right* but in the *heart*. If the day should ever come (may Heaven avert it!) when the affections of the people of these States shall be alienated from each other; when the fraternal spirit shall give way to cold indifference, or collision of interests shall fester into hatred, the bands of political associations will not long hold together parties no longer attracted by the magnetism of conciliated interests and kindly sympathies; and far better will it be for the people of the disunited states to part in friendship from each other, than to be held together by constraint."

**John Quincy Adams,** on the occasion of the 50th anniversary of the Constitution

The list of authorities that supported the principle that American states had the legal right to secede is impressive. Taken together, they amount to very serious evidence of the existence of such a right: Thomas Jefferson; John Quincy Adams; William Lloyd Garrison; William Rawle; and Alexis de Tocqueville, the great French observer of American affairs. Add to this that the New England states threatened secession several times in the early nineteenth century, and the result is practically unavoidable: The legitimacy of secession, although not held unanimously, had been taken for granted in all sections of the country for years by the time of the war.

## What a Famous Frenchman Said

The Union "was formed by the voluntary agreement of the states; and these, in uniting together, have not forfeited their nationality, nor have they been reduced to the condition of one and the same people. If one of the states chose to withdraw its name from the contract, it would be difficult to disprove its right to do so."

**Alexis de Tocqueville**

## Was the war fought to free the slaves?

No one who has studied the issue would dispute that for at least the first eighteen months of the war, the abolition of slavery was *not* the issue.

The U.S. Senate declared from the beginning that the purpose of the war was to restore the Union and that there was no other objective. They passed the following resolution on July 26, 1861:

> Resolved, That the present deplorable civil war has been forced upon the country by the disunionists of the southern and northern States, that in this national emergency Congress, banishing all feeling of mere passion or resentment, will recollect only its duty to the whole country; that this war is not prosecuted upon our part in any spirit of oppression, nor for

any purpose of conquest or subjugation, nor purpose of over-throwing or interfering with the rights or established institutions of those States, but to defend and maintain the supremacy of the Constitution and all laws made in pursuance thereof, and to preserve the Union, with all the dignity, equality, and rights of the several States unimpaired; that as soon as these objects are accomplished the war ought to cease.

In 1861, a proposed amendment to the Constitution would have explicitly stated that the federal government had no authority—ever—to interfere with slavery in the states where it existed. Lincoln supported this amendment, saying: "I understand a proposed amendment to the Constitution...has passed Congress, to the effect that the Federal Government shall never interfere with the domestic institutions of the States, including that of persons held to service.... Holding such a provision to now be implied Constitutional law, I have no objection to its being made express and irrevocable."

## Reality check: Lincoln's views on race

With all that has been written about Abraham Lincoln, his racial views should be well known to Americans. But they are not. In his fourth debate with Stephen Douglas in 1858, he declared:

I will say that I am not, nor ever have been, in favor of bringing about in any way the social and political equality of the white and black races, that I am not, nor ever have been, in favor of making voters or jurors of Negroes, nor of qualifying them to hold office, nor to intermarry with white people; and I will say in addition to this that there is a physical difference between the white and black races which I believe will forever forbid the two races from living together on terms of social and political equality. And inasmuch as they can not so live, while they do remain together there must be the position of superior and inferior, and I as much as any other man am in favor of having the superior position assigned to the white race.

Such views are evident throughout Lincoln's political career. While serving in the Illinois legislature Lincoln never challenged the anti-black legislation of his state, voting against black suffrage and refusing to sign a petition allowing black testimony in court. Lincoln was also a strong supporter of colonizing freed blacks, convinced that they could never be assimilated into American society. As president he favored a constitutional amendment authorizing the purchase and deportation of slaves, and he urged the State Department to look into possible areas of settlement in such places as Haiti, Honduras, Liberia (where a U.S. colony for freedmen already existed), Ecuador, and the Amazon.

## Lincoln fought to "save the Union"... and consolidate its power

Lincoln was a creature of his age. This was the decade in which Piedmont would forge Lombardy, Parma, Venetia, and the various Italian states into a single Italy, in which Prussia would unite the various German lands

## What America's Military Leaders Said:

"If I thought this war was to abolish slavery, I would resign my commission and offer my sword to the other side."

**Ulysses S. Grant,** Union general (a slaveholder until the Thirteenth Amendment abolishing slavery was ratified after the war)

(other than Austria and its holdings) into Germany, and in which political centralization was occurring in Japan. Lincoln was drawn to this spirit of nationalism, and, along with Daniel Webster, viewed the Union and the Southern secession through this ideological lens. He told Horace Greeley that if he could save the Union by freeing the slaves he would do so; if he could save the Union by freeing no slave he would do that; and if he could save the Union by freeing some slaves and leaving others in bondage, he would do that too.

## And then there was the practical side. . .

There were other motives as well, as some Northern newspapers admitted. If the South were allowed to secede and establish free trade, foreign commerce would be massively diverted from Northern ports to Southern ones, as merchants sought out the South's low-tariff or free-trade regime. "Let the South adopt the free-trade system," warned the *Daily Chicago Times*, and the North's "commerce must be reduced to less than half what it now is." Ohio congressman Clement Vallandigham believed that the tariff played a crucial role in persuading important sectors of Northern society to support war. As soon as the Confederate Congress adopted a low-tariff system, Vallandigham said, "trade and commerce . . . began to look to the South."

> The city of New York, the great commercial emporium of the Union, and the Northwest, the chief granary of the Union, began to clamor now, loudly, for a repeal of the pernicious and ruinous tariff. Threatened thus with the loss of both political power and wealth, or the repeal of the tariff, and, at last, of both, New England and Pennsylvania . . . demanded, now, coercion and civil war, with all its horrors, as the price of preserving either from destruction. . . . The subjugation of the South, and the closing up of her ports—first, by force, in war, and

afterward, by tariff laws, in peace, was deliberately resolved upon by the East.

Following John Brown's raid, Wendell Phillips's description of the North's Republican Party as a party pledged against the South took on a dangerous and disturbing significance. Some Southerners chose not to wait to see what a president from such a party had in store for them. And certainly some feared that Lincoln, despite his protestations to the contrary, might abolish slavery and thereby set Southern society on a path of social chaos and economic ruin.

But slavery was far from the only issue on Southerners' minds, particularly since the great majority of Southerners did not even own slaves. For their part, Robert E. Lee and Stonewall Jackson, two of the South's best-known generals, described slavery as "a moral and political evil." Lee had even been an opponent of secession, but fought on the side of Virginia rather than stand by as the federal government engaged upon the mad project of waging war against his state. Recall that Virginia, Tennessee, North Carolina, and Arkansas seceded only after Lincoln had called up 75,000 volunteers to invade the South and prevent its secession. These four states, therefore, certainly did not secede over slavery, but rather over Lincoln's decision to use *military force* to suppress Southern independence.

## Why did the soldiers fight? The soldiers speak...

Forget the politicians: What did ordinary soldiers of the North and South have to say about why they took up arms against their neighbors? Acclaimed Civil War historian James McPherson, in his 1997 book *For Cause and Comrades: Why Men Fought in the Civil War*, consulted a sizable quantity of primary sources, including soldiers' diaries and their letters to loved ones, to try to determine how the ordinary soldier on each side thought of the war.

★ ★ ★ ★ ★ ★ ★ ★ ★ ★

# The Cherokees support the Confederacy

**The so-called Five Civilized Tribes**—the Cherokees, Choctaws, Chickasaws, Creeks, and Seminoles—sided with the Confederacy. On October 28, 1861, the Cherokee Nation issued the *Declaration by the People of the Cherokee Nation of the Causes Which Have Impelled them to Unite Their Fortunes With Those of the Confederate States of America*, from which the selections below are taken. The Confederacy was delighted to have the Indians' support, and even promised them their own state, not a mere federal reservation.

**D**isclaiming any intention to invade the Northern States, they [Southerners] sought only to repel the invaders from their own soil and to secure the right of governing themselves. They claimed only the privilege asserted in the Declaration of American Independence, and on which the right of Northern States themselves to self-government is formed, and altering their form of government when it became no longer tolerable and establishing new forms for the security of their liberties....

But in the Northern States the Cherokee people saw with alarm a violated Constitution, all civil liberty put in peril, and all rules of civilized warfare and the dictates of common humanity and decency unhesitatingly disregarded. In the states which still adhered to the Union a military despotism had displaced civilian power and the laws became silent with arms. Free speech and almost free thought became a crime. The right of habeas corpus, guaranteed by the Constitution, disappeared at the nod of a secretary of state or a general of the lowest grade. The mandate of the chief justice of the Supreme Court [who had declared that the president had no right to suspend habeas corpus] was set at naught by the military power and this outrage on common right approved by a President sworn to support the Constitution. War on the largest scale was waged, and the immense bodies of troops called into the

> field in the absence of any warranting it under the pretense of suppressing unlawful combination of men....
>
> Whatever causes the Cherokee people may have had in the past to complain of some of the Southern States, they cannot but feel that their interests and destiny are inseparably connected to those of the South. The war now waging is a war of Northern cupidity and fanaticism against the institution of African servitude; against the commercial freedom of the South, and against the political freedom of the states, and its objects are to annihilate the sovereignty of those states and utterly change the nature of the general government.

In two-thirds of his sources—the same proportion among Northern and Southern fighting men—soldiers said it was due to patriotism. Northern soldiers by and large said they were fighting to preserve what their ancestors had bequeathed to them: the Union. Southern soldiers also referred to their ancestors, but they typically argued that the real legacy of the Founding Fathers was not so much the Union as the principle of self-government. Very often we see Southern soldiers comparing the South's struggle against the U.S. government to the colonies' struggle against Britain. Both, in their view, were wars of secession fought in order to preserve self-government.

## The rise of total war

F.J.P. Veale, in his classic study of the development of total warfare, described the American War Between the States as a historical watershed in that it broke deliberately and dramatically from the European code of warfare that had developed since the seventeenth century and that had forbidden targeting the civilian population. Although there were exceptions, says Veale, "[Robert E.] Lee was able to keep the Southern strategy in harmony with the European code." The same could not be said for Lincoln's forces.

Among the most notorious examples of assaults on civilians occurred in New Orleans, where General Benjamin Butler led the occupying Northern soldiers. The women of New Orleans did not respond well to his crude and coarse manner, and to the sexual advances by the soldiers. Enraged, Butler issued Order Number 28:

> As the officers and soldiers of the United States have been subject to repeated insults from the women calling themselves "ladies" of New Orleans in return for the most scrupulous non-interference and courtesy on our part, it is ordered that hereafter when any female shall by word, gesture or movement insult or show contempt for any officer or soldier of the United States she shall be regarded and held liable to be treated as a woman of the town plying her avocation.

In other words, Southern women were to be thought of as prostitutes. This "right to rape" order horrified the civilized states of Europe, and immediate protests were issued from Britain and France. The British prime minister declared, "I will venture to say that no example can be found in the history of civilized nations till the publication of this order of a general guilty in cold blood of so infamous an act as deliberately to hand over the female inhabitants of a conquered city to the unbridled license of an unrestrained soldiery."

The crimes of General William Sherman alone would involve a great many pages. In Vicksburg, Mississippi, Sherman's troops destroyed houses and stripped farmland of all crops. "The city was so heavily bombed," writes Thomas DiLorenzo, "that the residents had to resort to living in caves and eating rats, dogs, and mules." Similar tactics were followed in Jackson, which was bombarded relentlessly. The soldiers robbed and then destroyed homes. "The inhabitants are subjugated," Sherman observed. "They cry aloud for mercy. The land is devastated for thirty miles around." Describing what his men had done to Meridian, Mississippi, where no Confederate army presence existed at the time, Sherman wrote, "For five days, 10,000 of our men worked hard and with a will, in that work of destruction, with axes, sledges, crowbars, clawbars, and with fire, and I have no hesitation in pronouncing the work well done." Meridian, he said, "no longer exists."

And this is not to mention Sherman's better known atrocities, particularly in Georgia.

Now for many people today, this conception of war has grown so familiar, perhaps even crudely sensible, that it is difficult to conceive of the conduct of war in any other way. That only goes to show the extent of our moral captivity to twentieth-century ideas. This behavior was not considered normal or morally acceptable in the nineteenth century. Sherman himself put it best when he admitted that according to what he had been taught at West Point, he deserved to be executed for war crimes.

**What a Southern Soldier Said**

"Times may grow a great deal worse than they now are, and still we can stand it— And even then not go through what our Grandparents went through, when they were struggling for the same thing that we are now fighting for."

**What a Northern Soldier Said**

"We are fighting for the Union, a high and noble sentiment, but after all a sentiment. They are fighting for independence and are animated by passion and hatred against invaders."

What happened in the United States was a national tragedy. No one, of course, mourns the passing of the slave system. But consider Brazil's experience. Slavery collapsed in Brazil after being abolished in the Brazilian state of Ceará in 1884. Slaves escaped to Ceará, and a fugitive slave law that was hastily passed was largely ignored. The value of slaves fell dramatically, and within four years the

Brazilian government had acknowledged the reality of the situation by enacting immediate and uncompensated emancipation. This is exactly why abolitionist William Lloyd Garrison favored the secession of the North: to lure slaves away from the South and make the slave system untenable.

But those who can see nothing more than slavery at stake in this contest miss the insight of men like British libertarian Lord Acton, who saw in this victory for centralization a terrible defeat for the values of civilized life in the West. In a November 1866 letter to Robert E. Lee, Lord Acton wrote:

> I saw in States' rights the only availing check upon the absolutism of the sovereign will, and secession filled me with hope, not as the destruction but as the redemption of Democracy. The institutions of your Republic have not exercised on the old world the salutary and liberating influence which ought to have belonged to them, by reason of those defects and abuses of principle which the Confederate Constitution was expressly and wisely calculated to remedy. I believed that the example of that great Reform would have blessed all the races of mankind by establishing true freedom purged of the native dangers and disorders of Republics. Therefore I deemed that you were fighting the battles of our liberty, our progress, and our civilization, and I mourn for the stake which was lost at Richmond more deeply than I rejoice over that which was saved at Waterloo.

## A Quotation the Textbooks Leave Out

"The Gettysburg speech was at once the shortest and the most famous oration in American history…the highest emotion reduced to a few poetical phrases. Lincoln himself never even remotely approached it. It is genuinely stupendous. But let us not forget that it is poetry, not logic; beauty, not sense. Think of the argument in it. Put it into the cold words of everyday. The doctrine is simply this: that the Union soldiers who died at Gettysburg sacrificed their lives to the cause of self-determination—that government of the people, by the people, for the people, should not perish from the earth. It is difficult to imagine anything more untrue. The Union soldiers in the battle actually fought against self-determination; it was the Confederates who fought for the right of their people to govern themselves."

**H.L. Mencken** on the Gettysburg Address

★ ★ ★ ★ ★ ★ ★ ★ ★ ★

## Chapter 7

# RECONSTRUCTION

With the war over in 1865, what would be the federal government's policy toward the defeated Southern states? The Constitution had made no provision for anything like what the country faced. It was even a matter of debate whether the power to restore the Southern states rested with the president or with Congress.

## Lincoln, Johnson, and presidential Reconstruction

While the war was still going on, Lincoln was already thinking ahead to the restoration of the Southern states. (The terminology is important: Lincoln would not have spoken of the *readmission* of the Southern states, since he believed the Union to be perpetual and indestructible, and secession therefore a metaphysical impossibility. The Southern states may think they seceded, but in Lincoln's mind they never left at all; they had merely rebelled against the federal government.)

Lincoln's Reconstruction plan was relatively lenient. He granted amnesty to those who took an oath of loyalty to the Union and promised to abide by federal slavery laws. High Confederate officials would need presidential pardons to enjoy their political rights once again. Once 10 percent of a state's qualified voters took an oath of loyalty to the Union, that state could establish a government and send representatives to Congress.

Andrew Johnson, who became president following Lincoln's assassination in April 1865, pursued a roughly similar approach, though he added to the list of people requiring presidential pardons anyone who possessed wealth in excess of $20,000. This provision was intended to punish the planter class, which Johnson considered responsible for having persuaded Southerners to support secession. Although he favored the gradual introduction of black suffrage, like Lincoln, he did not insist upon it as an immediate requirement.

### Enter the Radical Republicans

These policies were not severe enough for the Radical Republicans, a faction of the Republican Party that favored a stricter Reconstruction policy. They insisted on a dramatic expansion of the power of the federal government over the states as well as guarantees of black suffrage. The Radicals *did* consider the Southern states out of the Union. Massachusetts senator Charles Sumner spoke of the former Confederate states as having "committed suicide." Congressman Thaddeus Stevens of Pennsylvania went further, describing the seceded states as "conquered provinces." Such a mentality would go a long way in justifying the Radicals' disregard of the rule of law in their treatment of these states.

President Johnson's Reconstruction plan had been proceeding well by the time Congress convened in late 1865. But Congress refused to seat the representatives from the Southern states even though they had organized governments according to the terms of Lincoln's or Johnson's plan. Although Congress had the right to judge the qualifications of its members, this was a sweeping rejection of an entire class of representatives rather than the case-by-case evaluation assumed by the Constitution. When Tennessee's Horace Maynard, who had never been anything but scrupulously loyal to the Union, was not seated, it was clear that no Southern representative would be.

## Were the Radical Republicans just in it for themselves?

A great many contemporary observers believed that the real purpose behind Radical Reconstruction was to secure the domination of the Republican Party in national political life through the newly freed population in the South. The Republicans took for granted that the freed slaves would vote Republican. Connecticut senator James Dixon, for example, argued that "the purpose of the radicals" was "the saving of the Republican Party rather than the restoration of the Union." This was also the view of General Sherman, who was convinced that "the whole idea of giving votes to the negroes" was "to create just that many votes to be used by others for political uses." He expressed his displeasure with a plan "whereby politicians may manufacture just so much more pliable electioneering material." And indeed, Radical Republican Thaddeus Stevens conceded that the votes of the freed slaves were necessary in order to bring about "perpetual ascendancy to the Party of the Union"—that is, the Republican Party.

Henry Ward Beecher, too, was concerned about the Radicals. Beecher, the brother of Harriet Beecher Stowe (author of *Uncle Tom's Cabin*), had been a fierce opponent of slavery, and had helped to arm opponents of slavery in Kansas. Yet even he warned his countrymen of the party spirit that animated the Radicals:

> It is said that, if admitted to Congress, the Southern Senators and Representatives will coalesce with Northern democrats and rule the country. Is this nation, then, to remain dismembered, to serve the ends of parties? Have we learned no wisdom by the history of the past ten years, in which just this course of sacrificing the nation to the exigencies of parties plunged us into rebellion and war?

Otto Scott, a twentieth-century Northern writer, observed that Radical vindictiveness following the war, including the Radical insistence that the South was out of the Union and not entitled to congressional representation, strongly suggested that the North's motives in going to war had not been so pure after all: "To win that war, and then to refuse to allow the South to remain in the Union was not only logically perverse, but a tacit admission that the war had not been about slavery, but—as in all and every war—power."

In 1866 President Johnson vetoed the Freedmen's Bureau Bill and the Civil Rights Act of 1866. His veto messages contained detailed critiques of what he considered the constitutionally dubious aspects of the legislation. As Ludwell Johnson explains, "The Freedmen's Bureau and Civil Rights bills proposed to establish for an indefinite time an extensive, extra-constitutional system of police and judicature with the opportunity, as Johnson correctly pointed out, for enormous abuses of power." Moreover, Johnson considered it neither fair nor wise to proceed on matters of such gravity while eleven states were still deprived of their representation in Congress.

## The South's black codes

Such legislation was said to be necessary on account of the "black codes" that had been imposed in some Southern states. These codes curtailed black liberty in various degrees and the Radicals described them as a continuation of slavery. But the codes were essentially based on Northern vagrancy laws and other restrictive legislation that was still on the books when the Reconstruction Acts were drawn up. Historian Robert Selph Henry contends that "there was hardly a feature of the apprenticeship and vagrancy acts of Mississippi, and of the other Southern states, which was not substantially duplicated in some of these Northern laws, while many of the Northern provisions were more harsh in their terms than anything proposed in the South."

In the northeast, as well as in Indiana and Wisconsin, the vagrancy laws were as broad as anything in the South, with more severe punishments for violating them. "[O]ne without employment wandering abroad, begging, and 'not giving a good account of himself,' might be imprisoned as a vagrant, for periods varying from ninety days to three years, in various Northern states."

Two modern scholars, H. A. Scott Trask and Carey Roberts, contend that the black codes have been misunderstood in their intent and exaggerated in their impact:

> Most granted, or recognized, important legal rights for the freedmen, such as the right to hold property, to marry, to make contracts, to sue, and to testify in court. Many mandated penalties for vagrancy, but the intention there was not to bind them to the land in a state of perpetual serfdom, as was charged by Northern Radicals, but to end what had become an intolerable situation—the wandering across the South of large numbers of freedmen who were without food, money, jobs, or homes. Such a situation was leading to crime, fear, and violence.

The sense of moral righteousness that dominated fashionable Northern opinion often blinded Northerners to their own problems. The *Chicago Tribune* protested the black codes of Mississippi without for a moment reflecting on the laws of its own state. In Illinois, any free black in the state who could not produce a certificate of freedom and who had not posted a bond of one thousand dollars was subject to arrest and to be hired out as a laborer for a year. Illinois continued to forbid the testimony of blacks in cases involving whites. And it was only in 1865 that the state had repealed the law imposing a fine of fifty dollars upon free blacks entering Illinois. (Blacks unable to pay had their labor sold to whoever paid the fine for them and demanded the shortest period of labor.)

### Southern states begin protecting blacks' rights

By early 1866 most Southern states had enacted statutes protecting blacks' right to hold property, to have recourse to the courts, and to testify in all cases in which at least one party was black. Voices could be found throughout the Southern states calling for the liberalization of state policy toward blacks—even in Mississippi, whose code was the most stringent. The Columbus *Sentinel* described the architects of the restrictive code as a "shallow-headed majority more anxious to make capital at home than to propitiate the powers at Washington.... They are as complete a set of political Goths as were ever turned loose to work destruction upon a State. The fortunes of the whole South have been injured by their folly." Other state papers took a similar view, including the Jackson *Clarion* and the Vicksburg *Herald*.

Even though Union generals Grant and Sherman declared the South loyal and deserving of prompt readmission to the Union, some still claimed that the South was not completely loyal. One of Thaddeus Stevens's friends professed shock that "while they acknowledge themselves whipped and profess future loyalty...Confederate Generals are their heroes—Confederate bravery, and endurance under difficulties, their pride and boast—Confederate dead their martyrs.... In all the stores of Richmond...I did not see the picture of a single Union general or politician, but any number of Rebels." Yet President Johnson, who had never sympathized with secession and had always been a Union man, nevertheless understood why a defeated people would have honored its heroes. "A people should be allowed to grumble who have suffered so much," said Johnson, "and they would be unworthy of the name of men if they did not respect the brave officers who have suffered with them, and honor the memory of their gallant dead who sleep on a hundred battle fields around their homes." Such remarks, of course, only further alienated Johnson from the Radicals.

## The Fourteenth Amendment and states' rights

Perhaps the most glaring example of the contempt for the rule of law that characterized Reconstruction involves the passage and ratification of the Fourteenth Amendment to the Constitution. The Radicals realized that the Civil Rights Act of 1866 could be legally challenged, so they sought to incorporate its provisions into a constitutional amendment. The amendment's most significant section was its first:

> All persons born or naturalized in the United States, and subject to the jurisdiction thereof, are citizens of the United States and of the State wherein they reside. No State shall make or enforce any law which shall abridge the privileges or immunities of citizens of the United States; nor shall any State deprive any person of life, liberty, or property, without due process of law; nor deny to any person within its jurisdiction the equal protection of the laws.

The first sentence extended American citizenship to all persons born in America and subject to its jurisdiction, reversing the *Dred Scott* decision that had declared blacks not American citizens. As for the remainder of the first section, controversy still exists with regard to its "original intent." Harvard's Raoul Berger devoted much of his career to proving that the amendment was modest in scope, intended simply to empower the federal government to ensure that the states did not interfere with the basic rights of the freedmen—the right to enter contracts, to sue, and to own property. Likewise, James E. Bond showed in the *Akron Law Review* in 1985 that according to supporters of the amendment, the "indispensable" civil rights that it protected were "the right to contract, to sue, to testify, and otherwise resort to the courts; to hold and transfer property; and to the full and equal benefit of all laws for the protection of person and property." The Radicals had hoped for something more sweeping, but this is what they got.

### Why would anyone oppose it?

Even with this relatively modest purpose, however, some Southerners believed that granting such powers of oversight to the federal government would tend over time to undermine America's federal system, and that the amendment would be only the beginning of a process that

★★★★★★★★★★

## Fourteenth Amendment Horror Show #1

An entire book needs to be written about the ways in which the Fourteenth Amendment has unjustly encroached upon the self-governing rights of the states. Here we can consider a few.

**I**n 1994 California passed a ballot initiative, Proposition 187, which would have denied "free" (that is, taxpayer-funded) social services to illegal aliens. Californians, under the delusion that they had the right to govern themselves, defied fashionable opinion—liberal and "conservative" alike—in passing the initiative. But they found out who really governed them when the federal courts prevented the implementation of 187, in the name of the Fourteenth Amendment. What does forcing a state to bankrupt itself by giving away "free" services to people who are in the country illegally have to do with the Fourteenth Amendment? Who knows. But this is why many people opposed it in the first place: Language in the amendment that meant something specific and finite when taken in its proper context became a recipe for federal domination of the states when torn from that context.

would ultimately emasculate states' rights. This concern was by no means unfounded; even some Northerners feared that Reconstruction was headed down this path. Orville Browning, Johnson's secretary of the interior, who had made his political career in Illinois, warned: "One of the greatest perils which threatens us now is the tendency to centralization, the absorption of the rights of the States, and the concentration of all power in the General Government. When that shall be accomplished, if ever, the days of the Republic are numbered."

Section 2 of the Amendment pertained to black suffrage, and was soon superseded by the Fifteenth Amendment in 1870. Section 4 repudiated the Confederate debt. Section 3 excluded from American politics anyone who had held any office in the Confederacy. Thus the natural leadership class of the South would be disqualified from office and disgraced

## What a Famous American Said

"The federal government is unfit to exercise minor police and local government, and will inevitably blunder when it attempts it....To oblige the central authority to govern half the territory of the Union by federal civil officers and by the army, is a policy not only uncongenial to our ideas and principles, but pre-eminently dangerous to the spirit of our government. However humane the ends sought and the motive, it is, in fact, a course of instruction preparing our government to be despotic and familiarizing the people to a stretch of authority which can never be other than dangerous to liberty."

**Henry Ward Beecher**
(brother of Harriet Beecher Stowe)

forever by having been dishonored in a constitutional amendment. This section alone, some observers believed, practically guaranteed that the South would reject the amendment. A New York gubernatorial candidate told a Northern audience, "This radical Congress knew as well as you know that there is no people on the face of the earth who would ever consent to a constitutional amendment which would proscribe their own brothers, fathers and friends—the men with whom they had labored and suffered."

### Ratify—or else! Was the Fourteenth Amendment really ratified?

The first time the Fourteenth Amendment was presented for their consideration, ten of the eleven states of the former Confederacy (the exception being Tennessee) failed to ratify it, for the reasons mentioned above, among others. For the Radical Republicans, this was really the last straw. Flush with victory in the 1866 congressional elections, the Radicals decided that the South should be punished. As Wisconsin's senator James Doolittle put it, "The people of the South have rejected the constitutional amendment and therefore we will march upon them and force them to adopt it at the point of the bayonet" and rule them with military governors and martial law "until they do adopt it." It was through coercion, then, that the Republicans determined to bring about the amendment's ratification.

In 1867 Congress passed a series of Reconstruction Acts over Johnson's vetoes. They declared that with the exception of Tennessee, no legal governments existed in any of the former Confederate states. The ten recalcitrant states would be divided into five military districts and ruled by military governors and martial law. For those states to take their places in the Union and gain representation in Congress once again, they would have to do the following:

* Elect delegates to state constitutional conventions to draw up new state constitutions.
* In those new constitutions, acknowledge the abolition of slavery, the unlawfulness of secession, and the introduction of black suffrage.
* Ratify the Fourteenth Amendment.

The president condemned the Reconstruction legislation. According to Johnson it was "in its whole character, scope, and object without precedent and without authority, in palpable conflict with the plainest provisions of the Constitution, and utterly destructive to those great principles of liberty and humanity for which our ancestors on both sides of the Atlantic have shed so much blood and expended so much treasure." Johnson argued that Radical Reconstruction showed such contempt for law and precedent that it proved the Southern secessionists' point at the time they withdrew from the Union: that their constitutional liberties would not be secure under the administration elected in 1860. He said:

> Those who advocated the right of secession alleged in their own justification that we had no regard for law and that the rights of property, life, and liberty would not be safe under the Constitution as administered by us. If we now verify their assertion, we prove that they were in truth fighting for their liberty, and instead of branding their leaders as traitors against a righteous and legal government, we elevate them in history to the rank of self-sacrificing patriots, consecrate them to the admiration of the world, and place them by the side of Washington, Hampden, and Sidney.

In his third annual message to the Union, Johnson went so far as to argue that Radical policy had destroyed the Union that the Framers established:

> Candor compels me to declare that at this time there is no Union as our fathers understood the term, and as they meant it to be understood by us. The Union which they established can exist only where all the States are represented in both Houses of Congress; where one state is as free as another to regulate its internal concerns according to its own will, and where the laws of the central Government, strictly confined to matters of national jurisdiction, apply with equal force to the people of every section.

The Republican approach was not only unconstitutional, but it was also contradictory. In 1865 Congress had accepted the Southern states' ratification of the Thirteenth Amendment, abolishing slavery. But in 1867, even though the Southern states had not changed in the interim, they were suddenly declared illegal when they dared to reject the Fourteenth Amendment. Simple consistency would require Congress to accept both decisions by the Southern states (that is, the decision to ratify the Thirteenth Amendment and the decision to reject the Fourteenth) or to reject both decisions. But consistency was not a conspicuous virtue of Reconstruction.

Moreover, there is clear evidence that the Fourteenth Amendment was unlawfully ratified. On the one hand, Congress declared ten of the eleven former Confederate states to be without legal governments, and therefore not entitled to representation. On the other, Congress demanded that these states, which were not entitled to the privileges of statehood (including the right to send representatives and senators to Washington), ratify an amendment to the Constitution in order to resume their proper place in the Union. If a state truly lacks a legal government, it would indeed be prohibited from enjoying representation in the U.S. Congress—but, logically, *it would also be excluded from the process of amending the Constitution.*

The Southern states eventually ratified the Fourteenth Amendment, but the ratification process was strewn with irregularities. In Tennessee, which had avoided Radical Reconstruction by ratifying the amendment the first time, opponents refused to be present for the vote so that a quorum would be prevented and ratification impossible. To overcome this difficulty, amendment supporters seized two Tennessee legislators and held them in an anteroom as the vote proceeded. In vain did the speaker attempt to proclaim the two men officially absent (they refused to answer the roll). The vote in favor of the amendment went ahead anyway.

Then there were the irregularities in Oregon. There the vote was taken on the amendment at a time when two Republicans' seats in the legisla-

★★★★★★★★★★

## Fourteenth Amendment Horror Show #2

**Thanks to California's** relatively high welfare payments, the Golden State attracts a large number of people who want to collect welfare. This has resulted in serious and persistent economic difficulties for the state. To cope with the strain, California adopted a policy in which new settlers, for the first year of their residence in California, were limited in the welfare benefits they could receive to what they would have had in their state of origin. In *Saenz v. Roe* (1999), however, the Supreme Court found—surprise!— that California's law violated the Fourteenth Amendment. This time it was the "privileges or immunities" clause that was cited. California, by limiting the amount of welfare money it paid out to settlers in the first year, apparently violated the "right to travel." By forcing California to increase its welfare payments to new residents, the Court had in effect raised taxes on Californians without their consent. (Wasn't there a revolution fought over that somewhere?)

ture were being challenged on legal grounds. The two Republicans provided the thin margin by which the amendment passed. But they were eventually removed from the legislature in that same session when it was determined that they had been illegally elected. Their seats were given to Democrats. Not surprisingly, the legislature voted to rescind its ratification of the amendment. But this was not allowed to stand, and Oregon was counted as having ratified the amendment.

Oregon was not alone in its decision to rescind; New Jersey, too, changed its mind as it observed Radical Republican behavior. The New Jersey state resolution warned that the amendment had been "made vague for the purpose of facilitating encroachment on the lives, liberties, and property of the people." New Jersey's rescission was not allowed to stand either.

A great many other procedural irregularities could be cited with regard to the ratification of the Fourteenth Amendment. The point, however, is clear. As Professor Forrest McDonald, a Jefferson Lecturer of the National Endowment for the Humanities, declared in his own study of the matter: "[T]he Fourteenth Amendment was never constitutionally ratified."

## The first impeachment of a president

In 1867 Congress passed the Tenure of Office Act, and again overrode a presidential veto. The act forbade the president to remove any civil official, including Cabinet members, without the consent of the Senate. It clearly had in mind secretary of war Edwin Stanton, a holdover from Lincoln's Cabinet who was in danger of being fired by Johnson. Stanton was a Radical Republican and functioned as a White House mole for his Radical allies. He even used the War Department's telegraph line to censor messages intended for or sent by the president. Thus the Tenure of Office Act was a brilliant Radical stroke: If Johnson abided by it, Stanton was safe; if he defied it, he could be impeached.

Johnson did in fact dismiss Stanton. That may seem foolish; did he not see that the Radicals were trying to trap him into doing just that, in order to devise grounds on which to impeach him? Johnson, however, was convinced that he would be vindicated when the constitutionality of the act was reviewed by the Supreme Court. And there was good reason to believe that he would prevail. In a congressional debate on the matter in June 1789, James Madison had made the argument that the power to remove a Cabinet official rested exclusively with the president, and that it would be unconstitutional for Congress to attempt to interfere with this power. Years later, the Supreme Court finally did vindicate Johnson when Chief Justice William Howard Taft declared in *Myers v. United States* (1926) that "the Tenure of Office Act of 1867, in so far as it attempted to prevent the President from removing executive officers who had been appointed by him and with the advice and consent of the Senate, was invalid." Such vindication came rather too late.

The Radicals believed they had grounds for impeachment in Johnson's violation of the constitutionally dubious Tenure of Office Act. Although they were strong enough by 1867 to override Johnson's vetoes consistently, they had come to detest him, and moreover they feared that as the head of the executive branch, which was charged with the responsibility of enforcing the law, Johnson might be lax in enforcing reconstruction legislation that he did not support. They promptly impeached him in the House, but the vote to remove him from office fell one short of the necessary two-thirds. But Johnson had been gravely weakened by the proceedings and by the stigma of being the first president ever to be impeached.

### Did Americans support the Radical Republicans?

Some readers may wonder if the American people supported all of this radicalism. They had, after all, handed the Radicals a substantial off-year victory in 1866. Howard Beale, in his 400-page study of that election,

★★★★★★★★★★

## Fourteenth Amendment Horror Show #3

**As legal scholar Gene Healy** points out, the case of *U.S. v. Yonkers* (1986) gives still more indication of where the Fourteenth Amendment can lead: Judge Leonard Sand declared the city of Yonkers, New York, guilty of "discrimination" in housing and education, and, usurping the power of the legislature, ordered hundreds of units of public housing to be built. He then imposed a fine for noncompliance that would have driven Yonkers to bankruptcy in just over three weeks.

wrote that such a conclusion would not be justified. There were, as Beale explains, many issues at stake in the 1866 election.

For Northerners, the key issues were economic. Having benefited from high tariffs, many Northerners were not eager to readmit to Congress Southern representatives who would favor lower tariffs. Ex-New York governor Horatio Seymour declared, "This question of tariffs and taxation, and not the negro question, keeps our country divided.... The men of New York were called upon to keep out the Southern members, because if they were admitted they would vote to uphold [i.e., hold up or obstruct] our commercial greatness."

Likewise, the Radicals had spread the idea that if Johnson's lenient Reconstruction plan were allowed to stand, disloyal Southern congressmen would vote to repudiate the federal debt—leaving U.S. bondholders with only worthless paper—and may even vote to honor the Confederate debt. That there was not the slightest prospect that such a thing would happen did nothing to prevent Radicals from using it to scare voters. Beale concludes from his study of the 1866 campaign "that the Radicals forced their program upon the South by an evasion of issues and the clever use of propaganda in an election where a majority of the voters would have supported Johnson's policy had they been given a chance to express their preference on an issue squarely faced."

In short, Reconstruction was very far from the cartoonish battle of good, noble Northerners against wicked, unrepentant Southerners that historians of the past several decades have suggested. It was neither as straightforward nor as morally unambiguous as such a simplistic view suggests. The troops were withdrawn from all the Southern states by 1877, and to that extent Reconstruction came to an end. But its legacy of federal supremacy over the states would live on, and come to dramatic fruition in the twentieth century.

**Chapter 8**

# HOW BIG BUSINESS MADE AMERICANS BETTER OFF

**N**istory textbooks love to highlight the villainous American businessmen who have "exploited" workers, taken advantage of the public, and wielded so much power. Government officials, on the other hand, are portrayed as benevolent, self-sacrificing crusaders for justice, without whom Americans would be working eighty-hour weeks and buying shoddy goods at exorbitant prices. This is what every student believes as he leaves high school (or college, for that matter), and it's hard to blame him. This kind of thing has been taught, day after day, for years.

We can speculate as to why secondary-school teachers and textbook authors are so eager to draw such a picture of American history; Ludwig von Mises came up with a lot of possible reasons in his short book *The Anti-Capitalist Mentality*. But regardless of how many times it has been repeated and how many otherwise sensible people have fallen for it, this little morality play is completely at odds with reality.

At the same time, we should be careful not to romanticize businessmen; they have moral foibles too. At times big business has entered into cozy relationships with government that helped it to take advantage of the public. Such arrangements are deplorable, of course, but they only prove the point: It is only with government help—in the form of subsidies, restrictions on potential rivals, and the like—that business can

## Guess what?

★ It's a myth that "predatory pricing" exploited American consumers and created business monopolies.

★ Thanks to government subsidies, many of America's railroads were often laid on inefficient, circuitous routes.

★ Rockefeller, Carnegie, Dow, and other great American businessmen did more for America than all the big-government programs combined.

"exploit" the public in any meaningful sense. That is why Professor Burton Folsom, in his study of some of the titans of American business, distinguishes between what he calls "market entrepreneurs," who grew wealthy because they improved people's standard of living and supplied them with goods more inexpensively than their competitors, and "political entrepreneurs," who amassed their fortunes thanks to various grants of government privilege.

## How government promoted waste and corruption in railroad construction

The transcontinental railroads in the latter half of the nineteenth century were typically built with substantial infusions of federal, state, and local government aid. This aid took two forms: loans and land grants. The railroads sold the land to settlers for cash. In the process, they also created a market for their services. Those who lived near their railroad now had livelihoods that hinged on the railroad's success, usually because they needed it to ship their freight.

The Pacific Railway Act of 1862 called for the laying of track by the Union Pacific (UP) and the Central Pacific (CP), the former going west from Omaha and the latter going east from Sacramento. The two roads would eventually link.

The project had more than its share of problems. The government subsidies introduced perverse incentives, all chronicled by Professor Folsom. Since the railroad companies received land and loans in proportion to the amount of track they laid, management had an incentive to lay track rapidly in order to collect as much federal aid as possible. There was much less emphasis on the quality of track laid or on following the shortest possible route than there would have been in the absence of these government handouts. To the contrary, circuitous routes meant more track laid and therefore more federal aid. Moreover, since low-

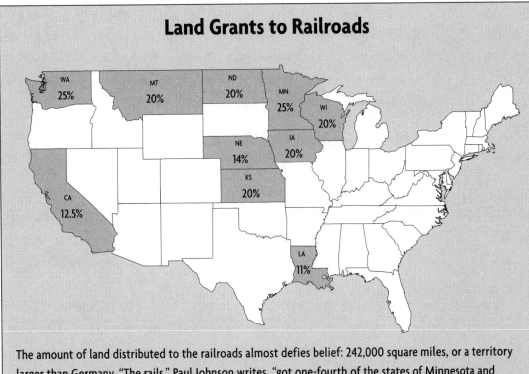

## Land Grants to Railroads

The amount of land distributed to the railroads almost defies belief: 242,000 square miles, or a territory larger than Germany. "The rails," Paul Johnson writes, "got one-fourth of the states of Minnesota and Washington, one-fifth of Wisconsin, Iowa, Kansas, North Dakota, and Montana, one-seventh of Nebraska, one-eighth of California, and one-ninth of Louisiana."

interest loans were granted in higher amounts for more mountainous terrain, the railroad companies had greater incentive to lay track over less suitable land than if they had had to lay track with their own resources.

As the two tracks approached each other in Utah in 1869, more serious troubles began. Seeing the end of subsidies looming, the two lines built track parallel to each other instead of joining, and both lines applied for subsidies on the basis of the parallel track. Worse, physical destruction and even death resulted when the mainly Irish UP workers clashed with mainly Chinese CP workers. The celebrations that took place on May 10, 1869, when the two lines finally met, obscured the often shoddy workmanship that government grants had inadvertently encouraged, and it was not until several years later that all the necessary repairs and rerouting were completed. Looking back on the construction process, UP chief engineer Grenville Dodge remarked, "I never saw so much needless waste in building railroads. Our own construction department has been inefficient."

### Did anyone prosper without government freebies?

Many people have supposed that the railroads could never have been built without government largesse. But this is untrue. For one thing, the entire English railway system was built with private funds. Second, the history of the Great Northern Railroad provides an outstanding example of a businessman who prospered without any government help: railroad magnate James J. Hill.

Hill was the entrepreneurial genius behind the Great Northern, which stretched from St. Paul to Seattle—the same market in which Henry Villard, equipped with the help of the federal government, would fail with his Northern Pacific railroad. Hill, who came from a very modest background, eventually joined a group of friends in purchasing the bankrupt line.

Hill prospered. When most of the transcontinentals went bankrupt in the economic downturn of 1893, Hill both reduced his rates and turned a sizable profit. He went on to build steamships to carry American products to markets in Asia. It was a tremendous success at first, until it ran into the stupidity and destructiveness of the Hepburn Act of 1906, which regulated rail rates and gave teeth to the Interstate Commerce Commission.

## How "fairness" crippled American farmers

American textbooks are unanimous in praising the Hepburn Act; the only occasional criticism is that it didn't go far enough. Among other things, the act enforced an older requirement that railroads charge the same rates to all shippers. No problem, right? "It's only fair!" says your high school teacher.

Well, here's at least one problem. In order to open Chinese and Japanese markets for American products like cotton and wheat, Hill had offered discounts for freight intended for export to Asia that was being shipped along the Great Northern. According to the Hepburn Act, Hill had to offer these discounts to all shippers or not offer them at all. Since it was not economically possible to offer discounts to everyone, he was forced to stop them altogether. As a result, American exports to Japan and China were substantially reduced in the wake of the act. Thus the regulation of rail rates, undertaken in the name of helping the common man, ended up sharply curtailing American agricultural sales in Asia—not exactly a recipe for helping American farmers. This is the kind of bumbling that should be recalled whenever a history text tries to speak of the wisdom of government bureaucrats.

### The myth of "predatory pricing"

One of the ways big business is said to have enriched itself and exploited the consumer was through "predatory pricing." According to this practice,

## What an Honest Businessman Said

The government "should not furnish capital to [railroad] companies, in addition to their enormous land subsidies, to enable them to conduct their business in competition with enterprises that have received no aid from the public treasury....
Our own line in the North...was built without any government aid, even the right of way, through hundreds of miles of public lands, being paid for in cash."

**James J. Hill** of the Great Northern Railroad

big business can use its economic clout to eliminate competition by offering goods at exceptionally low prices. They can afford to suffer losses for the time it takes to drive their competition from the field. With the competition eliminated, they can reap monopoly gains by raising their prices once again.

What your high school teacher doesn't mention is the substantial literature that exists debunking the alleged problem of predatory pricing. University of Chicago economist George Stigler has gone so far as to declare, "Today it would be embarrassing to encounter this argument in professional discourse." One of the many problems with the predatory pricing model is that it seems impossible to find an actual example. Antitrust scholar Dominick Armentano, reviewing scores of the most important antitrust cases of the twentieth century, could not find one. There is no shortage of examples of large stores offering low prices, but the enormous profits they are supposed to make when they raise prices again once they have the field to themselves seem to be the stuff of myth. (Readers interested in an economic refutation of "predatory pricing" are referred to works in the bibliography by Reisman and Armentano.)

## A Book You're Not Supposed to Read

*The Myth of the Robber Barons: A New Look at the Rise of Big Business in America* by Burton W. Folsom, Jr.; Herndon, Virginia: Young America's Foundation, 1991.

As Thomas DiLorenzo has shown, this myth has existed ever since the passage of the Sherman Antitrust Act in 1890, which was passed to prevent "anticompetitive practices" and to protect consumers from "predatory" firms and strategies. In the *International Review of Law and Economics*, DiLorenzo showed that the industries most frequently accused in the late nineteenth century of holding a "monopolistic" position—he investigated seventeen of them—were not acting like monopolies. A monopolistic firm, according to the standard definition, reaps an economic benefit by restricting output and raising prices. But the industries in which "monopoly" was supposedly a problem were neither restricting output nor raising prices. During the 1880s, for example, output of "monopolistic" industries grew seven times faster than the overall economy. And prices in these industries were generally falling—even faster than the 7 percent rate of decline that occurred in the economy as a whole.

### THE RESULTS OF "PREDATORY PRICING"

Commodity Prices from 1880–1890

| | |
|---|---|
| Steel | ↓58% |
| Zinc | ↓20% |
| Sugar | ↓22% |

Although John D. Rockefeller's Standard Oil is sometimes accused even today of having engaged in predatory pricing, honest scholars stopped making the accusation after John W. McGee's classic 1958 article in the *Journal of Law and Economics*. Rockefeller acquired his position, McGee showed, by means of mergers and acquisitions voluntarily entered into by his competitors, and not by predatory pricing. These opponents were browbeaten into accepting poor offers from Rockefeller, some say. To the contrary, Standard Oil typically employed the managers and owners of the firms they acquired, even making them shareholders. Had these managers and owners really been treated poorly, they would not have been desirable employees. "Victimized ex-rivals," McGee writes, "might be expected to make poor employees and dissident or unwilling shareholders."

McGee also provides examples of people who made excellent livings establishing refineries and selling them to Standard Oil. In most cases, competing firms approached Rockefeller and asked to be acquired. Knowing that his costs were lower than theirs, they chose absorption rather than being driven from the field altogether. (As another scholar explained,

"Critics also have accused Rockefeller of competing unfairly by selling below cost, but he wasn't selling below *his* cost, he was just selling below most competitors' costs.")

Standard Oil, typically excoriated and condemned in junior high and high school textbooks, was in fact an excellent example of American ingenuity and efficiency, and provided considerable benefits to the great mass of consumers. Until the 1850s, crude oil had been nothing but a nuisance to farmers who found it seeping from their soil. But when Yale University chemist Benjamin Silliman discovered in 1855 that it could be refined into kerosene, a better and potentially less expensive illuminant than the whale oil then in widespread use, the only question was whether it could ever be collected in sufficient quantities to make it marketable. When Silliman silenced skeptics by drilling for oil in 1859, this useless substance suddenly took on tremendous value.

## The "wicked" Rockefeller

John D. Rockefeller had managed to work his way up from stock boy to partner in a Cleveland store. In 1859, when he was twenty years old, oil had been discovered in northwestern Pennsylvania, not far from Cleveland. Rockefeller was intrigued at the possibilities of oil, but looked beyond the obvious venture of acquiring an oil well or two. He was convinced that the refinery business held out enormous opportunities. In 1862 he bought into a partnership in a Cleveland refinery.

### *How Rockefeller did more for the average American than any big government program*

Rockefeller was committed to streamlining production and eliminating waste. This paid off for him and for consumers: He managed to reduce the price of kerosene, which was a dollar per gallon when he began selling it, to a mere ten cents by the 1880s. Troubled by the disposal of the waste product that remained after the oil was refined, he eventually produced 300 products out of the waste. Thanks to Rockefeller's efficiency and low prices, millions of Americans who had previously gone to bed early to save money could now afford to illuminate their homes.

Prices declined throughout the period of Standard Oil's dominance. When the Russians struck some of the world's most oil-rich lands in 1882, they were poised to eclipse American oil production. In order to compete, Rockefeller would have to cut costs further. He did.

But despite Rockefeller's enormous service to American consumers and businesses (which could now produce their own products more cheaply), the federal government moved to dissolve Standard Oil during Theodore Roosevelt's presidency. But by the time the federal government dissolved Standard Oil in 1911, the company's market share had already been reduced to 25 percent as a result of normal market competition. Even the New Left historian Gabriel Kolko notes that from 1899, Standard Oil had "entered a progressive decline in its control over the oil industry, a decline accelerated, but certainly not initiated, by the dissolution." Standard's decline, Kolko explains, was "primarily of its own doing—the responsibility of its conservative management and lack of initiative." Thus even a Standard Oil must remain innovative and dynamic or lose market share.

## Andrew Carnegie and the American standard of living

Then there is Andrew Carnegie. His family came to America in 1848 from the Outer Hebrides islands off the northwestern coast of Scotland. At age twelve, Carnegie began work in a textile mill. He held a number of jobs in his youth, and as a young adult began to invest in a variety of businesses and projects. He eventually became convinced of the great potential of the steel industry, which in 1870 was in its infancy.

## What an Honest Businessman Said

"The man who dies thus rich dies disgraced."

**Andrew Carnegie**

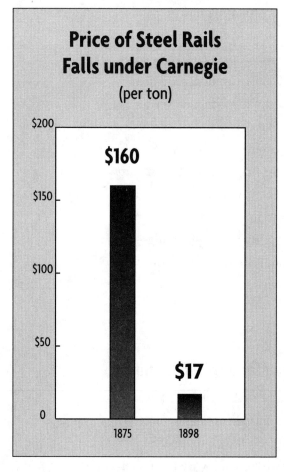

### Price of Steel Rails Falls under Carnegie
(per ton)

$160 — 1875

$17 — 1898

Carnegie opened his first plant in 1875. He was an organizational genius, devising incentive structures to ensure that each of his various departments worked conscientiously for the good of the company, practices that MBA students still read about in textbooks. Like Rockefeller, Carnegie was a master of efficiency. With 4,000 men at his Homestead Works in Pittsburgh, he could produce three times as much steel annually as could the 15,000 workers at Krupps steelworks, Europe's most modern and renowned facility.

The decrease in steel prices that occurred in the last quarter of the nineteenth century, which was largely due to Carnegie's labors, was another great benefit to ordinary Americans. Steel was absolutely fundamental to a modern economy, so a major cut in its production cost was a great boon. Any product or production process involving steel now cost less; these lower costs were in turn passed on to consumers.

Carnegie and Rockefeller were both great philanthropists, giving away nearly a billion dollars between them and establishing a great variety of charitable, educational, and cultural foundations. Both men criticized the idea of accumulating wealth for its own sake.

## Herbert Dow: Forgotten American hero

Despite the enormous benefits that Rockefeller and Carnegie brought to American consumers, the myth of "predatory pricing" dies hard. A useful counter-example, which shows the perils and the foolishness of attempting to dominate an industry through this practice, comes from the experience of the great chemical manufacturer Herbert Dow.

Dow was an exceptionally clever chemist who sought an inexpensive way to extract bromine from brine. (Bromine's uses included sedation and film developing.) He eventually succeeded, and after a couple of false starts established the Dow Chemical Company. Breaking into the industry was far from easy. Dow was known to work eighteen-hour days and even to sleep at his factory.

But here is where "predatory pricing" enters the picture. Dow was eager to provide bromine to Americans as well as to expand into the European market. But in Europe he would have to go toe-to-toe with a German cartel that dominated the European chemical market, and which had threatened to ruin any American firm that attempted to undersell the Germans in Europe. The German cartel vowed to flood the American market

## What the Press Said

"That so-called Anti-Trust law was passed to deceive the people and to clear the way for the enactment of this…law relating to the tariff. It was projected in order that the party organs might say to the opponents of tariff extortion and protected combinations, 'Behold! We have attacked the Trusts. The Republican party is the enemy of all such rings.'"

The *New York Times*'s interpretation of Senator John Sherman's motivation in drafting the Sherman Antitrust Act.

with cheap chemicals and drive the hapless upstart out of business. Dow ignored this threat and began selling bromine in England for thirty-six cents a pound, as opposed to the cartel's forty-nine cents.

In 1904 Dow received a visit from an angry representative of the German cartel, who reminded him to stay out of Europe. Dow refused to be intimidated, despite the man's threat to drive him out of business. When Dow continued to sell bromine in Europe, the German cartel attempted to make good on its threat by selling large quantities of bromine in the United States at the unheard-of price of fifteen cents per pound. In a fiendishly clever move, Dow instructed his purchasing agent in New York to buy up hundreds of thousands of pounds of the German consortium's cheap bromine. Dow then turned around and sold it in European markets at twenty-seven cents per pound—a price that the consortium could not match since it had to turn a profit in Europe in order to endure the losses it was running in America.

★ ★ ★ ★ ★ ★ ★ ★ ★ ★

## Reality check: Government— the true source of monopoly

To the extent that there really was a monopoly problem during America's Gilded Age and Progressive Era, the major culprit was the high protective tariffs that made it possible for big business to rip off American consumers. But all too few politicians wanted to face up to the problem, happy to win big business over to their side by supporting high tariffs. The Sherman Act gave such politicians cover, allowing them to claim that they were uncompromising opponents of big business while at the same time doing absolutely nothing about the tariff.

Dow would have the last laugh. In 1908, exhausted from the losses—at one point even reducing its price to an unthinkable 10.5 cents—the German cartel threw in the towel. They worked out a deal with Dow: If he stopped selling bromine in Germany, they would stop selling it in the United States—and the rest of the world would be open to free competition. Dow had met the German challenge, demonstrated the futility of "predatory pricing," and lowered the price of bromine forever.

## Antitrust idiocy: Should antitrust laws be repealed?

By the mid-twentieth century, the absurd and arbitrary character of antitrust law had become apparent to at least a small segment of the public. Speaking of regulations in general, the Federal Trade Commission's Lowell Mason declared: "American business is being harassed, bled, and even blackjacked under a preposterous crazyquilt system of laws, many of which are unintelligible, unenforceable and unfair. There is such a welter of laws governing interstate commerce that the government literally can find some charge to bring against any concern it chooses to prosecute. I say that this system is an outrage."

Supreme Court Justice Robert H. Jackson remarked while head of the Justice Department's Antitrust Division that "it is impossible for a lawyer to determine what business conduct will be pronounced lawful by the Courts. This situation is embarrassing to businessmen wishing to obey the law and to Government officials attempting to enforce it." Longtime Federal Reserve chairman Alan Greenspan condemned antitrust legislation in no uncertain terms four decades ago:

> It takes extraordinary skill to hold more than 50 percent of a
> large industry's market in a free economy. It requires unusual
> productive ability, unfailing business judgment, unrelenting
> effort at the continuous improvement of one's product and

technique. The rare company which is able to retain its share of the market year after year and decade after decade does so by means of productive efficiency—and deserves praise, not condemnation.

The Sherman Act may be understandable when viewed as a projection of the nineteenth century's fear and economic ignorance. But it is utter nonsense in the context of today's economic knowledge.... The entire structure of antitrust statutes in this country is a jumble of economic irrationality and ignorance.

Yet the antitrust juggernaut went forward. It destroyed Pan American World Airways by preventing it from acquiring domestic routes, thus depriving it of so-called feeder traffic for its international flights. IBM was harassed for thirteen years because it had 65 percent of the market; by the time the government finally gave up on the case the company had already been eclipsed by competitors. Beginning in 1937, General Motors actually made it company policy for the next two decades not to gain more than 45 percent of the automobile market out of fear of antitrust prosecution; some experts say that this self-imposed restriction partly explains why Americans lost so much market share to the Germans and Japanese in the latter half of the century.

### Punished for being the best: The case of ALCOA

Entire books have chronicled the damage that antitrust legislation has done to the economy and the absurd grounds on which American businesses have been prosecuted. Among the most ludicrous rationales ever provided for employing antitrust legislation against a private company appeared in the case against ALCOA, namely *United States v. Aluminum Company of America* (1945). Now ALCOA was indeed a monopoly in the crude sense—it was the only supplier of primary aluminum. But it could not for that reason simply have charged whatever it wished for aluminum, since abnormally high profits would have attracted competitors to the field and driven profits back down. (And contrary to what antitrust legislation seems to imply, there is no non-arbitrary way for an outside observer to determine how many firms should exist in a given industry.) In his decision against ALCOA, Judge Learned Hand declared:

> It was not inevitable that it [ALCOA] should always anticipate increases in the demand for ingot and be prepared to supply them. Nothing compelled it to keep doubling and redoubling its capacity before others entered the field. It insists that it never excluded competitors; but we can think of no more effective exclusion than progressively to embrace each new opportunity as it opened, and to face every newcomer with new capacity already geared into a great organization, having the advantage of experience, trade connections and the elite of personnel.

ALCOA's wickedness, according to this bizarre decision, came from its great skill and expertise in supplying its product! Alan Greenspan once remarked that the case against ALCOA revealed the true damage of antitrust legislation. Whatever destruction of wealth and efficiency it may have caused, whatever decrease in living standards it may have brought about, the worst aspect of antitrust law was that it led to "the condemnation of the productive and efficient members of our society *because* they are productive and efficient."

Antitrust activity has been every bit as irrational as its critics have claimed. And no wonder: It has primarily been an instrument by which

## Other Books You're Not Supposed to Read

*Antitrust and Monopoly: Anatomy of a Policy Failure* by Dominick T. Armentano; New York: John Wiley & Sons, 1982.

*Antitrust: The Case for Repeal*, 2nd rev. ed. by Dominick T. Armentano; Auburn, Alabama: Ludwig von Mises Institute, 1999.

less competent firms petition the government to punish rivals they couldn't outcompete in the marketplace. In its drearily predictable routine, the typical textbook rakes big business over the coals for its terrible "greed." But the real greed here is on the part of firms who want the government to punish and break up efficient firms that supply the goods people need at prices they can afford, all so that these complaining firms can survive and charge higher prices. There is, finally, a certain irony in the idea that we should want to be protected from "monopoly" by the government, the most truly monopolistic institution that has ever existed.

**Chapter 9**

★★★★★★★★★★

# WORLD WAR I

T he events surrounding the outbreak of World War I, perhaps the most terrifying and brutal conflict the world has ever seen, were so complicated and obscure that historians to this day continue to debate which country bore the greatest responsibility for starting the war. As of 1915, the major players were:

| The Allies | The Central Powers |
|---|---|
| Britain | Germany |
| France | Austria-Hungary |
| Russia | Bulgaria |
| Italy | The Ottoman Empire |

Immediately following the war, revisionist historians in America began to challenge wartime propaganda throughout the Allied countries that had placed the blame for the war squarely on Germany. Harry Elmer Barnes (1889–1968) went so far as to argue that of all the major belligerents Germany was actually the *least* to blame for starting the war. In the early 1960s the pendulum began to swing back toward German guilt with the work of historian Fritz Fischer. Not all scholars were persuaded by Fischer, and by the early twenty-first century, historian

## Guess what?

★ Woodrow Wilson's much-heralded "idealism" paved the way for World War II.

★ The Germans took out ads warning potential passengers that they would sink the *Lusitania*, but the British authorities assured people that it was safe.

★ Prominent American critics charged that America joined the war simply for the right to travel through a war zone on belligerent ships.

Niall Ferguson would argue in *The Pity of War* that the lion's share of the blame belonged to Britain.

Whatever the truth of the matter, none of it made a whit of difference to Americans in 1914. No American interest was at stake, and American security was not threatened in the slightest. As the war progressed and degenerated into a hopeless quagmire, Americans counted their blessings that their sons had been spared the senseless fate of European men, hundreds of thousands of whom were being sacrificed in battles that moved the front only a matter of yards. Injuries were unspeakable. It was this war, for instance, that introduced the term "basket case" into our vocabulary; it referred to a quadruple amputee. No American in his right mind was eager to involve his country in such slaughter.

President Woodrow Wilson, for his part, urged Americans to be neutral in thought, word, and deed. Yet the president was at heart pro-British. Wilson himself once remarked privately, "England is fighting our fight and you may well understand that I shall not, in the present state of the world's affairs, place obstacles in her way. . . . I will not take any action to embarrass England when she is fighting for her life and the life of the world."

## Where to Start

*The Western Front: Battle Ground and Home Front in the First World War* by Hunt Tooley; New York: Palgrave Macmillan, 2003. An outstanding, judicious, and enjoyable introduction to World War I.

Germany's violation of Belgian neutrality, which involved the passing of troops through Belgium on their way to France, became for the Allies a symbol of barbarity and militarism run amok and a reminder of the need to wipe autocracy from the face of the earth. In fact, Belgium was not neutral at all; it had agreements with France and Britain, and forts dotted its border with Germany (unlike its border with France, which had none). The Germans had made the same request of the Belgians that it had of Luxembourg, which accepted them without difficulty:

They wanted safe passage for German troops, and agreed to compensate Belgians for any damage or for any victuals consumed along the way.

## Propaganda in wartime? It can't be!

Allied governments won an important public relations victory in America with propaganda alleging widespread atrocities committed by German soldiers against Belgian civilians. Children with their hands cut off, babies tossed from bayonet to bayonet, nuns violated, corpses made into margarine—these were just some of the gruesome tales coming out of war-torn Europe. Americans on the scene, however, could not verify these stories. American reporters who had followed the German army insisted that they had seen nothing at all that would lend credence to the lurid tales making their way to the United States. Clarence Darrow, the lawyer who would become known for his work in the Scopes trial of 1925, offered to pay $1,000 (roughly $17,000 in 2004 dollars) to anyone who could show him a Belgian boy whose hands had been cut off by a German soldier. No one took him up on it. (After the war it was well established that the Belgian atrocities were largely fabricated, but the lies did their damage.)

Although Americans still favored staying out of the war, many had absorbed the message of Allied propaganda that Germany was evil incarnate and needed to be crushed for the sake of civilization.

## Starving civilians is against the law

Meanwhile, the British were involved in a real atrocity of their own: a deliberate attempt to starve the Germans with a naval blockade. The British hunger blockade of Germany violated the generally accepted norms of international law codified in several key international agreements of the nineteenth and twentieth centuries.

While a so-called close blockade, where a belligerent stopped traffic with its enemy's ports by stationing ships within a three-mile limit, was considered legitimate, a distant blockade of the kind in which Britain was engaged was not. In a distant blockade, one side simply declares whole areas of the seas to be off-limits. In this case, the British mined the North Sea so that even neutral ships would travel in peril. So while an opposing force had the right to search ships carrying cargo to its enemy, British mines indiscriminately destroyed anything with which they came into contact. "By sowing mines in international waters," historian John Coogan explains, "Britain deliberately replaced the belligerent right of visit and search in the North Sea with a new rule: explode and sink."

Moreover, food intended for civilian use was not considered contraband by anyone—except Britain. But given the relatively mild international response to Britain's conduct, the British government concluded that "the neutral powers seem to satisfy themselves with theoretical protest." It was in that spirit that the Germans expected their submarine policy to be accepted as well—but in the case of President Wilson at least, they were in for a surprise.

## The Germans strike back

On February 4, 1915, the German government announced that it would retaliate against the illegal British blockade:

All the waters surrounding Great Britain and Ireland, including the whole of the English Channel, are hereby declared to be a war zone. From February 18 onwards every enemy merchant vessel found within this war zone will be destroyed without it always being possible to avoid danger to the crews and passengers.

Neutral ships will also be exposed to danger in the war zone, as, in view of the misuse of neutral flags ordered on January 31 by the British Government, and owing to unforeseen incidents to which naval warfare is liable, it is impossible to avoid attacks being made on neutral ships in mistake for those of the enemy.

The reference to "the misuse of neutral flags" recalled the occasional British practice of decorating their ships with the flags of neutral countries to shield them from attack. By early 1915 Churchill was encouraging such a policy, and crews were being urged to don civilian clothing in order to lure German subs to the surface—where they would then be destroyed. For that reason, and because of the general danger that always exists during wartime, even neutral ships could not be assured of their safety when traveling through the war zone. Thus both the British and, in retaliation, the Germans, were guilty of violating the rights of neutral nations.

## Wilson's response to German submarine warfare

Woodrow Wilson refused to draw any connection between the German warning of submarine warfare and the British hunger blockade of Germany. His sympathies were always with the British. British violations of international law were met with little more than a slap on the wrist. So pro-British was the American administration that on one occasion, American ambassador to Great Britain Walter Hines Page read an American dispatch to British officials and then sat down to help them devise a reply to his own government! German misdeeds on the high seas, on the other hand, received immediate condemnation from Washington. As soon as the German policy on submarine warfare was announced, Wilson replied that the German government would be held strictly accountable for the loss of American vessels or lives on the high seas.

The realities of submarine warfare became particularly evident on March 29, 1915, when the British steamship *Falaba* was sunk by the Germans. According to British propaganda, the German U-boat captain had fired without warning, killing some 110 people, including one American. It was later discovered that the German captain had given the *Falaba* three warnings, and had fired only after a British warship had appeared on the horizon. The *Falaba* was also carrying some thirteen tons of ammunition, which helped to account for the severity of the disaster. Nevertheless, Wilson sent a note to the German government spelling out his policy that the United States had the duty to protect American citizens sailing on ships flying belligerent flags.

## Wilson's double standard

The double standard in Wilson's treatment of the British and the Germans played an important role in bringing United States to war. Columbia University's John Bassett Moore, the distinguished professor of international law who went on to serve as a judge at the International Court of Justice after the war, argued that "what most decisively contributed to the involvement of the United States in the war was the assertion of a right to protect belligerent ships on which Americans saw fit to travel and the treatment of armed belligerent merchantmen as peaceful vessels. Both assumptions were contrary to reason, and no other professed neutral advanced them." Two other scholars argued that the "persistent refusal of President Wilson to see that there was a relation between the British irregularities and the German submarine warfare is probably the crux of the American involvement." Wilson's position was "obviously unsustainable, for it is a neutral's duty to hold the scales even and to favor neither side."

It is obvious enough that bringing the United States into the war was a significant British aim. According to Churchill, "It is most important to attract neutral shipping to our shores in the hope especially of embroiling the United States with Germany. . . . If some of it gets into trouble, better still." Churchill later wrote that the policy he observed during the war was intended to make surface attack increasingly dangerous for German submarines. "The submerged U-boat," he explained, "had to rely increasingly on underwater attack and thus ran the greater risk of mistaking neutral for British ships and of drowning neutral crews and thus embroiling Germany with other Great Powers." Since all other Great Powers were already in the war at the time, Churchill could only have been referring to the United States.

## The sinking of the *Lusitania*

Although it did not bring the United States immediately into the war, the sinking of the *Lusitania* in May 1915 was among the most dramatic events from the American point of view prior to U.S. entry. This British cruise liner was perhaps the most famous ship in the world. The German government had published warnings in major newspapers not to book passage on the *Lusitania*. The morning it was to set sail, Count Johann von Bernstorff had issued an alert that British vessels were "liable to destruction," and cautioned that travelers sailing in the war zone "on ships of Great Britain and her allies do so at their own risk."

Passengers by and large ignored the warning. It was inconceivable to them that a ship with the speed of the *Lusitania* was in any danger, and those who inquired about potential risks were told not to worry and that the ship would be escorted by a naval convoy through the war zone. With their lives in the safe hands of the Royal Navy, the ship's passengers traveled with confidence.

Although a submarine attack seems scarcely to have been considered by either the Royal Navy or the Cunard Line (to which the *Lusitania* belonged), the assumption was that if the ship were indeed hit there would be ample time and opportunity for evacuation. It was, after all, a very substantial ship. The *Titanic* had remained afloat for some two and a half hours after suffering serious damage. But the torpedo that hit the *Lusitania* did an unexpected amount of damage, and it remains something of a mystery to this day why she went down so quickly, though some have attributed it to the munitions on board.

After the first shot, German submarine captain Walter Schwieger had held back from firing a second torpedo. Certainly he had not believed that a single torpedo would destroy the ship, and he was likely waiting for it to be abandoned before firing again. But he could see through his periscope just fifteen minutes after impact that the ship was in serious trouble. "It seems that the vessel will be afloat only a short time," he noted. He could not bear to witness the scene, and turned away from his periscope. "I could not have fired a second torpedo into this thing of humanity attempting to save themselves."

Some 1,195 of the ship's 1,959 passengers perished, including 124 of the 159 Americans on board. There is little sense in whitewashing the German attack on the *Lusitania*, but at the same time it is difficult not to convict both the British government and the Cunard Line of extreme recklessness. As one historian correctly put it, "With the sanction of the British Government, the Cunard Line was selling people passages through a declared war zone, under due notice that its ships were subject to being sunk on sight by a power which had demonstrated its ability and determination to do so."

### American reaction

The intensity of American reaction, primarily among politicians and in the press, was something to behold. Yet when the newspaper editorials are examined more closely, it turns out that hardly any of them were actually advising war as a response to the tragedy. Wilson himself chose to avoid war but wished to draft a stern note to Berlin, warning the Germans of serious consequences should this kind of submarine warfare continue.

Secretary of State William Jennings Bryan feared the potential consequences of so stern a message. Bryan was practically alone in the Wilson administration in attempting to balance the scales of the two sides. Bryan reminded Wilson of the results of an investigation that found that over 5,000 cases of ammunition had been on board the liner. He also noted an agreement accepted by Germany but rejected by Britain that would end the submarine warfare in exchange for the elimination of the starvation blockade. He addressed Wilson's double standard head on: "Why be shocked by the drowning of a few people, if there is to be no objection to starving a nation?"

But it was no use. In late May, Wilson sent another note to Berlin. Wilson's earlier note had spoken of the rights of Americans to travel aboard "unarmed" merchantmen; now Wilson changed "unarmed" to "unresisting." Americans now had the right to expect immunity from attack as they traveled aboard the armed ships of a nation at war. To paraphrase the memorable formulation of Professor Ralph Raico, Wilson believed that every American, in time of war, had the right to travel aboard armed, belligerent merchant ships carrying munitions of war through a declared submarine zone. No other neutral power had ever proclaimed such a doctrine, let alone gone to war over it.

During the Russo-Japanese War of 1904–1905, the British government's policy had been that British citizens traveled through the war zone at their own risk, and that Britain would not be drawn into war if a British citizen were killed as a result of his own reckless behavior. It was a sensible position, and it was the position that Wilson adopted during the Mexican civil war. But now, in Bryan's judgment, Wilson had become completely unreasonable. Convinced that he was part of an administration bent on war, Bryan resigned.

Bryan's replacement, Robert Lansing, was far more sympathetic to the pro-British stance that the ostensibly neutral Wilson had taken in practice. In his memoirs he spoke with an almost shocking candor about the British blockade, German submarine warfare, and United States policy. Following the sinking of the *Lusitania*, he explained, Britain "continued her policy of tightening the blockade and closing every possible channel by which articles could find their way to Germany."

When the United States sent notes of protest to Britain over these repeated violations of American neutral rights, the British knew perfectly well that they had no need to satisfy American demands. "In dealing with the British government," Lansing wrote, "there was always in my mind the conviction that we would ultimately become an ally of Great Britain and that it would not do, therefore, to let our controversies reach a point where diplomatic correspondence gave place to action." Once the United States did become a British ally, "we would presumably wish to adopt some of the policies and practices, which the British adopted" in order to "destroy the morale of the German people by an economic isolation, which would cause them to lack the very necessaries of life."

All the American notes of protest to Britain, Lansing admitted, were essentially for naught. "Everything was submerged in verbiage. It was done with deliberate purpose. It insured the continuance of the controversies and left the questions unsettled, which was necessary in order to leave this country free to act and even act illegally when it entered the war."

## American officials to Wilson: The right to travel through a war zone on belligerent ships isn't worth dying for

As the months passed following the *Lusitania* disaster, Wilson kept up the diplomatic pressure on the German government to a degree that alarmed some congressmen and other prominent Americans.

Senator Wesley Jones of Washington implored the president "to be careful, to proceed slowly, to make no harsh or arbitrary demands, to keep in view the rights of 99,999,000 people at home rather than of the 1,000 reckless, inconsiderate and unpatriotic citizens who insist on going abroad in belligerent ships." Senator Robert La Follette of Wisconsin spoke of the wisdom of Wilson's Mexico policy as compared with the president's policy regarding American sea travel into the European war zone. The policy of warning Americans that they traveled to Mexico at their own risk was, he said, "a small sacrifice on the part of the few to preserve the peace of the nation. But how much less sacrifice it requires for our citizens to refrain from travel on armed belligerent ships."

## The *Sussex* pledge

After the *Lusitania* disaster, the German government had privately decided to abandon the practice of firing upon passenger liners. But in March 1916, acting against orders, a German submarine fired without warning upon the French steamer *Sussex*, killing about eighty people. Four of the twenty-five Americans aboard were injured. The ship had not possessed the usual markings that indicated a passenger ship; it was painted black, and its bridge looked like that of a warship. When the German captain spied it traveling outside the routes that the British Admiralty had designated for passenger ships, he suspected it was a mine layer and fired a torpedo at the target.

### What an American Statesman Said

"Why should we enter a great war because some American wants to cross on a ship where he can have a private bathroom?"

**James Gerard,** American ambassador to Germany

The Germans had made a mistake, and would certainly have made reparation for the disaster. Wilson, however, took the opportunity to issue an ultimatum to Germany demanding that unless she abandoned submarine warfare entirely, the United States would sever diplomatic relations with her. The result was the *Sussex* pledge of May 1916, in which the German government made a major concession to Wilson. Although they would not abandon submarine warfare altogether, the Germans would not sink enemy merchant ships, armed or unarmed, without warning and without saving the lives of the people aboard, unless the ship in question opened fire or attempted to flee. This was an enormous concession, since the Germans, in effect, granted enemy merchant ships the opportunity to fire the first shot.

The pledge, however, was conditional. The German government expected Wilson to put pressure on the British government to abandon its hunger blockade and to allow food to make its way to Germany. Should the American government not achieve such a concession from the British, the German government would have complete freedom of action.

Not surprisingly, Wilson accepted the concession and refused the condition. Since America's neutral rights were absolute and inalienable, they were to be enjoyed regardless of the behavior of another belligerent. Wilson thus felt free to continue his policy, which he insisted on calling "neutrality," of holding one belligerent strictly accountable for its violations of international law but doing next to nothing about those of another belligerent.

### Impossible demands

The fact that British merchant ships were increasingly armed and prepared to take offensive action against German submarines put America in an awkward position. From early on, British ship captains had been warned by the admiralty that they would be prosecuted if they quietly surrendered their ships to the enemy. Submarines, which were notoriously frail, should be rammed or fired upon when possible. And since Churchill had said that the survivors of British attacks on German submarines would be treated as felons rather than as prisoners of war, U-boat captains understood very well that they could face death even if they managed to survive an attack.

Even Secretary of State Lansing could perceive the absurdity of the situation. The fact that British merchant ships were armed and capable of destroying submarines made it "difficult to demand that a submarine shall give warning and expose itself to the heavy guns carried by some of the British passenger vessels." Traditional "cruiser rules," now being applied to submarines, required them to give fair warning to an unarmed merchant vessel in their sights. The submarine could require that the ship submit to a search; if it turned out to be a belligerent merchant ship, the people on board became hostages and the ship itself, along with its cargo, could be confiscated or sunk.

But international law recognized *armed* ships not as peaceful vessels but as ships of war that could be destroyed. It was ridiculous even to Lansing to insist that German submarines be required to give notice before attacking *armed* merchant ships, since by giving such notice they would simply give the merchant ships the opportunity to sink them. British claims that their ships were only "defensively" armed were meaningless in the present context, since any of the arms in question were powerful enough to destroy a submarine. Lansing, with Wilson, wished to insist upon the American right to travel on belligerent ships through the war zone, but he believed that America's legal case would be much stronger if British merchant ships were unarmed. He believed that the traditional cruiser rules "could hardly be required justly of a submarine if the observation of the rule compels the submarine to expose itself to almost certain destruction."

Yet by early 1916, when it was clear that the British would not agree to disarm their merchant ships, Lansing and Wilson acted as if the issue had never been raised, going on record that the British could legitimately arm their merchant ships with "defensive" weapons, even if those weapons were powerful enough to destroy a submarine. In an official statement on February 15, Lansing insisted that such ships be treated as peaceful vessels that were entitled to receive notice from a submarine before it started firing.

### Congressmen: Americans travel on belligerent ships at their own risk
### Wilson: No way—they have a right!

Two days later, Texas congressman Jeff McLemore, working with Senator Thomas P. Gore, introduced a nonbinding resolution into Congress calling upon the president to warn Americans not to travel aboard armed ships, and that "in case Americans do travel on such armed belligerent ships . . . they do so at their own risk." It was a sensible and enormously popular position; the Speaker of the House said it would pass by a two-to-one margin. But when three influential Democratic legislators met with Wilson at the White House to discuss the issue four days later, the president urged the men to prevent a vote on the resolution. Senator William Stone, who was chairman of the Foreign Relations Committee, told Wilson, "Mr. President, I have followed you in your domestic policies, but—by God! I shall not follow you into war with Germany." McLemore's resolution did come to a vote after all, but Wilson used all the influence—and threats—at his disposal to defeat it.

German authorities scarcely knew what to make of the American position. The German kaiser himself scribbled his frustrated replies in the margins of another of Wilson's notes, this one sent in late April 1916. Wilson had appealed to the interests of "humanity" in opposition to German submarine warfare. This term, said the kaiser, meant to Wilson the unrestricted right "for real or hypothetical citizens of U.S.A. to cruise about on hostile & armed merchantmen whenever they like in the zone of war."

Britain's starvation policy, on the other hand, was "absolutely *not 'inhu-man'* in Wilson's eyes & quite right."

## The Germans make one last push

By January 1917 the German situation was becoming more and more difficult, with the starvation blockade taking a terrible toll on civilians. The German military managed to persuade the civilian leadership that it was necessary to engage in unrestricted submarine warfare, even if it meant war with the United States. They believed that Germany could sink enough enemy shipping that the war would be won by the time the Americans could send an expeditionary force to Europe.

Not surprisingly, fewer and fewer American ship captains dared venture into the war zone, not wanting to be sunk by a German submarine. Now for those historians who, out of a misplaced devotion to Wilson's memory, try to claim that the president was a lover of peace who desperately tried to avoid American involvement in the war, it is difficult to account for what Wilson did next. Breaking with all previous American tradition, the president called for arming merchant ships with U.S. Navy guns and staffing them with Navy crews, and instructing them to fire on any surfacing submarine they encountered. Bearing such instructions, American merchant ships headed for the war zone. Four of them had been sunk by the time Wilson requested a declaration of war from Congress in April.

## Why did Wilson favor war?

In February, Wilson had greeted Jane Addams and a group of peace activists at the White House. His guests caught a glimpse of his rationale for war. The president explained that "as head of a nation participating in the war, the president of the United States would have a seat at the peace table, but . . . if he remained the representative of a neutral country, he could at best only 'call through a crack in the door.' "

Persuaded that the European powers, left to themselves, would produce a vindictive and unworkable peace, Wilson believed that an impartial America could contribute much to the future peace of Europe and of the world. (Of course, the Congress of Vienna of 1814–1815, worked out by European powers without any American assistance, had produced a peace settlement that endured for a full century.) And in order to get a seat at the peace table, Wilson believed that he had to be the head of a nation that had taken part in the war.

### Wilson goes to war

In his speech calling for war, Wilson argued that the United States would fight for great moral principles. The struggle was not merely against Germany in particular but also against autocracy in general. Wilson believed that democratic regimes were inherently less warlike than regimes in which, as the president described them, grave matters of foreign policy were decided by a ruling cabal that was sheltered and aloof from public opinion.

Wilson also spoke of submarine warfare as "a war against all mankind." According to historian Thomas Fleming, this claim is not substantiated by America's experience in later wars:

> There is no moral onus for using it in the only way that gives submariners a decent chance for survival against their surface enemies—torpedoing enemy ships without warning. This surprise-attack approach was the policy adopted by the U.S. Navy during World War II. No one, including America's Japanese or German enemies, called the practice a war against mankind.

Wilson also promised in his war address to Congress that Americans' treatment of the ethnic Germans who lived among them would prove to the world that the United States had no quarrel with the German people, only with the German government. It did not work out that way. German-Americans were harassed and demonized. Symphony orchestras refused to perform works by Beethoven and other German-speaking composers; in many states it became illegal to teach German in schools (and in two states it was illegal to speak German in public); German-language books were burned; "disloyal" professors were dismissed; and sauerkraut was renamed "liberty cabbage."

## The peace conference: The disaster Wilson pretended not to notice

In January 1918, Wilson issued what became known as his Fourteen Points, outlining the principles of world order that he believed should inform any peace settlement. Wilson spoke of a "peace without victory," in which the victors would seek no unjust aggrandizement at the expense of the defeated nations. Among Wilson's principles were an end to secret diplomacy, which was thought to have contributed to the war's outbreak; reduction of armaments among victor and vanquished alike; the return of Poland to the map, in indisputably Polish lands; free trade; freedom of the seas; an impartial settlement of all colonial claims; and a League of Nations, an international body that Wilson believed could put an end to war once and for all. An additional principle informing Wilsonian diplomacy, though not expressly included in the Fourteen Points, was that of national self-determination: Every people should have the right to determine its own political fate.

Following the German surrender in November 1918, Wilson departed for the peace conference in Paris. In keeping with his uncompromising nature, he brought with him not a single influential Republican; the one Republican in the delegation, lifetime diplomat Henry White, had little connection to the party.

The diplomatic wrangling that took place at the peace conference has been the subject of countless detailed studies. The important point to take away is that Wilson's fond hopes of a "peace without victory"—a peace concerned more with justice than with vengeance, a peace taking into account all just claims, whether of victor or vanquished—were quickly dashed. In the closed-door negotiations among the Big Four (Britain, France, Italy, and the United States), Wilson saw only revenge and self-aggrandizement.

So wedded was Wilson to the idea of a League of Nations that the British and French delegations knew that all they had to do to persuade the American president to abandon any of the other Fourteen Points was to threaten not to join his beloved League. For his part, Wilson persuaded himself that as long as he got his League, that institution could modify any objectionable aspects of the peace treaty. Ultimately, for Wilson, it was the League that mattered.

## Ignorance, inconsistency, absurdity

Wilson's principle of national self-determination led to problems in practice. Intended to give national minorities (primarily those in the now-defunct Austro-Hungarian Empire) nations of their own, when carried out in practice it simply wound up creating more minorities. In the new nation of Czechoslovakia, for example, there were three million Germans—a fact that surprised the hapless Wilson when it was pointed out to him. This minority population, which the League of Nations concluded in later years was suffering from discrimination, would later be exploited by German leader Adolf Hitler, who would appeal to the principle of national self-determination to justify annexing Czechoslovakia's Sudeten region, where the vast bulk of these Germans lived.

In fact, for all his alleged commitment to national self-determination, Wilson was far from consistent in applying it. Portions of German-speaking Europe were parceled out not only to Czechoslovakia but also to Poland, Italy, and France; Germany even lost the port city of Danzig, which was 95 percent German. Austria was essentially reduced to its German-speaking core. And despite the overwhelming popular support that existed for a union of Germany with this smaller Austria, Wilson expressly forbade any such union in the treaty.

Other aspects of the treaty enraged the Germans, who insisted that they had surrendered on the basis of the Fourteen Points. Wilson had called for general disarmament, for example, but the treaty sought only to disarm Germany, which was to be without an air force, tanks, submarines (naturally), and restricted to an army of 100,000 (which put her on par with Lithuania). The amount that Germany would be expected to pay in reparations was not spelled out in the treaty and would not be settled until a special reparations commission reached a precise figure several years later. But based on what the Germans were hearing, they believed that the bill would take decades, even centuries, to repay.

The war guilt clause stung with particular force. German honor was impugned, her leaders said, by the suggestion that she alone bore the burden for the outbreak of war. Count Ulrich von Brockdorff-Rantzau, who headed the German delegation, was especially adamant on this point, insisting that while his country did not disclaim all responsibility for the outbreak of the war or the way it was conducted, Germany could not accept that she alone was guilty. Pointing to the ongoing hunger blockade, which continued for four months after the German surrender, he added: "The hundreds of thousands of noncombatants who have perished since November 11 by reason of the blockade were killed with cold deliberation after our adversaries had conquered and victory was assured to them. Think of that when you speak of guilt and punishment."

## Opponents say we can't police the world!

With the drafting of the treaty complete, Wilson had to persuade the U.S. Senate to ratify it. Although in his public remarks Wilson insisted that the

American people favored the treaty and that it was only an obstructionist minority in the Senate that objected, the reality was rather different. Huge crowds turned out for rallies against the treaty. There were German-Americans who considered it too harsh on Germany, Italian-Americans stunned that Wilson had rebuffed Italy's demands, Irish-Americans aghast that Irish independence had not been secured at the conference, and liberals who considered it a betrayal of Wilson's own principles.

The primary source of contention among Americans, however, was the covenant of the League of Nations, which had been included as part of the treaty. In particular it was Article 10, which obligated League members to preserve the territorial integrity of other member states, that caused the controversy. Opponents were concerned that it might erode American sovereignty—that is, they feared that League membership could obligate the United States to become militarily involved in conflicts involving the obscure border disputes of other League members.

Many opponents of the Covenant were not "isolationists," as supporters of American neutrality are misleadingly described, but were themselves internationalists, Senator Henry Cabot Lodge of Massachusetts being among the best examples. Far from arguing that the United States should retreat from the world stage, they argued simply for written guarantees that Americans would have the right to decide when and where they would take action.

The Lodge Reservations state: "The United States assumes no obligation to preserve the territorial integrity or political independence of any other country... under

★★★★★★★★★★

## Article 10 of the Covenant of the League of Nations, 1919

**The Members** of the League undertake to respect and preserve as against external aggression the territorial integrity and existing political independence of all Members of the League. In case of any such aggression or in case of any threat or danger of such aggression the Council shall advise upon the means by which this obligation shall be fulfilled.

the provisions of Article 10, or to employ the military or naval forces of the United States under any article of the treaty for any purpose"—except in any particular case in which Congress, which possessed the exclusive right to declare war, shall so provide. The preamble to the list of reservations also provided that American ratification of the Treaty of Versailles would not take effect until at least three of the four major Allied powers should officially accept the reservations.

Wilson remained convinced that any watering down of Article 10 would be fatal to the League. He explained to his fellow Americans, "I am not one of those who, when they go into a concert for the peace of the world, want to sit close to the door with their hand on the knob and constantly trying the door to be sure that it is not locked. If we want to go into this thing—and we do want to go into it—we will go in it with our whole hearts and settled purpose to stand by the great enterprise to the end."

> ## Good Grief!
>
> To those who feared that the League of Nations would compromise American sovereignty, **Woodrow Wilson** replied that he looked forward to the day "when men would be just as eager partisans of the sovereignty of mankind as they were now of their own national sovereignty."

## "Bizarre" and "wild-eyed": The Wilsonian program

Wilson, crisscrossing the nation to gain support for the treaty, routinely accused his opponents of ignorance or malice, even when all they sought was to modify the treaty to ensure the integrity of American sovereignty. Former president William Howard Taft, who supported the League, was aghast at Wilson's behavior: "It is impossible for him [to] . . . explain the League without framing contemptuous phrases to characterize his opponents. . . . The president's attitude in not consenting to any reservations at all is an impossible one." "The more the president talked," writes

## Wilson's Mania and Freud's Diagnosis

"[Wilson] was rapidly nearing that psychic land from which few travelers return, the land in which facts are the products of wishes, in which friends betray and in which an asylum chair may be the throne of God....

"The man who faces facts, however unpleasant they may be, preserves his mental integrity....[Wilson] had called his countrymen to follow him on a crusade and they had followed...he had promised them and the enemy and, indeed, all mankind a peace of absolute justice based upon his Fourteen Points; he had preached like a prophet who was ready to face death for his principles; and he had quit. If...Wilson had been able to say to himself, I broke my promises because I was afraid to fight, he would not have disintegrated mentally after April 1919. His mental life from April to September 1919, when he collapsed completely and permanently, was a wild flight from fact."

**Sigmund Freud**

Thomas Fleming, "the more he convinced a majority of the senators that the treaty needed these reservations to protect the country against a League of Nations run by a leader like Woodrow Wilson—a wild-eyed idealist who would embroil the country in bizarre attempts to perfect the world, without the consent of Congress or the American people."

Wilson's mental instability was perhaps reflected in his increasingly grandiose portrayals of a treaty that amounted to a repudiation of so many of his own principles. As he traveled the country to drum up support for the treaty (which still needed approval by the Senate), he spoke of this fatally flawed document as the "incomparable consummation of the hopes of mankind"; at one point it even became an "enterprise of divine mercy." "The Treaty of Versailles is an unparalleled achievement of thoughtful civilization," Wilson insisted. "It is the first treaty ever made by great powers that was not made in their own favor."

When Wilson refused to accept the treaty as revised by the Senate, it was doomed. He ordered his own supporters to vote against it and the treaty went down to defeat. Under Wilson's successor, Warren Harding, Congress passed a resolution officially declaring the war over, bringing closure to a conflict that had cost 120,000 American lives.

## Setting the stage for World War II

Wilson managed to persuade himself that the German kaiser was the epitome of evil in the world. Getting rid of him and abolishing Germany's constitutional monarchy, it was assumed in Wilsonian circles, would lead to a more peaceful world in the long run, as the expansionist Germany of the kaiser gave way to the representative and moderate Weimar regime.

Historians have pointed to the punitive Treaty of Versailles, which established peace terms with Germany at the end of World War I, as a major contributing factor to World War II. Hitler appealed to the patriotism and honor of the German people, who detested the Versailles Treaty, for support of his foreign policy. Woodrow Wilson, who had genuinely wanted to make the world safe for democracy, did not. An even more terrible conflict would erupt two decades later.

Chapter 10

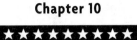

# THE MISUNDERSTOOD TWENTIES

Warren Harding and Calvin Coolidge usually wind up near the bottom in presidential rankings compiled by the votes of historians. This is no surprise; these presidents engaged in no large-scale social engineering, embarked on no vast legislative program like the New Deal or the Great Society, and involved the United States in no major foreign war. Since most historians favor an activist government committed to "social justice" at home and abroad, they have little sympathy for chief executives who simply leave the American people alone.

Yet America prospered during the 1920s. American business set production records. Wages increased and working hours declined. And as if to underscore yet again the irrelevance of labor unionism, these outcomes occurred at a time when labor union membership was undergoing a rapid decline.

## Voting for the anti-Wilson

Harding had earned the Republican nomination in 1920 partly because he was utterly unlike Wilson. He had no grandiose plans to remake the world, and no particular desire to strengthen and enlarge the office of the presidency along Wilsonian lines. As Massachusetts senator Henry Cabot Lodge explained, "Harding will not try to be an autocrat but will do his

## Guess what?

★ Without grand programs, Harding and Coolidge presided over one of the most economically prosperous times in America's history.

★ Under Treasury secretary Andrew Mellon, the top income tax rate fell from 73 percent to 40 percent and later to 25 percent, but the greatest proportional reductions occurred in the lower income brackets, where people saw most of their income tax burden eliminated altogether.

best to carry on the government in the old and accepted Constitutional ways." As for foreign affairs, Harding favored a modest and independent course: "Confident of our ability to work out our own destiny and jealously guarding our right to do so, we seek no part in directing the destinies of the Old World. We do not mean to be entangled. We will accept no responsibility except as our own judgment and conscience may determine." Although certainly no genius, Harding was not the bumbling idiot that unsympathetic historians have made him out to be. His private papers reveal how well read he was; his favorite writers included Carlyle, Dickens, Pope, and Shakespeare.

### Scandals

None of this is intended to suggest that either of these men was squeaky clean, either personally or politically. Harding, although loved by the American population—the train carrying his deceased body from San Francisco to Washington was at times prevented from making progress by the mobs of people who had come out to pay their last respects—was personally at least as unsympathetic a character as scholars have said.

**What a President Said**

"Perhaps one of the most important accomplishments of my administration has been minding my own business."

**Calvin Coolidge**

Although he may not in fact have fathered the child of Nan Britton as was alleged (recent research tends not to corroborate her story), he was nevertheless involved in his share of amorous affairs. His private papers reveal that on one occasion he even paid for a woman's abortion. He carried on a fifteen-year affair with Carrie Phillips, who had been his wife's best friend. Phillips later blackmailed him. Harding's campaign supporters responded by raising $20,000 to pay her to leave the country until after the election; when news of the incident later appeared in a book, the Bureau of Investigation was sent to destroy the plates and the copies.

Politically he left his mark primarily in the scandals that became forever attached to the memory of his administration, but even here the scandalous behavior typically did not involve Harding himself, and most of the time he was genuinely unaware of what had been going on. The day after Harding's confrontation with Jess Smith, a bureaucrat who had been selling government favors, Smith committed suicide. Two months earlier, Charles Cramer, counsel for the Veterans Bureau, had killed himself after Harding had discovered that the bureau's director had been profiting by selling government medical supplies.

## The truth about the Twenties

According to the conventional wisdom, the 1920s were a time of dramatically reduced levels of government activity, both domestically and internationally. Harding and Coolidge are typically said to have been strict supporters of laissez-faire economics and of nonintervention in foreign affairs. Again, however, liberal historians have overstated their case.

It is true that both domestically and internationally the 1920s represented a time of decreased government intervention when compared with the previous decade. But the previous decade, after all, included World War I. So although government spending and foreign involvement did indeed decrease in the 1920s when compared with the previous decade, they were both much higher than they had been before the war. This is what economic historian Robert Higgs has called the "ratchet effect": although government is inevitably scaled back in the aftermath of an emergency, it never reaches pre-emergency levels. Its scope, its spending, and its taxation are lower than during the emergency, but higher than before the emergency.

## *Lower taxes...*

During World War I, the top income tax rate had been increased from 7 percent to an incredible 73 percent. Andrew Mellon, secretary of the Treasury under both Harding and Coolidge, believed that such suffocating rates were damaging the economy. He also believed that such a high rate was actually yielding less revenue to the federal government than would a lower rate. (Mellon thereby anticipated the argument of economist Arthur Laffer and his "Laffer Curve," which gained attention in the late 1970s.) The excessively high rates were causing the wealthy to shelter their incomes rather than expose themselves to such punishing taxation. If they invested their money and did well, the federal tax code allowed them to keep twenty-seven cents of every dollar earned, but if they invested their money and failed, they would lose 100 cents of every dollar. No thanks, said many Americans.

A great many wealthy Americans were putting their money into tax-free state and municipal bonds—not an extraordinarily lucrative avenue, of course, but they yielded at least some return, *and they were not taxable.* Meanwhile, businesses were starved for capital. Money that might have been devoted to business investment was tied up in state bonds. The states were awash with cash to fund various projects of dubious merit, but the private sector was in trouble.

Mellon therefore considered tax relief essential to the nation's economic health. Under his influence, rates were reduced across the board, for all tax brackets, throughout the course of the decade. The top rate, since it was so high, saw the greatest absolute reduction, from 73 to 40 and later to 25 percent, but the greatest proportional reductions occurred in the lower income brackets, where people saw most of their income tax burden eliminated altogether.

As a result, not only did federal revenue actually increase—the unfortunate aspect of Mellon's policy—but, much more important, economic activity multiplied many times over. These tax reductions undoubtedly played a role in bringing about the prosperity of the 1920s. In 1926, unemployment reached the incredible low of 1 percent.

No, Harding and Coolidge did not establish a Square Deal, a New Deal, a New Frontier, a Great Society, or a New Covenant. For the most part they simply stayed out of the economy and out of people's lives. But the results speak for themselves. By the end of the decade, the United States could boast an incredible 34 percent of total world production, followed by Britain and Germany, each with just over 10 percent. No wonder historians loathe Harding and Coolidge; these presidents' success goes to show how much better off the country might be if ambitious politicians with their grandiose plans would just shut up and leave us alone.

It is next to impossible to imagine an unassuming man like Calvin Coolidge being elected today. He made no campaign promises to enrich some citizens at the expense of others through taxation or any other government program. He understood the damage that "well-intentioned" government programs can do, and he understood the limited nature of American government as envisioned by the Framers of the Constitution. Nothing could be further from the message heard from present-day presidential candidates.

## What a President Said

"Nothing is easier than the expenditure of public money. It doesn't appear to belong to anyone. The temptation is overwhelming to bestow it on somebody."

**Calvin Coolidge**

The America that elected Calvin Coolidge was decent and good. Their president was a man of character who initiated no grandiose programs of economic and social reconstruction, and had no interest in meddling in all the world's problems. H. L. Mencken said of him, "There were no thrills while he reigned, but neither were there any headaches. He had no ideas, and he was not a nuisance." If only the same could be said of his successors.

# Chapter 11

# THE GREAT DEPRESSION
# AND THE NEW DEAL

The stock market crash of October 1929 brought the prosperous 1920s to a dramatic end. Real GNP per capita fell by 30 percent between 1929 and 1933. At its worst, unemployment reached an incredible 25 percent. It's been said that if all the unemployed stood in a line a yard apart, the line would stretch from New York to Seattle to Los Angeles and all the way back to New York, and would still leave some 280,000 people out of the line. Corporate profits, after taxes, were actually negative in 1931, 1932, and 1933. Net private investment during the 1930s was also negative—that is, plant and equipment wore out faster than they could be replaced.

What caused the downturn of 1929 is a complicated question. Most historians, from Marxists to the center-right, have blamed the Depression on capitalism, claiming that the boom-bust cycle is an inherent part of a market economy. Yet the most persuasive explanation, offered by the Austrian school of economics, argues the opposite: The boom-bust cycle isn't a necessary feature of a market economy; it's really set in motion by the central bank (in America's case, the Federal Reserve System)—a distinctly non-market institution. Interested readers are urged to consult Murray N. Rothbard's *America's Great Depression* for a sound and reliable treatment of the subject.

## Guess what?

★ While many Americans were hungry and destitute, FDR ordered the slaughter of six million pigs and the destruction of ten million acres of cotton.

★ Public-sector jobs "created" by the New Deal displaced or destroyed private-sector jobs.

★ World War II didn't end the Great Depression; a return to free-market activity after the war did.

## Hoover: A "do nothing" president? If only!

Most people believe that Hoover stood by and did nothing as the Depression ravaged the country, and that it was Franklin Roosevelt's vigorous intervention into the economy that finally brought recovery. Nothing could be further from the truth.

First, it's not true that Hoover sat idly by during the Depression. He did plenty—more than any peacetime president had ever done. Rexford Tugwell, an important figure in FDR's New Deal programs, later acknowledged, "We didn't admit it at the time, but practically the whole New Deal was extrapolated from programs that Hoover started." In fact, Hoover's incessant meddling with the economy made the situation worse. He managed to turn the recession in 1929 into the Great Depression.

While the economic picture was poor in 1929 and 1930, it was only in 1931, after a year of government intervention, that the situation seriously deteriorated.

### Guaranteeing unemployment

In the month following the stock market crash, Hoover summoned key business leaders to the White House. He implored them to refrain from cutting wages, arguing that high wages were a way out of the Depression since they gave workers the means to purchase goods.

To be sure, Hoover's philosophy is superficially plausible, and virtually every American history textbook dutifully adopts it; the economic downturn, the argument goes, was caused by "underconsumption." But this view is fallacious. For one thing, if the cause of the Depression had been a reduction in consumer spending, we would

---

★ ★ ★ ★ ★ ★ ★ ★ ★ ★

## Hoover Should Have Learned From Harding

Harding's strategy for the downturn of 1920–21 was to do nothing at all—except to tighten the government's purse strings by cutting spending. The economy was hopping within the year.

expect the hardest-hit segments of the economy to be those industries that make pots and pans, toothbrushes, or apple pies. But as historian Gary Dean Best points out, it was industries that produced durable and capital goods that suffered the most. "Increased consumer spending," Best explains, "would largely assist the consumer goods industries, where the volume of business showed the least decline from predepression levels; it did little or nothing for the heavy industries that had been most affected by the depression and where the bulk of unemployment was concentrated."

Hoover's theory neglected an important consideration—wages are a cost of doing business. By demanding high wages, *particularly at a time when prices were rapidly declining*, he was making it more difficult for businesses to hire people. Big business, however, honored the president's request. The result was sadly predictable: mass unemployment.

Hoover's mistake was to presume that high wages were the cause of American prosperity rather than a reflection of that prosperity. If high wages could produce prosperity on their own, we could eliminate world poverty simply by enforcing a minimum wage of $100 an hour. Only a lunatic would support such a policy, since the result would be unheard-of levels of unemployment and utter devastation to the economy.

### *Meddling in agriculture*

Hoover's agricultural policy was another disaster. Since the end of World War I, farmers had argued for government assistance of one kind or another, including help to prop up farm prices. (Translation: The farmers wanted the government to make food and clothing more expensive for everyone in order to benefit themselves.) Farmers were having problems making a living because there were too many of them—far more than made any economic sense. The American agricultural sector had expanded dramatically during World War I when production in Europe had been disrupted. With the war over, it was unreasonable to expect that America's bloated agricultural sector could remain the same size. People and resources had to be shifted to industries that produced goods that Americans really needed.

Hoover established a Federal Farm Board (FFB) to improve the lot of American farmers. The FFB made loans to farm cooperatives so that farmers could keep their crops, particularly wheat and cotton, off the market until their prices rose. Whenever this approach did manage to get prices up, however, farmers gleefully produced more the following year, making the surplus problem even worse. Eventually the Farm Board authorized, through its Grain Stabilization Corporation, massive purchases of wheat from American farmers at prices well above the world price. Farmers thus sold their wheat to the Grain Stabilization Corporation instead of exporting it. Government farm bureaucrats were sure that by keeping American wheat off the world market, a world shortage of wheat would ensue and foreigners would soon be begging for American wheat. Instead, Canadian and Argentinean wheat producers grabbed America's share of the world market.

Federal bureaucrats were in fact able to raise the grain price for a brief period, but the huge surpluses, bought up by the government, depressed prices even more since the world knew they would eventually be dumped on the world market. The British economist Lionel Robbins observed several years later: "The grandiose buying organizations by which Hoover tried to maintain agricultural prices had the effect of demoralizing markets altogether, by the accumulation of stocks and the creation of uncertainty."

Given this problem, some government officials were honest enough to admit that for a program like this to work, strict limits would have to be imposed on how much farmers would be allowed to produce. Requests that farmers voluntarily cut back their acreage of wheat and cotton fell on deaf ears. Desperate to increase prices, the FFB's chairman went so far as to call upon state governors to "induce immediate plowing under every third row of cotton now growing."

## *More brilliance: Tax increases*

The notorious Smoot-Hawley Tariff was originally intended to provide tariff protection for American agriculture, but it turned out that there was no politically feasible way to limit that protection to one sector of the economy. Pressure groups from countless industries descended upon Washington to argue for tariff protection. Virtually all American economists united in urging Hoover to veto Smoot-Hawley, but Hoover ignored them all and signed it into law in June 1930. It raised tariffs an average of 59 percent on more than 25,000 items.

The tariff hit American export industries hard. America's trading partners inevitably retaliated when their products were shut out of U.S. markets. For instance, the Italian government responded by doubling its tariffs on American cars—whereupon American automobile sales in Italy fell by 90 percent. The French practically shut American products out of their country altogether. Spain retaliated by raising tariffs on American cars to a level that practically guaranteed that no American cars would be sold there.

There were other tax increases—lots of them. In December 1931 Andrew Mellon, who championed lower tax rates in the 1920s, suddenly did an about-face and wanted a massive tax increase. Congress and the president listened, and the result was the disastrous Revenue Act of 1932. It was the largest peacetime tax increase in United States history up to that point. Income tax rates were increased dramatically and surtaxes on

★ ★ ★ ★

**New or
Higher Taxes**

Corporate

Estate

Gifts

Cars

Tires

Gasoline

Toiletries

Electric energy

Luxury items

Bank checks

Telephone, tele-
graph, and radio
messages

★ ★ ★ ★

the highest incomes soared from 25 to 63 percent. This meant that in the midst of the Depression, when private investment was desperately needed, it was made much less attractive.

### Hoover the big spender

Hoover also vastly increased spending on public-works projects. More money was spent on such projects in four years than in the previous thirty. He subsidized the shipbuilding industry at a time when shipping services were less in demand thanks to the shrinkage in international trade brought about by Smoot-Hawley. Hoover's Reconstruction Finance Corporation (RFC) supplied failing businesses, mainly railroads and banks, with emergency low-interest loans. By the latter half of 1932 the RFC was no longer simply bailing out businesses in trouble but was also lending money to the states for unemployment relief and to fund public-works projects.

The president's attempts to prop up failing businesses were of dubious effect. "The businesses he hoped to save," writes one historian, "either went bankrupt in the end, after fearful agonies, or were burdened throughout the 1930s by a crushing load of debt."

The one area in which Hoover differed from FDR was that Hoover hesitated to provide direct federal relief, preferring instead to rely on voluntary organizations and, eventually, to make loans to states. He believed that voluntary organizations as well as state and local government were the appropriate institutions for giving aid.

Looking back upon his tenure, Hoover congratulated himself for his bold action. "We might have done nothing," the president said in 1932. "That would have been utter ruin. Instead, we met the situation with proposals to private business and to Congress of the most gigantic program of economic defense and counterattack ever evolved in the history of the Republic." The result was ongoing economic catastrophe.

## FDR comes to town

In 1932, Democrat Franklin Delano Roosevelt defeated Hoover in a landslide. Along with Washington and Lincoln, FDR is routinely listed in polls as among the "great" presidents. Many Americans believe his New Deal programs rescued the country from the grips of the Depression. In fact, under FDR, unemployment averaged a whopping 18 percent from 1933 to 1940.

One biographer said that there was no one more ignorant of economics than FDR. It showed. FDR knew nothing about how wealth was created. The legislation he called for was a patchwork of absurdities, sometimes at odds with each other, and sometimes even at odds with themselves.

### *Seeking prosperity through central planning*

The National Industrial Recovery Act (NIRA), which established the National Recovery Administration, was an enormous contradiction. On the one hand, it sought to keep wage rates high to give the consumer greater "purchasing power." On the other hand, it established hundreds of legally sanctioned, industry-wide cartels that were allowed to establish standard wages, hours of operation, and *minimum* prices. The minimum prices meant that businesses would be largely prevented from underselling each other; everyone's price had to be *at least* the prescribed

## A Charity that Refused Government Handouts

In 1931 the **Red Cross** turned down a proposed federal grant of $25 million, arguing that it had all the money it needed and that such government grants to private charities would "to a large extent destroy voluntary giving."

minimum. The artificially high wages meant continuing unemployment, and the high prices meant hardship for nearly all Americans. Some strategy for recovery.

## Let's help starving people by destroying food!

FDR's agricultural policies were in a class of genius all their own. Not content with setting high prices for other goods, FDR moved on to food. He proposed to pay farmers for cutting back on production or producing nothing at all. The decrease in supply, he believed, would raise farm prices. But in the meantime, he had to deal with the existing bounty. The administration decided to destroy much of what had already been produced to create a shortage and thereby raise farm prices. Six million pigs were slaughtered and ten million acres of cotton were destroyed.

Agriculture secretary Henry Wallace, as thoroughgoing a Soviet dupe as this country has ever seen, described the wholesale destruction of crops and livestock as "a cleaning up of the wreckage from the old days of unbalanced production." Wallace, of course, had special insight into precisely what quantity of production would bring things into "balance."

★★★★★★★★★★

## PC Today

**eorge Tindall and David Shi**, the authors of a standard U.S. history text, assure us that "for a while these farm measures worked." Well, if by "worked" they mean that these measures succeeded in their goal of raising the prices of food and clothing at a time when people were desperately poor, then indeed they did "work." Slaughtering animals and destroying crops did tend to increase the prices of these items. Congratulations.

Shortly after the American Agriculture Administration (AAA) was established, the Department of Agriculture released the findings of its study of the American diet during these difficult years. The study constructed four sample diets: liberal, moderate, minimum, and emergency (below subsistence). It found that America was not producing enough food to sustain its population at the minimum (subsistence) diet. It took a special kind of mind to conclude that the best approach to this disaster would be to make food more expensive.

Meanwhile, the evidence proving that FDR's approach was fundamentally flawed continued to mount. In 1936, the Bureau of Agricultural Economics reported that in the case of cotton, farm income would have been at least as high and perhaps even higher in the absence of the AAA. The following month, Cornell University's James E. Boyle argued in the *Atlantic* that the AAA had been responsible for the joblessness of at least two million Americans, especially sharecroppers and farm laborers. And although the AAA was intended to increase farm income, historian Jim Powell observes that farmers "actually found themselves worse off because FDR's National Recovery Administration had been even more successful in forcing up the prices that consumers, including farmers, had to pay for manufactured goods."

## FDR's legacy in agriculture

Unfortunately, massive government intervention in agriculture never went away. Even in the 1980s, a decade people associate with government

### What One of Our "Greatest" Presidents Said

"Are we going to take the hands of the federal government completely off any effort to adjust the growing of national crops, and go right straight back to the old principle that every farmer is a lord of his own farm and can do anything he wants, raise anything, any old time, in any quantity, and sell any time he wants?"

**FDR** when the Supreme Court struck down his agricultural program

## Three Books You're Not Supposed to Read

*The Roosevelt Myth* by John T. Flynn; 50th anniversary edition, San Francisco: Fox & Wilkes, 1998. (This one is occasionally unsound on economics, but is still a good read.)

*FDR's Folly* by Jim Powell; New York: Crown Forum, 2003.

*Out of Work: Unemployment and Government in Twentieth-Century America* by Richard K. Vedder and Lowell E. Gallaway; New York: Holmes & Meier, 1993.

retrenchment and a commitment to market principles, farm programs were eating up $30 billion annually, two-thirds of which took the form of subsidies and the other third in higher prices to consumers. The principal device behind these programs is the price support: The federal government offers to pay farmers a certain amount per product and at that price will buy whatever amount the farmers are willing to sell. Farmers, therefore, will not sell on the market if the price offered by the federal government is higher than the market price. So the government often winds up with enormous amounts of various agricultural products on its hands. It then has to figure out how to get rid of them without driving prices back down. Often, the government simply destroys them. FDR's legacy in agriculture continues to be felt today.

In the 1980s, the USDA ordered the annual destruction of:

- ❀ 50 million lemons
- ❀ 100 million pounds of raisins
- ❀ 1 billion oranges

Quotas on peanuts have had the effect of doubling the price of peanuts and peanut butter. Dairy subsidies are still more absurd, with every dairy cow in America subsidized to the tune of $700 per year—"an amount greater than the income of half the world's population," Professor Eric Schansberg points out. Indeed, for most of the twentieth century the price of sugar to Americans was 500 percent higher than the world price, thanks to government price supports. This is certainly a boon to sugar producers, who receive an average of $235,000 a year from the policy. But it costs consumers well over $3 billion per year, and it puts all American industries that use sugar at a competitive disadvantage vis-à-vis foreign producers who are not forced to pay such an inflated price for sugar.

## FDR's anti-business zealotry delays recovery

Other aspects of the New Deal damaged the economy. New Deal labor laws, as well as the increased labor costs associated with Social Security, further contributed to the unemployment problem—to the tune of an additional 1.2 million unemployed by 1938, according to economists Richard Vedder and Lowell Gallaway.

Economic historian Robert Higgs has argued that "regime uncertainty" also hindered recovery. Businessmen and investors, unsure of what the federal government would do next and what additional punitive measure would be imposed on them, simply stopped investing. Higgs also noted that long-term investment was particularly hard hit in the 1930s. In the bond market, long-term bonds carried a substantial risk premium, indicating that business leaders were very uncertain about the future. Higgs collected polling data from the 1930s suggesting that this uncertainty about the future boiled down to an uncertainty about *future government policy*. Businessmen took seriously the various ravings of the anti-business zealots who occupied the White House.

## The consequences of labor legislation

FDR gave a tremendous boost to organized labor with the National Labor Relations Act, better known as the Wagner Act of 1935. The standard textbook takes for granted that what is good for unions is good for workers (even though the whole purpose of a modern union is to exclude people from a trade in order to raise the wages of union workers). The facts say otherwise.

The ways in which labor unions impoverish society are legion, from distortions in the labor market to work rules that discourage efficiency and innovation. In a study published jointly in late 2002 by the National Legal and Policy Center and the John M. Olin Institute for Employment Practice and Policy, economists Richard Vedder and Lowell Gallaway of Ohio University calculated that labor unions have cost the American economy a whopping *$50 trillion* over the past fifty years alone. That is not a misprint. "The deadweight economic losses are not one-shot impacts on the economy," the study explains. "What our simulations reveal is the powerful effect of the compounding over more than half a century of what appears at first to be small annual effects." Not surprisingly, the study did find that unionized labor earned wages 15 percent higher than those of their nonunion counterparts, but it also found that *wages in general* suffered dramatically as a result of *an economy that is 30 to 40 percent smaller than it would have been* in the absence of labor unions.

## A Book You're Not Supposed to Read

*Making America Poorer: The Cost of Labor Law* by Morgan Reynolds; Washington, D.C.: Cato, 1987.

Labor historians and activists would be at a loss to explain why, at a time when unionism was numerically negligible (a whopping 3 percent of the American labor force was unionized by 1900), real wages in manufacturing climbed an incredible 50 percent in the United States from 1860–1890, and another 37 percent from 1890–1914, or why American workers were so much better off than their much more heavily unionized counterparts in Europe. Most of them seem to cope with these facts by neglecting to mention them at all.

## The disaster of "public works"

The New Deal's admirers assure us that FDR's massive spending projects provided jobs and economic stimulus. But such jobs are funded by taking money from some people (taxpayers) and giving it to others, so there is no net stimulus. In fact, such programs are positively bad in that they divert capital from the private sector and inhibit healthy job creation. Economists John Joseph Wallis and Daniel K. Benjamin found that the public-sector jobs "created" by New Deal spending programs either simply displaced or actually destroyed private-sector jobs. The various public-works programs that FDR established and the billions of dollars he devoted to them only dried up capital in favor of government projects that were inherently wasteful, since they lacked the kind of profit-and-loss test that guides entrepreneurs in their investment decisions.

### Buying votes with make-work jobs

FDR's public-works projects were rife with corruption. Economic historians have been at pains to account for the distribution of these projects around the country—why, for example, did the South, where people were the poorest, receive the *least* assistance from FDR's Works Progress Administration (WPA)?

A number of scholars, noting the rather curious preponderance of WPA projects in western states where FDR's electoral margin had been thin in 1932, believe political considerations played an important role in how these projects were distributed. Researchers like Gavin Wright, John Joseph Wallis, Jim F. Couch, and William F. Shughart II found a significant correlation between New Deal spending and FDR's political needs. Wright, for instance, contended that political factors could account for 80 percent of the difference in New Deal spending among the states. FDR spent more on western states than on southern ones because the South, which had given him 67 percent of the vote, was much more politically secure than the west, and he had little need to buy their votes.

WPA workers were often pressured into supporting FDR's favored candidates, changing their party affiliations, or "contributing" to FDR's re-election campaign. An investigation by a Senate committee found case after case of WPA employees being instructed to contribute a portion of their salaries to the president's reelection campaign if they wished to remain employed; of people being thrown off the relief rolls for refusing to pledge their support for a favored candidate; and of demands that registered Republicans on relief register as Democrats in order to keep their jobs.

This was by no means the only example of political intimidation that occurred during the FDR years. The standard textbook provides all the details of Watergate and of Richard Nixon's abuse of power (as indeed it should), but not a word about FDR as the pioneer of this activity. When the Paulist Catholic radio station of poor Father James Gillis in Chicago criticized FDR's court-packing scheme, the FCC took its license away. As early as 1935, FDR requested that the FBI initiate a series of investigations into a variety of conservative organizations, and later in the decade secretly sought proof (which, of course, never came) that prominent members of the America First Committee, routinely smeared as Nazis and traitors, were receiving Nazi money.

## Not so fast, Court tells FDR

It is heartwarming to recall a time in American history when programs such as those of the New Deal were actually criticized on constitutional grounds. In the 1930s there were still enough Supreme Court justices committed to an honest interpretation of the Constitution that programs like the National Industrial Recovery Act and the Agricultural Adjustment Act were actually declared unconstitutional.

Needless to say, the Court's decisions infuriated FDR. He denounced the "nine old men" of the Court, whose constitutional interpretation was appropriate only to "horse-and-buggy days." But he went well beyond denunciations. In 1937, FDR proposed that when any Supreme Court justice who had reached age seventy did not resign or retire, one additional justice could be added to the Court. Since six of the nine Supreme Court justices at the time were over seventy the proposed legislation would have allowed FDR to add six more justices to the Court.

At first, the president tried to claim that his plan was intended simply to provide assistance to elderly justices, but even some of his own supporters were insulted by this obvious lie. Eventually, FDR became more forthright about his intentions: He believed that the current slate of justices was wedded to an old-fashioned jurisprudence, and that a more flexible view of the Constitution needed to be introduced into the Court for the sake of preserving his New Deal programs.

Opposition to the plan was intense, and included many of FDR's fellow Democrats. Thankfully, the bill was rejected. But FDR's intimidation of the Court may have had its effects. In particular, some suspect that the president's pressure accounts for why Justice Owen Roberts suddenly became much friendlier to the administration in his decisions. It turns out, however, that FDR would get his chance to influence the Court after all, and not through such crude manipulation. Over the next four years

## A Quotation the Textbooks Leave Out

"We recommend the rejection of this bill as a needless, futile, and utterly dangerous abandonment of constitutional principle.... Its practical operation would be to make the Constitution what the executive or legislative branches of the Government choose to say it is—an interpretation to be changed with each change of administration. It is a measure which should be so emphatically rejected that its parallel will never again be presented to the free representatives of the free people of America."

**Senate Judiciary Committee,** on FDR's court-packing plan

the president was able fill seven vacancies on the Court caused by resignations, retirements, and death.

### What the new Court was like

What was the new jurisprudence like once FDR had made his imprint on the Court? Consider the case of *Wickard v. Filburn* (1942). The Court ruled that a farmer growing wheat for his own use on his own property fell under the heading of "interstate commerce" and was subject to federal regulation under the Constitution's interstate commerce clause. Homegrown wheat, in the Court's words, "supplies a need of the man who grew it which would otherwise be reflected by purchases in the open market. Homegrown wheat in this sense competes with wheat in commerce." So someone who supplies himself with wheat, since he is not purchasing wheat on the market, therefore affects interstate commerce. Under this standard, anything would qualify as interstate commerce—and therefore be subject to federal regulation.

The Court became an instrument for justifying federal action and for reducing the states to a condition of subordination. In *Currin v. Wallace* (1939) the Court suggested that the federal government could extend its power over virtually any area that might contribute to the "general welfare."

## Did World War II lift America out of the Depression?

So if the New Deal didn't get us out of the Great Depression, what did? Forced to acknowledge the failure of the New Deal, some people—including many professors—say World War II. It has become part of the conventional wisdom that World War II was a time of great economic prosperity in the United States, and even that the war rescued the country from the Depression. This is simply not true. If it were, then it might be a good idea to be at war all the time. Think of all the people we'd put to work producing raw materials, building planes, and assembling missiles.

Historians have made much of the substantial production figures that were attained during the war. But most of this increase was due to the construction of armaments and military equipment and payments to military personnel. This production was not geared toward things that ordinary people needed. It made consumers worse off by diverting capital and other resources to goods that no consumer would want to buy. Between 1943 and 1945,

## What Economists Said

War prosperity is like the prosperity that an earthquake or a plague brings.

**Ludwig von Mises**

some two-fifths of the labor force—including the armed forces, civilian employees of the armed forces, people who worked in the military supply industries, and the unemployed—was producing neither consumer goods nor capital goods. That was not all, of course; the tax monies of the remaining 60 percent went to fund the activities of the 40 percent that were not producing things consumers needed. All of this amounted to a dramatic *loss* of material wealth.

## The military draft reduces unemployment!

Unemployment did virtually disappear, it is true. But it disappeared primarily because eleven million people were added to the armed forces, mostly by conscription. It is not exactly clear why this should be impressive. As Robert Higgs explains, "During the war the government pulled the equivalent of 22 percent of the prewar labor force into the armed forces. Voilà, the unemployment rate dropped to a very low level. No one needs a macroeconomic model to understand this event." In a healthy economy, there is always a desire for more labor to produce more goods. The sick economy of the New Deal, however, could make a dent in the unemployment problem only by conscripting over a fifth of the labor force into the military.

Meanwhile, the average work week in manufacturing increased by seven hours between 1940 and 1944, and by a full 50 percent in bituminous coal mining. And it was more difficult, and sometimes even impossible, to acquire the goods people needed. No one during the war could buy a new car, house, or major appliance, since the government had forbidden their production entirely. A great many other goods were either unavailable or very difficult to obtain, from chocolate bars and sugar to meat, gasoline, and rubber tires. As economist George Reisman explains:

> People believed they were prosperous in World War II because they were piling up large amounts of unspendable income—in the form of paper money and government bonds. They confused this accumulation of paper assets with real wealth. Incredibly, most economic statisticians and historians make the same error when they measure the standard of living of World War II by the largely unspendable "national income" of the period.

Needless to say, this is not prosperity. What finally brought the Depression to an end was neither economic legislation nor World War II. Instead, it was the return to normal conditions following the war and the removal of the uncertainty that had haunted business during the FDR years. Prosperity would have returned much sooner had it not been for the destructive and foolish policies of Hoover and Roosevelt.

## Chapter 12

# YES, COMMUNIST SYMPATHIZERS REALLY EXISTED

Generations of Americans have been told that only the paranoid and delusional believe that many of America's cultural and intellectual elite once sympathized with the Soviet Union, or that key departments of our government were infiltrated by Communist spies. This was all, in fact, true.

In 1921, the American dancer Isadora Duncan, elated at the news of the Bolshevik Revolution four years earlier, pointed to her red scarf and proclaimed to a Boston crowd at the end of one of her performances, "This is red! So am I! It is the color of life and vigor. You were once wild here. Don't let them tame you!" Mayor James Curley, among the most colorful in Boston's history, announced that Duncan would never be given a license to dance in Boston again "in view of the duty the city owes to the decent element." She decided to move to Soviet Russia "to dance for the people," and later described her years there as the happiest of her life.

Now consider the condition of Russia in 1921. It was a complete shambles politically, economically, and morally. Vladimir Ilyich Lenin had shut down the newly elected Constituent Assembly because Bolsheviks had won only a small minority of seats. Lenin's economic policies, including a half-baked attempt to run a modern economy without money, had led to utter chaos and ruin. Things got so bad that even Lenin himself, an ideologue to the last, conceded that a temporary, tactical retreat

## Guess what?

★ Walter Duranty of the *New York Times* actually covered up Stalin's strategy to starve Ukrainians.

★ Intercepted Soviet intelligence messages reveal that at least 350 Americans had secret relationships with the Soviets.

★ Senator McCarthy had nothing to do with investigations into Hollywood, which were carried out by the House of Representatives; he was concerned with Communists or Communist sympathizers *in government*.

from pure communism was necessary—hence the so-called New Economic Policy introduced in 1921. Famine threatened the lives of countless millions of Russians, and would certainly have consumed more souls than it did had it not been for the American assistance dispensed by Herbert Hoover, who had famously coordinated food relief during World War I. (Recent archival discoveries reveal that the Russian government diverted some of the American assistance to secret weapons purchases from Germany.)

By 1921 there were already 70,000 people confined in concentration camps. The czars had a secret police force, the Okhrana, of 15,000; by his death in 1924, Lenin had established a secret police *sixteen times* as large. The churches were already undergoing terrible persecutions.

This is the society that American leftists considered so "progressive," and a model for their own country.

## "I have been over into the future—and it works!"

It is not easy to decide which American intellectual merits the dubious honor of having been the first Soviet dupe, but journalist Lincoln Steffens is certainly in the running. As part of the "muckraking" journalistic tradition, Steffens had (and for some reason continues to have) a reputation for being alert to corruption and injustice. *McClure's* magazine serialized his writing on the cozy relationship between businessmen and politicians in several major cities, and these writings were eventually published as a book, *The Shame of the Cities* (1904). He later fixed his critical eye upon state governments. But there was no criticism to be found when Steffens traveled to Russia in 1919. "I have been over into the future," he proclaimed to Bernard Baruch upon his return, "and it works!" According to some historians, Steffens composed that line on his way to Russia, apparently prepared to utter it no matter what he saw. A great moral exemplar for us all.

## The Soviet experiment: A model for America?

Steffens was far from the only American intellectual to make a sojourn into the future. A great many noted American political activists and intellectuals followed in his footsteps, including Jane Addams (who called the Russian Revolution "the greatest social experiment in history"), Stuart Chase, John Dewey, Rexford G. Tugwell, and Edmund Wilson. These and other American visitors to the Soviet Union typically came back impressed, and convinced that the United States had much to learn from the great Soviet experiment. Books and articles poured forth, from Dewey's *Impressions of Russia* and Sherwood Eddy's *The Challenge of Russia* to George S. Counts's *The Soviet Challenge to America* and Maxwell Stewart's "Where Everyone Has a Job."

These various trips by American intellectuals to Soviet Russia formed a major component of the ideology behind President Franklin Roosevelt's New Deal. According to Professor Lewis Feuer of the University of California at Berkeley:

> The whole conception of a "social experiment," the whole notion of planned human intervention into social processes to raise the welfare of the people, had become linked in the minds of America's intellectual and social leaders with the practice of the Soviet Union. This transformation in American thought was largely the work of a small number of several hundreds of travelers to the Soviet Union during the previous decade. If there was no De Tocqueville among them, the reports which they published affected the American political consciousness more deeply nonetheless than any other foreign influence in its history.

Progressive educator John Dewey, in a series of articles for *The New Republic* in 1928, could hardly contain his enthusiasm for Soviet Russia.

"I have never seen anywhere in the world such a large proportion of intelligent, happy, and intelligently occupied children," he recalled. Other progressive educators were equally impressed; William Kilpatrick was flattered to see that his own writing on education had been translated into Russian and used to train Russian teachers.

## Labor unions speak: The merits of the Soviet system

Professor Paul Douglas of the University of Chicago was part of a trade union delegation that visited the Soviet Union in 1927. Professor Douglas later proclaimed that in Russia, people's "real rights, that is their economic rights, are much better protected than in any other country." Speaking on behalf of that delegation, John Brophy told Soviet leader Joseph Stalin: "The presence of the American delegation in the USSR is the best reply, and is evidence of the sympathy of a section of the American workers to the workers of the Soviet Union."

Labor leader Sidney Hillman, who headed the Amalgamated Clothing Workers, shared this positive view of the Soviet Union. "My conviction is that Russia is in an era of great economic reconstruction," he said. "I have never met a group of people that is so realistic, so practical, so courageous, and so able to handle the greatest job, as the group of people who have charge of the destinies of the Russian nation today." The president of the International Ladies Garment Workers' Union announced that the Soviet Union's workers "appear to be ready to undergo all kinds of misery as a necessary sacrifice for the attainment of the ideal communistic state, which, they believe, is on the way now."

For his part, social thinker Horace M. Kallen reported: "All, regardless of party, acknowledge that the revolution has awakened the millions, that the government, 'dictatorship' though it be, has liberated their energies, animated them with an altogether unprecedented sense of personal dignity and inward worth, [and] opened to them hitherto

## A Communist's Second Thoughts

One of the great twentieth-century historians of the American South, **Eugene D. Genovese** was an open Marxist for much of his career, going so far as to declare in 1965 that he would "welcome" a Communist victory in Vietnam. By the 1990s he was having second thoughts. In a 1994 article in *Dissent*, he discussed left-wing cover-ups of Communist crimes and explored the relationship between leftism and the totalitarian horrors to which Marxism had given birth. "Having...scoffed at the Ten Commandments and the Sermon on the Mount," said Genovese, "we ended a seventy-year experiment with socialism with little more to our credit than tens of millions of corpses."

According to Genovese, mainstream liberalism had provided indispensable support to people like himself: "[H]ow could we have survived politically were it not for the countless liberals who, to one extent or another, supported us, apparently under the comforting delusion that we were social reformers in rather too much of a hurry—a delusion we ourselves never suffered from."

"The horrors," Genovese explained, "did not arise from perversions of radical ideology but from the ideology itself. We were led into complicity with mass murder and the desecration of our professed ideals not by Stalinist or other corruptions of high ideals...but by a deep flaw in our understanding of human nature—its frailty and its possibilities—and by our inability to replace the moral and ethical baseline provided by the religion we have dismissed with indifference, not to say contempt."

In 1996, he reentered the Catholic Church, which he had left at age fifteen.

sealed worlds of science and art and personal advancement." (Note the quotation marks around "dictatorship.")

## Lighten up: It's all for "the good of the masses of the working people"!

*The Nation* was also spellbound by Soviet economic policy. Editor Oswald Garrison Villard, in a 1929 article called "Russia from a Car Window," could hardly contain himself in his endorsement, despite speaking no

Russian and never having met a Russian peasant: "This, I repeat, is the most stupendous governmental feat ever undertaken—the social, moral, political, industrial, economic emancipation of a people and its reorganization upon the basis of service to the society and to the nation, with the profit-making motive suddenly removed from the individual." He was sure that "the minority which controls the destiny of Russia is on its way with extraordinary and completely unselfish devotion, with the fiercest determination to succeed at any cost." To the charge that the Russian communists were fanatics he shot back: "Who else but fanatics would have the course for the task or could be relied upon to drive through to the end without essential compromise?" Such a task required something more than "timid or half-way reformers." The Soviet dictatorship wasn't really so bad, since the ruling party was "working for the good of the masses of the working people."

Perhaps the most notorious figure in this context is *New York Times* reporter Walter Duranty, the most truly iniquitous of the whole pathetic bunch, who covered up one of the greatest atrocities of the twentieth century.

## How Stalin starved his own people

Stalin wanted control of the food supply to feed the battalion of workers that would carry out his "Five Year Plan" of rapid industrialization. Communist ideology also had to be enforced, which meant private land ownership had to be abolished. In order to collectivize agriculture, Stalin herded private farmers onto large, state-owned farms where they would supposedly work for the common good instead of private gain.

Needless to say, the Russian peasantry resisted. When they did accept collectivization, it resulted in dramatic inefficiencies. Concessions had to be made early on; people were allowed to own tiny plots. By the 1980s it was an open secret that the 2 percent of Soviet farmland that was privately owned was producing 30 percent of Russia's agricultural output.

At the same time that Stalin forced collectivization, he also revived the campaign against Ukrainian national culture that had been dormant since the early 1920s. It was in Ukraine, which had been forcibly incorporated into the Soviet Union, that Stalin's collectivization policy met its fiercest resistance (though the process was largely complete even there by 1932). He decided to deal with what he saw as the problem of divided loyalty in Ukraine once and for all. First, he arrested and jailed thousands of Ukrainian intellectual and cultural leaders. Having deprived Ukrainians of people who might have spearheaded a resistance movement, Stalin then moved against the peasantry, where the real locus of Ukrainian traditions could be found.

Even though the collectivization process was largely complete, Stalin's battle against the wicked *kulak* (the large landowning peasant and "class enemy" of the countryside) was not yet over. They were "defeated but not yet exterminated." But by this point, anyone who had been a *kulak* had long since been driven away, killed, or sent into slave labor camps. The campaign was really targeting ordinary peasants. They would be broken, physically and spiritually, and their identity as a people would be drained from them by force.

Stalin began issuing delivery quotas for grain that the Ukrainians could not meet without themselves dying of starvation. Failure to meet the requirements was chalked up as deliberate sabotage. Eventually Stalin

## What the Intellectuals Said

The Soviet experiment proved the need for "no further incentive than the burning zeal to create a new heaven and a new earth which flames in the breast of every good Communist. It is something—this flame—that one has to see to appreciate. There is nothing like it in the world today."

**Stuart Chase,**
Economist

authorized seizure of the peasants' grain in order to meet the targets. Communist activists claimed that Ukrainian saboteurs were everywhere, systematically withholding food from Soviet cities and defying Stalin's orders. They made sweeps through private homes, the kinder agents leaving a modicum of food behind for the family's use but the more ruthless ones taking everything.

The result was predictable enough. The people began to starve in greater and greater numbers. A peasant who did not appear to be starving was considered suspect by Soviet authorities. At least five million people perished in Ukraine alone, a count that does not include Stalin's atrocities against peasants elsewhere in the Soviet Union.

Robert Conquest's book *The Harvest of Sorrow*, which tells the story of the terror-famine, reads like a novel. But the story is real. It should be read by everyone, not only as an example of man's inhumanity to man,

★★★★★★★★★★

## PC Today:
## A Missed Opportunity to Right a Wrong

n 2003, Columbia University historian Mark von Hagen was asked to review the reporting for which *New York Times* reporter Walter Duranty won the Pulitzer Prize, in response to an international campaign demanding that it be revoked. He found that Duranty's pattern of deception and of slavishly repeating Soviet propaganda was already in evidence at that time, even before the terror-famine of 1932–33. "For the sake of the *New York Times*' honor," he told the Associated Press, "they should take the prize away." The Pulitzer Board decided not to withdraw the prize.

but also to see the kind of crime that considerable segments of the political Left in the United States and throughout the West were willing to cover up or ignore in order not to cast Communism in a bad light.

## The *New York Times* reporter who covered up Stalin's crimes

Walter Duranty, desperate to maintain his access to Stalin, could consistently be counted on to portray the regime sympathetically. In November 1932, he claimed that "there is no famine or actual starvation nor is there likely to be." In June 1933, with death everywhere in Ukraine, Duranty reported: "The 'famine' is mostly bunk." In August he wrote that "any report of a famine in Russia is today an exaggeration or malignant propaganda."

Malcolm Muggeridge, a great British journalist who attempted to report the truth about the grisly events unfolding in Ukraine, later described Duranty as "the greatest liar of any journalist I have met in fifty years of journalism." Muggeridge chose his words carefully. Duranty was no ignoramus. He knew full well the terrifying nature and scope of what was occurring, as we know from his own private comments to others. In one letter he estimated the number of deaths at seven million; in another he guessed ten million.

*The Nation* magazine praised Duranty in the early 1930s for composing "the most enlightening, dispassionate and readable dispatches from a great nation in the making which appeared in any newspaper in the world." For *The Nation*, as for so many other American "progressives," Stalin's Russia was "a great nation in the making." Duranty even won the Pulitzer Prize for his reporting from Russia in 1931.

Some people did manage to get the word out about what was happening in Ukraine. But when a paper with the prestige of the *New York Times* denied the existence of the famine, doubts remained. As Conquest explains, "This lobby of the blind and the blindfold could not actually prevent true accounts by those who were neither dupes nor liars from reaching the West. But they could, and did, succeed in giving the impression that there was at least a genuine doubt about what was happening."

Why the cover-up? Conquest cites one Communist as saying that the Soviet Union could hope to attract support around the world for its Marxist system only if the human costs of its policies were kept from the public eye. You have to break some eggs to make an omelet, you see.

## Stalin's show trials genuine, say bootlickers

Prominent Americans could even be found to defend Stalin's show trials, a spectacle of political theater so transparent that it would have taken genuine effort *not* to see through it. In order to terrorize Communist Party members into absolute submission and at the same time eliminate potential rivals, Stalin put on a series of high-profile trials in which prominent Communists confessed to treachery against the Soviet Union. In some cases, people were coaxed into making these confessions by threats against their families if they refused. One by one some of the most loyal Communists, dating back to the days of the 1917 Bolshevik Revolution, solemnly admitted to counterrevolutionary activity. George Orwell could hardly have improved on this eerie and macabre spectacle.

Yet there were those on the American Left who supported Stalin and vouched for the authenticity of the trials. In 1938, some 150 Americans prominent in the entertainment industry signed a statement in support of the verdicts reached in "the recent Moscow trials." According to the expert opinion of these Broadway stars and assorted glitterati, the trials had "by sheer weight of evidence established a clear presumption of the guilt of the defendants." As if this weren't bad enough, people who knew better said the same thing. The U.S. ambassador to the Soviet Union, Joseph Davies, insisted to the American government that the trials were genuine, a claim he stood by in his 1941 book *Mission to Moscow*. He told the *New Republic*, "We see no reason to take the trial at other than its face value." The proceedings, he said, had uncovered the "virus of a conspiracy to overthrow the [Soviet] government." Duranty, for his part, described it as "unthinkable" that Stalin could have sentenced his friends to death "unless the proofs of guilt were overwhelming," and wrote of his conviction that "the confessions are true."

## Yes, Soviet spies were a problem

With the collapse of the Soviet Union and the opening of part of the Soviet archives to Western scholars, it was inevitable that our knowledge of Soviet espionage in America would grow deeper and more precise. In 1995, the Venona Project files were declassified and made available to the general public. These transcripts consist of thousands of Soviet intelligence messages that the U.S. government intercepted in the 1940s. In 1943, American cryptologists figured out there was a flaw in the Soviet code and within a few years began decoding some of these transmissions. The project went on for three decades. Although even by the 1970s only a fraction of the Venona cables had been successfully decoded, the brief window of Soviet intelligence vulnerability proved enormously enlightening in sketching at least part of the story of Soviet espionage during a crucial moment in history.

Thanks to Venona, we now know that at least 350 Americans had secret relationships with Soviet intelligence. Since only about 10 percent

### Anti-Soviet Historian Was Right

**Robert Conquest**, an outstanding American historian of the Soviet Union, was routinely pilloried by leftists for being too harsh on the Soviets and for "exaggerating" Soviet crimes. To this day, a few holdouts continue to deny or minimize those crimes, but by and large Conquest has been vindicated. He was recently asked by his publisher to prepare a new edition of his book *The Great Terror*, incorporating Soviet archival materials now available to scholars. They asked for a new title for the updated edition. Conquest suggested *I Told You So, You [expletive deleted] Fools*.

## A Book You're Not Supposed to Read

*The Venona Secrets: Exposing Soviet Espionage and America's Traitors* by Herbert Romerstein and Eric Breindel; Washington, D.C.: Regnery, 2000.

of the intercepted messages were decoded, we can only assume that the real figure was considerably higher. Although some of the conclusions drawn from Venona remain controversial, evidence suggests that Soviet agents could be found in some particularly sensitive and high-level positions. Harry Dexter White, assistant secretary of the treasury, was an influential figure in the creation of the World Bank and the International Monetary Fund. Laurence Duggan coordinated American relations with Latin America, and Lauchlin Currie was a special assistant to FDR.

## Joe McCarthy was a paranoid idiot, right?

Have the Venona cables vindicated Wisconsin senator Joseph McCarthy, who in the early 1950s famously called attention to a major security problem within the American government? (Senator McCarthy had nothing to do with investigations into Hollywood, which were carried out by the House of Representatives; he was concerned exclusively with Communists or Communist sympathizers *in government*.) It is simply impossible to do the subject justice here. Books on McCarthy, in fact, tend toward the enormous: David Oshinsky's book *A Conspiracy so Immense*, for example, is itself immense. In particular, McCarthy's accusations against Owen Lattimore, Philip Jessup, and John Stewart Service remain a source of contention. But we can at least raise a few suggestive points.

By the time McCarthy emerged on the scene, internal security was a major issue, and an unresolved one. There is little doubt, as one scholar puts it, that "many U.S. officials whose job it was to guard against subversion took a strangely casual view of their assignment." Repeated attempts, including two by FBI director J. Edgar Hoover, to persuade government officials to act on evidence of Soviet infiltration were ignored. The situation grew so bad that in mid-1947, members of the Senate Appropriations Committee, in a confidential report sent to Secretary of State George Marshall, observed in exasperation:

> It is evident that there is a deliberate calculated program being carried out not only to protect Communist personnel in high places, but to reduce security and intelligence protection to a nullity. . . . On file in the Department is a copy of a preliminary report of the FBI on Soviet espionage activities in the United States, which involves large numbers of State Department employees. . . . This report has been challenged and ignored by those charged with the responsibility of administering the department with the apparent tacit approval of [secretary of state] Mr. [Dean] Acheson.

## *A mysterious cover-up*

One of the cases that McCarthy investigated involved *Amerasia*, a small pro-Communist journal whose personnel included a host of well-known Soviet apologists. In early 1945, *Amerasia* published what turned out to be a nearly verbatim classified report on American and British policy in Southeast Asia. How had they accessed this secret report?

In June 1945, after a considerable period of surveillance, the FBI arrested several of the journal's staffers and three officials of the U.S. government—naval intelligence official Lieutenant Andrew Roth, State Department employee Emmanuel S. Larsen, and diplomat John Stewart Service—who had supplied them with secret information, largely dealing with American policy toward Asia. More than 1,000 government documents were seized.

Surely something would come of a bombshell like this, right? J. Edgar Hoover described the case against the defendants as "airtight," and preparations were made in the Justice Department to begin prosecution.

Then, suddenly, Justice backed off. Two of the figures involved received fines, while the others suffered no penalty at all. The Tydings Committee, a Senate committee established to investigate McCarthy's charges, dismissed the matter as overblown.

But FBI wiretaps at the time that were made public only in the 1990s reveal a conspiracy to bury the case on the part of Lauchlin Currie, Democratic lobbyist Thomas Corcoran, and officials from the Justice Department. Harvey Klehr and Ronald Radosh, two scholars of the subject, describe what all of this meant: "Three government employees were meeting regularly with a magazine publisher who had devoted his career to promoting the Stalinist line and who, as it turned out, had cultivated these contacts in the first place because it was his life's ambition to become a full-fledged Soviet agent.... One did not have to be a right-wing crank to find this unacceptable and to feel isolated and suspicious when the whole mess was swept under a rug." Stanton Evans concludes:

> Suffice it to note that the *Amerasia* case displayed, to the fullest, every kind of security horror, and federal crime: Theft of documents, policy subversion, cover-up, perjury, and obstruction of justice—to name only the most glaring. In short, everything McCarthy had said about the subject was correct, while his opponents were not only wrong, but lying; the Tydings "investigation," for its part, was a sham—the cover-up of a cover-up, not an investigation.
>
> Though all of this is now nailed down beyond all question, it apparently avails McCarthy nothing.

### Liberal historian: McCarthy "closer to the truth than those who ridiculed him"

Evidence from Venona was so considerable that even the liberal author Nicholas von Hoffman admitted in the *Washington Post* in 1996 that, much as he still detested McCarthy, the age of McCarthy "was not the simple witch hunt of the innocent by the malevolent, as two generations of high school and college students have been taught." He admitted that the weight of the available evidence now proved that "Ethel and Julius Rosenberg, executed in June 1953 for atomic espionage, were guilty; Alger Hiss, a darling of the establishment, was guilty; and that dozens of lesser known persons such as Victor Perlo, Judith Coplon and Harry Gold, whose innocence of the accusations made against them had been a tenet of leftist faith for decades, were traitors, or, at the least, ideological vassals of a foreign power." And even though von Hoffman believed that McCarthy had not pinpointed the correct people, he nevertheless admitted that the Wisconsin senator "was still closer to the truth than those who ridiculed him."

**A Quotation the Textbooks Leave Out**

"Thank God somebody's doing it."

**J. Edgar Hoover** on McCarthy's work

McCarthy supposedly terrified the nation, but his opponents spoke freely as a matter of routine, denouncing him from the pages of the most influential periodicals in the country. A 1954 Gallup poll found him to be the fourth most admired man in America. As one commentator puts it, if McCarthy was so beyond the pale then "why did Joe Kennedy back him, the Kennedy girls date him, Robert Kennedy work for him and JFK defend him as a 'great patriot' in his year of censure? And why was McCarthy asked to be the godfather to Bobby Kennedy's firstborn?"

But let us suppose for the sake of argument that all of the standard criticisms of Joe McCarthy are valid, in particular that he made reckless charges against people who had innocently belonged to Communist front groups without themselves being Communists. Even so, these deeds are rather minor compared to the deeds of other Americans who lived at about the same time that are not mentioned in a single mainstream American history text. McCarthy, for example, did not cover up one of the greatest atrocities in the history of mankind, as did Walter Duranty. But while the denunciations of McCarthy continue half a century later, *no one has even heard of Walter Duranty.*

None of what we have seen in this chapter is particularly flattering to the American Left, and in fact is rather embarrassing. By an interesting coincidence, it is mysteriously left out of standard histories.

## Chapter 13

# THE APPROACH OF
# WORLD WAR II

dolf Hitler, who had come to power in Germany in 1933, over the course of the decade unilaterally overturned a great many provisions of the Treaty of Versailles imposed on Germany at the end of World War I. Hitler:

* ❋ Rearmed Germany in violation of treaty's disarmament provisions
* ❋ Remilitarized the Rhineland, the buffer zone between France and Germany
* ❋ United Austria with Germany

Hitler also bullied the West into allowing him to annex the Sudetenland, a largely German-inhabited region of Czechoslovakia, and alienated Western opinion by going on to occupy nearly all of Czechoslovakia.

When Germany began making demands on Poland in 1939—such as the return of the city of Danzig, whose loss the British had long considered one of Germany's most understandable grievances from the Versailles Treaty—Britain and France decided to give the Poles a fateful war guarantee. Bolstered by British and French encouragement, Poland remained obstinate in the face of German demands, and on September 1, 1939, Germany invaded Poland. In practice, there was nothing the British or French could do to save Poland. By the following year Hitler had

## Guess what?

★ While telling Americans he was trying to keep the country out of war, behind the scenes FDR was trying to draw America in.

★ FDR's refusal to negotiate with the moderate Japanese prime minister weakened the moderates in Japan and helped bring the military to power.

★ Many prominent Americans were against the war: Sinclair Lewis, Charles Lindbergh, H. L. Mencken, Henry Miller, JFK, Herbert Hoover, and Gerald Ford.

acquired quite a list of European conquests, though the only militarily significant power he had defeated was France.

During the nearly two and a half years of World War II in which the United States was not involved, President Franklin Roosevelt portrayed himself as engaged in a strenuous effort to keep America out of the war. He said so as soon as the war broke out in 1939, and he continued to say so as the months and years passed. He famously declared in October 1940, "I have said this before, but I shall say it again and again and again: Your boys are not going to be sent into any foreign wars." "The first purpose of our foreign policy," he assured Americans several days later, "is to keep our country out of war."

Nothing could have been further from the truth. FDR was busy making secret pledges to the British, provoking Germany into attacking the United States (and then lying about it), and assisting the British in ways that violated at least the spirit of American neutrality legislation and which, according to international law, effectively made the United States a belligerent.

## FDR tries to neutralize neutrality laws

To involve America in the war, FDR had to overcome two major obstacles: American public opinion and a consistent body of neutrality legislation. By the 1930s, 70 percent of Americans polled said that U.S. involvement in World War I had been a mistake. When war broke out again in 1939, Americans were determined to stay out of the affairs of its quarrelsome neighbors across the Atlantic.

FDR's other problem was the pesky neutrality laws from the 1930s that were designed to prevent the United States from being lured into war, and which especially sought to avoid the circumstances that had led to U.S. entry into World War I. Thus, for example, Americans on belligerent ships were at first told that they traveled at their own risk, and neutrality legislation later in the 1930s prohibited such travel altogether. The neutrality legislation also prevented the United States from selling weapons to countries at war. America could sell other goods to belligerents, but only on a cash-and-carry basis and transported in the recipient country's ships. America's ships could not venture into war zones to conduct wartime trade.

FDR sought to change the part of the neutrality legislation that stopped the United States from selling weapons to nations at war. As of 1939, therefore, it became legal for a belligerent (Britain, in this case) to acquire weapons from the United States on a cash-and-carry basis. The prohibition on lending of *money* to belligerents was preserved; and the requirement that the equipment be transported in the belligerent's own ships meant that American ships would not be exposed to danger.

## The imperial presidency takes shape: Did FDR break the law?

Even after Hitler had abandoned his plans to invade Britain, FDR continued to lend support to the British. In September 1940, FDR gave the British government fifty American destroyers in exchange for ninety-nine-year leases on several military bases in the Western Hemisphere. It was a significant move, yet the president was not exactly forthcoming when questioned by reporters about the agreement. Did it require congressional approval? The reply: "It is all over; it is all done." What were the details of the agreement? It involved "all kinds of things that nobody here would understand, so I won't mention them." And the president never let on that the deal might in fact provoke Germany against the United States. Assistant secretary of state Breckinridge Long wrote in his diary that "Germany may take violent exception to it and declare war on us." He added that Secretary of State Cordell Hull "realizes that—specifically said he did, and says the President does, too."

A number of experts pointed out that FDR's actions were illegal. According to Yale University's Edwin Borchard, an expert in international law, "There are constitutional understandings which require that agreements of great importance, particularly involving the question of war and peace, shall not be concluded by executive power alone." In response to Attorney General Robert Jackson's contrived defense of FDR's actions, the distinguished political scientist Edward Corwin wondered: "Why not any and all of Congress's specifically delegated powers be set aside by the President's 'executive power' and the country be put on a totalitarian basis without further ado?" More recently, longtime Democratic senator Daniel Patrick Moynihan of New York wrote in *On the Law of Nations* (1992) that FDR "actually subverted the law" and "was clearly subject to impeachment." Robert Shogun's *Hard Bargain* (1995), a 320-page study of this single exchange, argues that the way FDR carried out this deal, without the consent of Congress, changed the presidency forever, setting the legal stage for ever more activist presidents and less and less accountability to Congress or the people.

## The end of neutrality

In March 1941 the Lend-Lease Act was enacted. The United States could lend ships and other military equipment to a belligerent (primarily to Britain and China, and later to the Soviet Union). By this point the old cash-and-carry provision introduced in 1939 had lost its usefulness for the British, who by now had no cash with which to make purchases. The Lend-Lease Act technically observed some of the neutrality requirements, since once again it did not involve *the lending of money*, though it seemed to disregard the previous requirement of cash payment for war matériel.

The ensuing months saw more departures from neutrality. Naval patrols were established in the Atlantic in April to alert British warships to the presence of German submarines. American troops occupied Iceland in July. The Atlantic Conference of Roosevelt and Churchill in August issued what was in effect a statement of war aims despite the fact that the United States was not actually in the war.

## How FDR got Americans into war

By 1941 it was clear that FDR was desperate to involve the United States in the war. On September 4, a German submarine torpedoed the *Greer*, an American warship that according to FDR had been on a peaceful mail run to Iceland. This was, said the president, an outrageous act of "piracy." But what in fact took place is that the *Greer* had been tracking the German submarine for several hours, signaling its location to British air forces that dropped depth charges on the sub—as, in turn, did the *Greer* itself. As Winston Churchill confided privately to aides, the president had made clear to him that he intended to become more and more provocative, and that, in Churchill's words, "everything was to be done to provoke an incident."

That FDR used deceptive means to try to draw his country into the war is acknowledged by everyone except, apparently, most textbook authors. One popular textbook's *entire discussion* of the *Greer* incident consists of this single sentence: "The first attack on an American warship occurred on September 4, when a German submarine fired two torpedoes at a destroyer."

In fact, Hitler instructed his submarine captains not to fire on American ships, well aware of the pretext that such attacks had provided for American entry into World War I. One week later, FDR ordered American warships to fire upon German subs on sight. The president's claims that he was working day and night to keep the United States out of the war were at this point becoming farcical. His accusations against Germany continued, this time with regard to a German attack on the USS *Kearny* in

October. But again it was the U.S. ship that had opened hostilities. Late that month, an exasperated FDR tried to frighten Americans with claims that he possessed a "secret map" showing a Nazi invasion plan for South America, from which the Germans would be in a position to launch an attack on the United States. Americans were expected to believe that Hitler's forces, which could not get across the English Channel, were poised to cross the Atlantic Ocean and take over an entire continent. Few Americans bought that scenario. And their instincts were right: FDR had made the whole thing up.

There are some who say that FDR was justified in lying to the American people. The American public, the argument goes, was too shortsighted to appreciate the threat posed by Nazi Germany. FDR biographer John T. Flynn answered that one in 1948: "[I]f Roosevelt had the right to do this, to whom is the right denied? At what point are we to cease to demand that our leaders deal honestly and truthfully with us?"

## "People historians love to hate" department: The America First Committee

The America First Committee (AFC) has not typically received the same kind of hearing that American historians have had no problem giving to the New Left of the 1960s, to the American Communist Party, or to the mass-murdering Mao Tse-Tung. America Firsters wanted to avoid American involvement in another savage European war. Consider the view later taken by *New York Times* military expert Hanson Baldwin, who wrote in his 1949 book *Great Mistakes of the War*:

> There is no doubt whatsoever that it would have been to the interest of Britain, the United States, and the world to have allowed—and indeed, to have encouraged—the world's two great dictatorships to fight each other to a frazzle. Such a struggle, with its resultant weakening of both Communism and

Nazism, could not but have aided in the establishment of a more stable peace.

What hostile scholars are rarely in any hurry to point out is just how many prominent and admired Americans belonged to or sympathized with the AFC, from both the left and the right.

A young John F. Kennedy sent in a donation to the AFC with a note: "What you are doing is vital." Future president Gerald Ford was described as an "enthusiastic recruiter" for the AFC while at Yale Law School. At its height the AFC had some 850,000 members, along with millions of sympathizers.

FDR launched a vicious campaign against America Firsters, having repeated recourse to the FBI and the IRS. America Firsters found their telephones tapped, and some of them even wound up before grand juries. No one ever found the Nazi "secret agents" that FDR claimed were lurking in America, and the president's instructions to the FBI that they comb the records for any evidence of Nazi funding of the AFC yielded nothing. Strangely, those delicate souls who are so troubled by Joe McCarthy's campaign to expose Communists and Communist sympathizers in the 1950s fall oddly silent when it comes to the victims of FDR's witch hunt.

## Did FDR make war with Japan inevitable?

The Asian theater of the war was entirely distinct from the European, though Japan did join the defensive Tripartite Pact with Germany and Italy in 1940. In the early 1930s, the United States had studiously avoided involvement in Japanese affairs. Herbert Hoover had remained aloof when Japan occupied the northern Chinese province of Manchuria in 1931–32, arguing that no vital American interest was at stake and that he had no intention of sacrificing American lives. Moreover, since the Japanese argued that they needed a security buffer against Stalin's Russia, it

★ ★ ★ ★

**America Firsters Who Opposed War**

Sherwood Anderson

Charles Beard

e.e. cummings

Theodore Dreiser

Gerald Ford

Herbert Hoover

John F. Kennedy

Sinclair Lewis

Charles Lindbergh

Alice Roosevelt Longworth (daughter of Theodore)

Hanford MacNider (former American Legion chairman)

Edgar Lee Masters

H. L. Mencken

Henry Miller

Kathleen Norris

Gore Vidal

Robert Wood, chairman of Sears, Roebuck and army quartermaster general under Wilson

Frank Lloyd Wright

★ ★ ★

was unlikely that anything short of all-out war with Japan would have dislodged them from Manchuria.

FDR would have a much more interventionist outlook in the Pacific. In 1937, when Japan and China went to war, FDR made his displeasure with the Japanese clear, and even authorized the sale of weapons to China. (He was able to evade the neutrality legislation since its prohibition on the sale of weapons to belligerents went into effect only when the president declared a war to be under way in a particular area; FDR simply refrained from officially finding a war to be in progress in China.)

As Japanese brutalities continued and Japan began to extend her influence throughout the Pacific, particularly in Korea and Indochina, FDR decided to take active measures against Japanese expansion. By 1941 he had not only frozen Japanese assets in the United States but had also coordinated a boycott of key goods, especially oil, that Japan needed to acquire from abroad. By cutting off oil shipments to Japan, FDR had dramatically increased the likelihood that the United States would one day find itself at war with Japan. But he never explained the implications of his policies to the American people.

The Japanese originally had three ways in which they could have dealt with the crippling embargo. One was to surrender to American demands and lose face. Another was negotiation, but FDR refused to negotiate despite the fact that Joseph C. Grew, the American ambassador to Japan, thought that negotiations would succeed. "We in the Embassy," he later wrote, "had no doubt that the Prime Minister would have agreed, at his meeting [which fell through] with the President, to the eventual withdrawal of all Japanese forces from all of Indochina and from all of China with the face-saving expedient of being permitted to retain a limited number of troops in North China and Inner Mongolia respectively." Washington had closed off that option. The final possibility was war: The Japanese could strike out further into the Pacific by expanding into British and Dutch colonies where they could acquire the resources they needed. But Japan would first have to take out the American naval installation at Pearl Harbor. The Japanese gambled that swift action on these fronts would pay off. Japanese prime minister Fumimaro Konoye fell from power and was replaced by General Hideki Tojo (who had been minister of war) on October 16, 1941.

War seemed increasingly inevitable to administration officials. Secretary of War Henry Stimson wrote in his diary on November 25, 1941, that the question had now come down to how "to maneuver them [the Japanese] into the position of firing the first shot." The administration was "doing everything they can to get us into war through the Japanese back door," said former President Hoover in 1941.

The first shot came, as Americans well know, on December 7, 1941, in the form of a Japanese attack on the American naval installation at Pearl Harbor, Hawaii. More than 2,000 servicemen and civilians perished. The following day, the United States declared war on Japan. Several days later, Adolf Hitler rashly declared war on the United States. America had entered World War II.

## Chapter 14

# WORLD WAR II: CONSEQUENCES AND AFTERMATH

orld War II was won by the Allies at the enormous cost of fifty million lives and unimaginable destruction. Germany, Italy, and Japan were defeated, to be sure, and their fascistic and militaristic governments overthrown. But when considered *in light of the Allies' original goals*, the balance sheet at the end of the war remained ambiguous.

Poland—which Britain and France had gone to war to save—had been liberated from the Nazi tyranny of Hitler only to be handed over to the Communist tyranny of Stalin. By 1948, Czechoslovakia, whose takeover by Germany had aroused such outrage a decade earlier, was also firmly in the Soviet orbit. A considerable Jewish population was rescued from Nazi concentration camps, to the joy and relief of all civilized people, but the Jews' terrible fate had largely occurred already by the time the Allied victory against Hitler came.

In Asia, Japan was defeated, but the American government's hostility toward Japan had originally stemmed from that country's invasion of China. What, then, was the fate of China? By 1949 it was living under the Communist tyranny of Mao Tse-Tung, perhaps the greatest mass murderer of all time. American interventionists who had sought to oust Japan from China (and who had spurned peaceful means of doing so) now discovered that there was indeed something worse than Japanese control of China.

## Guess what?

★ At Fort Dix, New Jersey, 200 Russians were tear-gassed, forced aboard a Soviet ship, and returned to the Soviet Union.

★ The Marshall Plan didn't help get Europe back on its feet; free markets did.

For nearly half a century following the war, the United States and Britain discovered that the price of siding with Stalin was having to live with the consequences of a hostile (and, by 1949, nuclear-capable) Soviet Union. The Cold War that pitted the United States and the West against the Soviet Union resulted in trillions of dollars in military spending, large and small wars across the globe, the deformation of the Constitution, and the threat of nuclear annihilation.

## FDR and Uncle Joe—
## How friendly was FDR toward Stalin?

Since late 1941, FDR had been guilty of gross ignorance, willful deception, or outright lying in his favorable remarks about the Soviet Union. In November of that year, for example, he claimed that freedom of religion was a fundamental right in Stalin's Russia, even though he knew that it had virtually ceased to exist under the violently atheistic Communist regime. When former U.S. ambassador to the Soviet Union William Bullitt spoke frankly to FDR about the true nature of the Soviet regime and of Stalin himself, just before the president was about to meet with Stalin and Winston Churchill at the Teheran Conference of 1943, FDR replied:

> Bill, I don't dispute your facts. They are accurate. I don't dispute the logic of your reasoning. I just have a hunch that Stalin is not that kind of a man. Harry [Hopkins] says he's not, and that he doesn't want anything but security for his country. And I think that if I give him everything I possibly can and ask for nothing from him in return, noblesse oblige, he won't try to annex anything and will work with me for a world of democracy and peace.

At that Teheran conference, FDR suggested that Eastern European governments ought to be "friendly" to the Soviet Union. But he asked Stalin not to make this concession public, since he did not wish to jeopardize the Polish vote in the 1944 election—"as a practical man," FDR "didn't want to lose their votes." (Shortly before the Teheran conference, FDR had absurdly claimed in a meeting with New York Archbishop [later Cardinal] Francis Spellman that the population of eastern

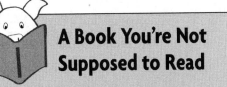

### A Book You're Not Supposed to Read

*Roosevelt and Stalin: The Failed Courtship* by Robert Nisbet; Washington, D.C.: Regnery Gateway, 1988.

Poland "wants to become Russian.") He also said of Estonia, Latvia, and Lithuania—the Baltic states that Stalin was in the process of forcibly incorporating into the Soviet Union—that he was "personally confident that the people would vote to join the Soviet Union." Stalin never bothered to ask them.

In a May 1944 article in the *Saturday Evening Post* that was published with FDR's approval, Forrest Davis described the president's negotiating stance:

> The core of his policy has been the reassurance of Stalin. That was so, as we have seen, at Teheran. It has been so throughout the difficult diplomacy since Stalingrad.... Suppose that Stalin, in spite of all concessions, should prove unappeasable.... Roosevelt, gambling for stakes as enormous as any statesman ever played for, has been betting that the Soviet Union needs peace and is willing to pay for it by collaborating with the West.

At the Yalta conference of February 1945, the second meeting of the Big Three, Stalin got practically everything he wanted, including a free hand in Eastern Europe. Yet Harry Hopkins, FDR's close aide, told the president, "The Russians have given us so much at this conference that I don't think we should let them down." What the Russians had granted was their willingness for the Soviet Union to have three votes in the proposed United Nations instead of the sixteen that they had originally demanded. (How generous.) Stalin had been somewhat forthcoming on the issue of the United Nations since he could see the importance that FDR attached to it, and realized that he was likelier to win concessions for himself on other issues if he made conciliatory gestures on this one, which he considered of relatively little significance.

Admiral William Leahy, who had been at Yalta, later told FDR that the arrangement that had been agreed upon was "so elastic that the Russians can stretch it all the way from Yalta to Washington without ever technically breaking it." FDR protested that it was "the best that I could get." FDR's defenders have typically argued that there was nothing the president could have done to prevent Eastern Europe from going Communist in the power vacuum left by the annihilation of Germany. But Professor Richard Ebeling is probably on to something when he concludes: "Based on his comments to Cardinal Spellman and other Americans, and from his explicit giving of a free hand to Stalin in Poland and the Baltic States at the Tehran Conference, in fact FDR really did not give a damn whether the people in these countries got anything more." Sociologist Robert Nisbet argued in his book *Roosevelt and Stalin* that what Yalta and particularly the Declaration on Liberated Europe did for Stalin was to provide moral legitimation for his Eastern European conquests.

In order to persuade Stalin to enter the war against Japan, FDR granted the Soviet Union control of Manchuria, the province of China whose occupation by Japan in the early 1930s had provoked the wrath of American interventionists. There Stalin was able to provide safe haven for the Chinese Communists and to outfit them with captured Japanese military

## What Our Statesmen Said

PIG

FDR "told me that he didn't care whether the countries bordering Russia became communized."

**Averell Harriman,**
U.S. ambassador to the
Soviet Union, May 1944

equipment, thus paving the way for the Communist takeover of China in 1949. After the Yalta meeting FDR maintained his sanguine view of Stalin (or "Uncle Joe," as the president affectionately referred to him). He suspected that some of Stalin's early seminary training—Uncle Joe had briefly pursued the Russian Orthodox priesthood—must have stayed with him. "I think that something entered into his nature of the way in which a Christian gentleman should behave," said FDR.

The White House's favorable view of Stalin went on longer than people realize. Roosevelt died in April 1945. He was replaced by vice president Harry Truman, who is usually thought to have been more skeptical of the Soviet Union than FDR. But when in 1946 Winston Churchill delivered his famous "iron curtain" speech in Michigan, noting that human freedom was being extinguished as a result of Soviet domination of Eastern Europe, Truman actually apologized to Stalin, and offered to bring him to the United States for a rebuttal.

## American presidents send a million Russians back to Stalin

Among the most egregious and shameful examples of placating Stalin was Operation Keelhaul. As part of the Yalta agreement of 1945, Russian prisoners of war liberated from German camps by British or American troops were returned to Russia, just as American and British POWs liberated by the Russians were returned to their respective countries. But unlike British and American prisoners, the Russian prisoners did not want to go home. They would have to be coerced or tricked into doing so. Some Russians had donned German uniforms and fought to rid their country of Stalin; many more had sympathized with those who did so. Although this decision might disturb some readers, it is certainly no more difficult to understand than Churchill's decision to side with the mass-murdering Stalin against Hitler. The Russian soldiers tried to free their country of Communism. And in order to ingratiate themselves to Stalin, FDR and then Truman betrayed at least a million anti-Communist Russians by delivering them into the hands of the Soviet dictator.

Repatriation of Russian POWs turned out to be a ghastly and grisly process. Some of the men simply committed suicide rather than return. The world hardly knew what was happening, though details managed to trickle out here and there.

## An atrocity on American soil:
## Russians drugged and returned home

Operation Keelhaul was not confined to Europe, where most of the Russian prisoners were; it was also carried out on American soil. About 200 Soviet nationals were among the prisoners of war at Fort Dix, New Jersey, in mid-1945; they had been in German uniform when Americans captured them. They were taken prisoner with the solemn promise that under no circumstances would they be repatriated to the Soviet Union, where they faced certain death. That promise was betrayed so that the American president might be faithful to Uncle Joe. These men, according to historian Julius Epstein, "had already experienced the determination of American military authorities to violate the Geneva Conventions [an international declaration pertaining to the treatment of prisoners of war] and the traditional American right of political asylum." Epstein was referring to an incident in Seattle in which these men had been ordered at gunpoint to board a Soviet ship. When the prisoners offered intense resistance, the decision was made to ship them to Fort Dix for the time being.

At Fort Dix another attempt was made to return the men to the Soviet Union by force. They were tear-gassed and forced aboard a Soviet ship, at which point the stunned men fought with all their strength, and even began to damage the ship's engines to the point at which the vessel was no longer seaworthy. Finally, a sergeant came up with the idea of drugging the prisoners, which he did by spiking their coffee with barbiturates. In the coma-like sleep that the drugs induced, the men were finally returned to the Soviet Union.

When Epstein attempted to acquire whatever government records existed on this particular incident, he was first greeted with denials. Finally, he received a letter from the Department of the Army, Office of the Chief of Information and Education, instructing him that "the records you requested permission to see...are part of a group of documents determined by a recent study as requiring indefinite maintenance of their current high security classification."

A thorough chronicle of Operation Keelhaul remains to be written, since the governments that perpetrated this unconscionable deed have refused to release the pertinent documents.

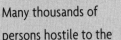

## What the Press Said

Many thousands of persons hostile to the present regime in the Soviet Union are being forcibly sent there by Americans and the British under the Yalta Agreement, Eugene Cardinal Tisserant asserted today and he said the Catholic Church constantly received appeals from "displaced persons" terrified of being sent back to territory now controlled by Russia, though they cannot be classified as traitors.

The Cardinal gave the writer [reporter Sam Pope Brewer] the permission to quote him, saying "It will compromise me, but the world must know of these things."

The **New York Times**,
March 1946

## Was the Marshall Plan a great success or another failed giveaway program?

One of the enduring myths of early Cold War history involves the so-called Marshall Plan, laid out by Secretary of State George Marshall in 1947. With Western Europe in economic ruin, some American policymakers suggested that massive injections of aid were necessary in order to jump-start those economies. An anti-Communist rationale was also offered for the program: Since Communism was thought to thrive amid conditions of poverty and despair, economic recovery in Western

Europe would undercut whatever attraction Communist propaganda might hold there.

The fact is that this program worked no better than any other government giveaway program. France, Germany, and Italy began their economic recoveries before any Marshall aid was disbursed. Austria and Greece, which received sizable amounts of Marshall aid per capita, began to recover only as it was being phased out. Britain received twice the Marshall aid that Germany did, yet British economic growth lagged far behind Germany's over the next decade.

West Germany's postwar economic recovery was so explosive, in fact, that the Germans actually coined a word—*Wirtschaftwünder*—to describe it. Naturally, Marshall Plan propagandists have attempted to take credit for the West German economic miracle. But the *Wirtschaftwünder* was the result not of Marshall Plan giveaways but of the market reforms that the Germans introduced.

Indeed, the return to some semblance of a market economy was what contributed to European prosperity. As economist Tyler Cowen points out, "In nearly every country occupied by Germany during the war, the stringent system of Nazi economic controls was continued even after the country was liberated. And in each case, rapid economic growth occurred only

★ ★ ★ ★ ★ ★ ★ ★ ★ ★

## The Real Reason Germany Got Back on its Feet

**We decided upon and reintroduced** the old rules of a free economy, the rules of laissez-faire. We abolished practically all controls over allocation, prices and wages and replaced them with a price mechanism controlled predominantly by money.

**Ludwig Erhard,** German economic minister

after the controls were lifted and sound economic policy established."
Marshall aid sometimes served to postpone the drastic economic measures that recipient nations would otherwise have had to make but which
could be indefinitely delayed as long as American money kept coming.

### The Marshall Plan's disastrous legacy

The real legacy of the Marshall Plan was the wrongheaded approach it
inspired in United States foreign aid programs for the rest of the century.
Foreign aid, beginning with Truman's "Point Four" program, has been
based on the idea that the Marshall Plan, which consisted of infusions of
money into poor economies, had been a success, and that the appropriate response to Third World poverty was therefore something similar.

As economist Peter Bauer pointed out, these Western aid programs
proved disastrous for the Third World. Since, like the Marshall Plan, they
took the form of government-to-government grants, they entrenched in
power some of the most brutal and repressive regimes in the world.
Thanks to infusions of United States and other Western aid, these regimes
could prosper without having to institute market reforms. Not surprisingly, Taiwan, South Korea, and Chile engaged in economic reform only
when U.S. aid was about to be cut off. As a result, they at last prospered.
The aid also produced disorder and even violence, as competing interest
and ethnic groups fought tooth and nail for control of the state apparatus
in order to get their hands on the grant money.

The Marshall Plan gave the impression that outside infusion of capital was what was necessary for a nation to prosper. The message that
*should* have been sent was that prosperity follows from the rule of law,
respect for private property, and the other institutional mechanisms on
which the market order rests.

That was the lesson of Hong Kong. With shortages of land and water,
no local power sources (such as coal or oil), and few raw materials, Hong
Kong seemed like the classic example of a society that needed foreign aid

to prosper. Instead, Hong Kong simply embraced the free market, and ultimately created such a successful export sector that by the 1980s Britain and the United States actually began asking Hong Kong to limit their exports, since the British and Americans found it so hard to compete with them!

The myth dies hard that Marshall aid encouraged "capitalism." The fact that the program was financed by taxation, a non-market institution, makes it suspicious from the start. And consider that for every dollar of Marshall aid sent to a recipient government, that government was required to devote a dollar to public works and "investment" projects. Thus Marshall aid had the direct effect of taking from the private sector to expand the public sector and the state apparatus of recipient nations— not exactly a recipe for "capitalism."

## Truman disregards the Constitution

In 1947, the president called for aid to Greece and Turkey as part of an overall strategy to assist nations that were in danger of Communist takeover by internal subversion or external aggression. This became known as the Truman Doctrine. Some conservatives, like Senator Robert A. Taft (who was known as "Mr. Republican"), sharply criticized Truman's approach. Not only would it potentially involve the United States in countless conflicts around the globe, but it was also, in his view, founded more in hysteria and paranoia than in a rational and sober appraisal of Soviet capabilities. To these budget-minded conservatives, Truman's policy seemed typically liberal: utopian, unrealistic, partial toward big government, and thoughtless of cost.

### Who authorized the Korean War, the U.S. Congress or the United Nations?

In the Korean War (1950–1953), Communist North Korea—with Stalin's knowledge and support, we now know—invaded the non-Communist

South. Despite a public statement by Secretary of State Dean Acheson in January 1950 that had placed Korea outside the U.S. defense perimeter, Truman decided to send American troops to defend South Korea and repel the aggressor. Significantly, Truman denied that he needed a declaration of war from Congress to authorize him to send troops to fight what he called a "police action" that had been authorized by the United Nations.

Here, then, was exactly what Woodrow Wilson's opponents had feared over three decades earlier: a president who took his country into war without fulfilling his constitutional obligation of consulting Congress, all on the pretext that his obligations to the League of Nations (or, in this case, the United Nations) rendered congressional consultation superfluous. (And since Truman said that he would send the troops even without United Nations authorization, he was going so far as to claim the right to send troops anywhere in the world without any authorization whatever from anyone or anything but himself.)

Mr. Republican, Senator Taft, objected to the president's unilateral decision. The president, Taft said, "has brought that war about without consulting Congress and without Congressional approval....So far as I can see...I would say that there is no authority to use armed forces in support of the United Nations in the absence of some previous action by Congress."

In fact, from the Korean War onward, Congress would never again officially declare war. It was one way in which the struggle against Communism would change America, perhaps forever.

# Chapter 15

★ ★ ★ ★ ★ ★ ★ ★ ★ ★

# CIVIL RIGHTS

Historical overviews of the civil rights movement of the 1950s and 1960s inevitably focus on certain well-known events: Rosa Parks and the Montgomery bus boycott; the forced integration of Little Rock's Central High School; the desegregation drive in Birmingham in 1963; and other important episodes. This chapter will focus instead on the legal ramifications of the civil rights movement, which are less widely known but have proven perhaps just as significant.

The landmark 1896 case *Plessy v. Ferguson* introduced into the American legal vernacular the famous "separate but equal" doctrine. According to that ruling, the Fourteenth Amendment's requirement that the state extend to all citizens the equal protection of the laws did not require that whites and blacks be permitted to use the same facilities. As long as separate facilities for whites and blacks were equal, then the state would be in compliance with the demands of the Fourteenth Amendment.

This was the judicial precedent that the Supreme Court had to reckon with when reaching its decision on school desegregation in 1954. The justices were obviously anxious to declare segregated schooling, which existed by law throughout the South, to be unconstitutional. But the Court could not simply argue that the Fourteenth Amendment's equal protection clause prohibited segregated schools, since 1) the Court had ruled in *Plessy* that it did not, and 2) the same Congress that drafted and

## Guess what?

★ A 1983 survey by the Department of Education could not turn up a single study that found integrated schooling to have had any appreciable effect on black educational achievement.

★ In *Regents of the University of California v. Bakke*, the student who was accepted into medical school instead of Allan Bakke was later suspended by California's medical board because of his "inability to perform some of the most basic duties required of a physician."

passed the Fourteenth Amendment had also approved segregated schooling in the District of Columbia. If anyone should know the intent of the amendment, it would be those who had voted on it. Another line of argument would have to be pursued.

## Instead of law, sociology

The argument that lawyers for the National Association for the Advancement of Colored People (NAACP) settled upon involved the use of sociological data to show that segregated schools were inherently unequal because they instilled in blacks a feeling of inferiority. In particular, a series of studies carried out by sociologist Kenneth Clark were cited to support the idea that segregated schooling had had negative effects on black self-esteem. Black students in segregated schools were shown a white doll and a black doll and asked which one they preferred. When a majority of black students indicated their preference for the white doll, Clark concluded that segregated schooling decreased black self-esteem.

But Clark was not entirely honest, since by 1954 he knew from his own research involving schoolchildren in Massachusetts that black students in integrated schools were even more likely to choose the white doll than were black students in segregated Southern schools. He did not provide this information to the Court.

### A Quotation the Textbooks Leave Out

"I may have used the word 'crap.'"

NAACP lawyer **Jack B. Weinstein** on the Kenneth Clark doll studies

Whatever the value of the doll studies, however, they had their intended effect. The Court declared segregated schooling unconstitutional, arguing that the *Plessy* requirement of separate but equal facilities could not be met in the case of education. Segregated schools, the Court argued, were *inherently* unequal, since the very act of separating the races in education scarred black students with a sense of inferiority that negatively impacted their ability to learn. The Court avoided the charge that it had brazenly defied precedent by claiming that the justices who had decided the *Plessy* case could not have known of the sociological information that "modern authority" had now made available about the effects of segregation on blacks' ability to learn. As the Court put it, "[I]n the field of public education the doctrine of 'separate but equal' has no place. Separate educational facilities are inherently unequal."

The conclusion reached by the social science literature cited in *Brown* remained the conventional wisdom among intellectuals for years afterward. But when Chinese and Japanese students were segregated by law in California in the early twentieth century, they outperformed white students. Why weren't they overcome by a lack of self-esteem? Still other studies have shown that no connection exists between self-esteem and educational performance. For example, in a study of mathematics skills among thirteen-year-olds in various countries, Koreans came in first and Americans last. Yet when asked if they considered themselves "good at mathematics," only 23 percent of the Koreans did. But *two-thirds* of the American students said they were good at math. American students had lots of self-esteem, but less mathematical knowledge than any other country surveyed.

## *Was* Brown *necessary?*

Scholarly opinion has even begun to suggest that the *Brown* decision was not necessary in order to bring about desegregation. According to Paul Craig Roberts and Lawrence Stratton:

A July 1944 survey of college students found that 68 percent agreed that "our postwar policy should be to end discrimination against the Negro in schools, colleges and universities." Georgia's progressive governor, Ellis G. Arnall, accomplished the repeal of the poll tax in 1945 and thereby knocked down a barrier to black voting. Jackie Robinson broke the color line in baseball in 1947, and black entertainers such as Lena Horne found increased access to Hollywood and Broadway. In response to the Truman civil rights committee's report, ordinary people, such as citizens of Montclair, New Jersey, took community inventories to expose and challenge local segregation. The Red Cross eliminated the racial designation of blood donors in 1950. Oklahoma high school students ignored traditional prejudices and elected a seventeen-year-old black to lead the state's Hi-Y clubs in January 1952.

Writing in the *Journal of American History*, Michael Klarman provides further evidence of such trends. He discusses the cases of blacks in the 1940s who won local political offices, often with substantial white support. He cites polling data showing increasingly favorable Southern attitudes toward integrated transportation facilities and other forms of desegregation. For these reasons and more, Klarman could conclude that "*Brown* was not necessary as an impetus to challenge the racial status quo."

## From race neutrality to race obsession

But decisions even more sweeping than *Brown* were still in store. In 1968 the Supreme Court handed down its ruling in the case of *Green v. County School Board of New Kent County*. The case involved a Virginia school district that had a "free choice" system in which transportation would be provided to any student to attend the school of his choice. In practice, none of the white children decided to attend the black school, and only a small number of black students chose to go to the white school.

The district believed that it had complied with the Court's ruling in *Brown* since access to schools was available without regard to race. Whether people actually took advantage of this policy was irrelevant; they had the opportunity to choose schools, and that was what everyone thought mattered. But in its 1968 ruling in *Green*, the Court decided that when it came to schools, desegregation programs were to be evaluated not by the opportunities they opened up but by the results they achieved. If the races continued to be largely segregated, the district was held to be in breach of its requirement to desegregate, even though it had given all students the right to attend whatever school they wished.

Some have argued that *Green* represented a radical departure from the reasoning employed in *Brown*. *Brown* had been a desegregation measure that called upon school districts to assign students to schools without

## Down the Memory Hole: Black Skeptics of *Brown*

Black author **Zora Neale Hurston**, author of *Their Eyes Were Watching God* and many other novels, refused to get caught up in the excitement of *Brown*. She could not muster much enthusiasm for what she described as "a court order for somebody to associate with me who does not wish me near them." The Court's reasoning—that all-black schools were inherently inferior, and that blacks could succeed only if whites were at their side—she found to be "insulting rather than honoring" members of her race. ("It never ceases to amaze me," Supreme Court Justice Clarence Thomas observed in 1995, echoing Hurston, "that the courts are so willing to assume that anything that is predominantly black must be inferior.") Polls found that only about half of Southern blacks approved of the Court's decision.

regard to race; *Green* was an integration measure that was obsessed with race. Yet the reasoning employed in *Green* was already implicitly contained in *Brown*. According to *Brown*, what made segregated schools inherently inferior was precisely that blacks did not have white classmates. *Green*, nearly a decade and a half later, merely took up where *Brown* had left off. Now that purely voluntary means of mixing the races had been tried and had not brought about the desired outcome, *Green* seemed to say that coercive measures could not be ruled out. The bottom line was that in order for the education of the races to be equal, there must be racial mixing of the schools. *Green* was simply more straightforward about what would need to be done: forcing parents, against their wills, to send their children to schools chosen by the state.

## Let's force those kids together—even if they have to be bused two hours a day!

One of the most notorious ways of doing that was by means of forced busing, which was upheld by the Supreme Court in *Swann v. Charlotte-Mecklenburg Board of Education* (1971). Although Swann envisioned forced busing being carried out only in the South, where school segregation had once had the force of law, later court decisions made clear that busing could also be imposed in Northern school districts that had never officially discriminated against blacks in the past. Parents all over the country, from Boston to Denver to Los Angeles, found their children being bused all over the city to accommodate a social engineer's plan. In Los Angeles, the average bused child spent nearly two hours on the bus every day.

### What were the consequences of forced busing?

Busing was overwhelmingly opposed by the vast majority of white parents, and supported by only a slim majority of black parents. (And black parents often changed their minds after their experiences with busing.) The policy's opponents undoubtedly understood that such forced mixture would increase racial animosity, not alleviate it. They also recognized that sending one's children to the local school was what encouraged community spirit, local patriotism, and civic virtue, and that tearing children away from their familiar surroundings in order to bus them hours each way to a school chosen for them by an education bureaucrat was morally wrong. As Professors Stephan and Abigail Thernstrom explain, parents wanted their kids, especially the youngest ones, in schools close by.

> Families who had scrimped and saved to buy housing in what seemed to them orderly, clean, safe neighborhoods naturally looked with great dismay at the prospect of having their children bused to schools on the other side of town in neighborhoods that not even their own residents celebrated. And then, too, parents took for granted that they had choices about their children's education.... As a result of desegregation suits, basic decisions about how the schools operated were removed from officials responsive to majority opinion and put in the hands of just one person, a federal judge who was politically protected by lifetime tenure and had no educational expertise.

It is hard to imagine how forced busing, particularly when undertaken in the manner of U.S. District Court Judge W. Arthur Garrity, Jr., in Boston, could *not* have resulted in increased racial tension and animosity. In 1974, in response to a suit brought by the NAACP, Judge Garrity decided upon a massive citywide busing plan to bring about greater racial mixture in the schools. One of the most controversial and ill-considered aspects of the plan involved a student exchange between Roxbury High, deep within the ghetto, and South Boston High, whose mainly working-class white students belonged to what has been described as "Boston's most insular Irish Catholic neighborhood." The entire junior class of South Boston High would be bused to Roxbury High, and half of South Boston's sophomore class would be composed of students from Roxbury.

South Boston parents protested immediately, often adopting the non-violent methods of civil disobedience associated with the civil rights movement. It was a question of getting their lives and communities back, explains writer Matthew Richer:

> Boston's neighborhood high schools, like South Boston High and Charleston High, produced few college-bound graduates, but they did form the nucleus of neighborhood pride. Young boys and girls were eager to grow up and play sports or cheer-lead for their local schools. The annual Thanksgiving Day "Southie-Eastie" football game between South Boston and East Boston high schools was an age-old ritual, typically thronged by crowds of more than 10,000. But these community traditions died and the people of South Boston and Charlestown could not understand why. It was these communities, what-ever their flaws, that people were defending when fleets of buses began rolling past their front stoops in 1974.

For the next three years, it took as many as 300 state police officers per day patrolling the school to maintain order. One teacher said that getting up in the morning was "like getting up to go to prison." And this was just one example of the busing fiasco in Boston.

### Blacks resist busing

No wonder black parents themselves came to question the wisdom of bus-ing. Loretta Roach, who chaired Boston's Citywide Educational Coalition, argued that busing had damaged black life as well as white. Busing, she said, undermined parental involvement in the "often faraway schools their children are bused to every morning." She also regretted the disappear-

## ★★★★★★★★★★

# PC Today:
# Did busing improve black performance?

**A**fter ten years of busing in Mecklenburg County—forever associated with the *Swann* case that had authorized busing in the first place—the gap in reading achievement between whites and blacks was as high or higher than it had been before busing. A 1983 survey by the Department of Education of all the relevant studies could not identify a single one that found integrated schooling to have had any appreciable effect on black educational achievement.

A prominent constitutional law text (Stone, Seidman, Sunstein, and Tushnet, *Constitutional Law*, 1991) concurs, arguing that there is "no proof…that [school integration] has aided blacks in any demonstrable fashion." In the 1990s, the Boston public schools ranked a dismal 275 out of Massachusetts' 279 cities and towns on a standardized reading test. Even Lawrence, a city with a large immigrant population often unskilled in English, had higher reading scores than Boston. And although some narrowing of the racial gap in reading is apparent, just as much progress has been made in essentially all-black schools as in mixed-race schools.

ance of community support for public schools, which "evaporated since schools are no longer part of their communities. Busing destroyed the neighborhood passion for those schools that previously existed." Another resident agreed: "Busing took away the community feeling we had for our neighborhood schools, the feeling of 'It's our school and we love it.'"

What this forced integration did accomplish was to drive white families out of the cities. President Eisenhower has been called a "racist" for arguing that people couldn't be forced to like each other, and that increased social interaction between the races involved the passage of time more than it did the passage of legislation. But hundreds of millions of dollars later (just in Boston alone), that is exactly what the experience with busing so clearly proved.

Meanwhile, whites abandoned the city schools in droves; the 62,000 white students in 1970 became an anemic 11,000 in 1994—only 18 percent of the total, despite the fact that whites comprised 58 percent of the city's population. By any measure, forced busing worsened the very condition its proponents had claimed to want to improve. With whites practically disappearing from Boston public schools, undaunted city officials nevertheless continued to forge ahead, devoting $30 million in 1994 to racially motivated busing—a reminder that nothing is more guaranteed to attract government money than repeated failure. Although busing was more coercive in some cities than in others, and other factors contributed to the disappearance of whites from urban schools, a non-Hispanic white majority is not to be found in the public school system of a single big city in America today. That is what government programs intended to mix the races have to show for themselves.

By the mid-1990s, the courts had begun granting permission in city after city to discontinue busing.

## The Kansas City fiasco

Kansas City, Missouri, never enacted forced busing. It found another way to spend over $1 billion on desegregation—and had the same results as everyone else.

Following the *Brown* decision, Kansas City had put forth a race-blind plan in which students attended the school closest to them. Since the races tended to live in separate neighborhoods, the plan did not portend a great deal of race mixing, but it was nevertheless color blind in principle.

Three decades later, Judge Russell Clark declared that the way to achieve racial balance in the schools, particularly given the movement of so many whites to the suburbs, was to establish a magnet school system in Kansas City so lavishly funded and impressive that it would attract whites to the city for their education. In a brazen act of judicial despotism, Clark doubled property taxes and ordered the state to pay as well. The money went toward a dozen new schools full of computers, and featuring such unheard-of amenities as radio and television studios equipped for real broadcasting, movie-editing rooms, a planetarium, greenhouses, a moot court with a jury room and judge's chambers, a model United Nations wired for simultaneous translation, Olympic-size pools, and still other features. By 1995 the program was spending an additional $36,111 for *each* of the 36,000 students in the system.

And what does this experiment have to show for itself? Not a thing. White enrollment in city schools continued to decline over the next decade, and black performance still showed no improvement. Dropout rates increased and attendance rates decreased. The racial gap in educational achievement remained unchanged. As of this printing, Judge Clark has not apologized.

## The Civil Rights Act of 1964

### How necessary or desirable was antidiscrimination legislation?

The Civil Rights Act of 1964 was one of the most momentous and far-reaching pieces of legislation in American history. The act prohibited segregation in public facilities and private establishments catering to the public, particularly restaurants and hotels. It also prohibited discrimination in private employment on the basis of race, creed, sex, or national origin. It extended federal authority over private behavior to an extraordinary degree; that power would continue to grow in the ensuing years.

Does the 1964 Act deserve the credit for improved black employment opportunities? Economist Thomas Sowell isn't so sure. He points out that in the decade *prior* to its passage, blacks had more than doubled their representation in professional, technical, and other high-level positions. "In other kinds of occupations," moreover, "the advance of blacks was even greater during the 1940s—when there was little or no civil rights policy—than during the 1950s when the civil rights revolution was in its heyday." The increase in black employment in professional and technical occupations in the two years following the passage of the act was smaller than the increase in the single year from 1961 to 1962, before the act was passed. "[T]he Civil Rights Act of 1964," he observes, "represented no acceleration in trends that had been going on for many years." The percentage of blacks employed as managers and administrators was no higher in 1967 than it had been in 1964 or 1960.

The affirmative action programs started in 1971 (under President Richard Nixon, contrary to popular belief) were accompanied by an improvement in the condition of blacks at the higher end of the earning spectrum, while those least advantaged lagged further behind. Similar stories could be told about Asian and Hispanic employment. Their prospects had already been improving for years, and the 1964 Act inaugurated no acceleration of trends that were already in effect.

### The 1964 Act could never lead to affirmative action!

Some observers feared that the legislation might give rise to preferential policies, like affirmative action. Proponents of the legislation denied that this could ever happen. Senator Hubert Humphrey famously promised a skeptical Senate colleague: "If the senator can find in Title VII [of the Civil Rights Act of 1964]...any language which provides that an employer will have to hire on the basis of percentage or quota related to color, race, religion, or national origin, I will start eating the pages one after another, because it is not there." Senators Joseph Clark and Clifford

Case wrote a memo on the subject in which they insisted that the legislation contained no requirement that an employer "maintain a racial balance in his work force. On the contrary, any deliberate attempt to maintain a racial balance, whatever such a balance may be, would involve a violation of [the legislation] because maintaining such a balance would require an employer to hire or refuse to hire on the basis of race." Republican Senator Harrison Williams added that "to hire a Negro solely because he is a Negro is racial discrimination, just as much as a 'white only' employment policy.... Those who say that equality means favoritism do violence to common sense."

## Or could it?

We know perfectly well, however, how the story turns out: Preferential policies, or "affirmative action," soon became entrenched throughout American society, in defiance of the 1964 Act. At the same time, though, it is probably a waste of time to argue that affirmative action violates Title VII of that act when the very logic of antidiscrimination legislation leads in that direction. Since it is impossible to read minds, it cannot be known whether a private employer is engaged in "discrimination," or if he is perfectly unbiased but in the course of hiring failed to employ various minority groups in proportion to their representation in the general population. In order to prove they have not discriminated, employers must now establish quota systems in hiring to protect themselves from government lawsuits. Thus *the logic of antidiscrimination legislation leads directly to affirmative action.*

## How did the Courts interpret the 1964 Act?

That point was not obvious to people at the time, however, and indeed antidiscrimination law took a number of twists and turns that most Americans had not expected. Consider the case of *Griggs v. Duke Power Company* (1971). The Supreme Court found the Duke Power Company guilty of discrimination because its requirements for promotion had a "disparate impact" on blacks and whites. By requiring that employees seeking promotion possess a high school diploma or pass an intelligence test, the company was indirectly discriminating against blacks, who were less likely than whites to have a high school diploma or pass the intelligence test.

The case was important for two reasons. First, it meant that *any* criterion that an employer used in choosing candidates for employment or promotion would be subject to a similar scrutiny; if it had a disparate racial impact, it was impermissible unless the employer could prove that the criterion was specifically job-related. This was not always easy to do, and few employers relished the prospect of being dragged into court and forced to justify their employment and promotion criteria. Therefore, it could now be illegal to inquire whether a prospective employee had not only a high school diploma but also an arrest record, a dishonorable military discharge, or any other characteristic that might have a racially disparate impact.

The case was also significant because in *Griggs*, the Court conceded that Duke had not *intended* to discriminate against its black employees. But the company was still found guilty of discrimination. The idea of discrimination as an intentional act, therefore, as the 1964 Act had conceived it, was essentially abandoned.

Among the most prominent (if ambiguously decided) civil rights cases since 1964 has been *Regents of the University of California v. Bakke* (1978). It involved Allan Bakke, an applicant to the medical school at the University of California at Davis. Despite his impressive academic credentials he was rejected twice, in 1973 and 1974. At the same time, though, the school had set aside places for "economically and/or educationally disadvantaged" students—in reality a minority set-aside program, since no white student was ever awarded one of these special slots. The academic credentials of the students admitted through this set-aside program were leagues below those of Bakke. Bakke's Medical College Aptitude Test (MCAT) scores placed him in the top 10 percent of test-takers; students admitted under the set-aside program were in the bottom third. Bakke's undergraduate grade average was A−, while that of the minority candidates was C+. Since the university was a state institution receiving

---

★ ★ ★ ★ ★ ★ ★ ★ ★ ★

# Fast Forward:
# Who was admitted instead of Allan Bakke?

**Patrick Chavis was one** of the five black students admitted to the medical school at UC Davis instead of the more qualified Allan Bakke. He later opened a successful OB/GYN office in the Compton, California ghetto. Champions of affirmative action happily contrasted Allan Bakke's relatively undistinguished medical career with that of Chavis, the applicant who had been admitted over Bakke despite the latter's higher scores.

What the vast majority of media outlets never bothered to report is that Chavis's medical license was later suspended by California's medical board, which pointed to his "inability to perform some of the most basic duties required of a physician." After botching Yolanda Mukhalian's liposuction, for example, Chavis hid her in his home for forty hours, during which time she lost 70 percent of her blood. Another patient also suffered severe bleeding following her surgery. According to Michelle Malkin, after the patient's sister brought her to the emergency room, Chavis "barged in and discharged his suffering patient—still hooked up to her IV and catheter—and also stashed her in his home."

A third patient wasn't so lucky. Tammaria Cotton bled to death and suffered a heart attack after Chavis "performed fly-by-night liposuction on her and then disappeared."

A tape recording of what was described as "horrific screaming" in Chavis's office included Chavis barking, "Don't talk to the doctor while he is working" and taunting the patient with "liar, liar, pants on fire."

federal funds, Bakke argued that the minority set-aside program deprived him of the equal protection of the laws.

The state court that originally heard his case agreed with Bakke, whereupon the university appealed to the California Supreme Court, which upheld the lower court's decision. At that point the university took its case all the way to the U.S. Supreme Court.

Allan Bakke did get to attend medical school after all, thanks to the Court. But the Court's decision nevertheless did little to overturn the race-obsessed admissions policies of universities receiving federal funds. Although there was no single majority decision, Justice Lewis Powell has been viewed as the pivotal figure. On the one hand, Powell sided with four of the justices in finding Davis's admissions policies to be racially discriminatory in a way that violated the principle of the equal protection of the laws. But he then sided with the other four in arguing that race could be considered by Davis or by anyone else as a factor—as long as it was not the only factor—in the decision to admit a student, on the grounds that the university had an interest in promoting a "diverse student body." Needless to say, affirmative action programs were quite safe under such a ruling.

A less ambiguous decision in favor of preferential policies came the following year in a case involving a preferential seniority policy adopted by the Kaiser Aluminum Company and the United Steelworkers of America in 1974. Responding to pressure from the Office of Federal Contract Compliance, Kaiser had decided to overturn its policy of admitting people to its on-the-job training program (through which one had to pass in order to gain entrance to the skilled crafts) on a seniority basis. Admission would now be based partially on seniority, but at least half the openings would be reserved for blacks regardless of seniority.

The test came when Brian Weber, a white worker who had been turned down for the program in favor of blacks with less seniority, suspected that his rights had been violated. He went back and read the text of the Civil

Rights Act and, sure enough, it said that any kind of discrimination on the basis of race was illegal. He was sure he had a case. He sued on the basis of Title VII, arguing that the company's policy (which the government itself had pressured it into adopting) violated federal law. The Supreme Court had upheld affirmative action programs supposedly intended to rectify past discrimination (by discriminating against whites in the present), but since not even Kaiser's opponents denied that it had been scrupulously fair in its hiring practices since opening in

> ## Two Books You're Not Supposed to Read
>
> *Civil Rights: Rhetoric or Reality?* by Thomas Sowell; New York: William Morrow, 1985.
>
> *The New Color Line: How Quotas and Privilege Destroy Democracy* by Paul Craig Roberts and Lawrence M. Stratton; Washington, D.C.: Regnery, 1995.

1958, Kaiser's program could not claim that it was rectifying a company history of discrimination.

A federal district court had sided with Weber, as had the Fifth Circuit Court. But in a 5–4 decision in *U.S. Steelworkers of America v. Weber* (1979), the Supreme Court ruled against him. Justice William Brennan argued that the real meaning of the 1964 Act was to be found in the *spirit* of the text. Since the "spirit" animating the legislation was one that aimed to help blacks, it was not strictly a violation of the legislation to institute preferential policies that discriminated against whites—*even if the wording of the legislation specifically forbade such policies.* Nothing in the 1964 Act, he said, did or could prevent private firms from adopting voluntary affirmative action programs along the lines of what Kaiser Aluminum had done.

The fiction that affirmative action programs in the private sector are "voluntary" dies hard, but fiction it is. Private firms and organizations typically adopt affirmative action programs in order to protect themselves from federal lawsuits alleging "discrimination" on the basis of innocent and unintentional disparities between the proportion of minority employees they have on the payroll and the proportion of minorities in the surrounding population. There is nothing "voluntary" about doing something in order to prevent the federal government from bringing you up on charges and destroying your business.

A final note: Over the past twenty years, net black migration has been overwhelmingly away from the North and toward the South, the only region of the country where a majority of blacks polled say they believe they are treated equally. Yet another fact that the standard textbook mysteriously fails to mention.

★★★★★★★★★★

## Chapter 16

# JFK AND LBJ

wight D. Eisenhower, first elected president in 1952, served two eventful terms in the White House. He was fairly typical of postwar Republicans: He slowed the rate of government growth without actually rolling back the federal apparatus, and he belonged to the internationalist wing of the party, which by the early 1950s had eclipsed its more isolationist wing.

## Who was the real John F. Kennedy?

Eisenhower was succeeded in 1960 by John F. Kennedy. By that year the young senator from Massachusetts had served three terms as a congressman and eight years in the U.S. Senate. For many years after his untimely death in 1963 he was treated with such reverence that few could bring themselves to say an unkind word about him. But in recent years his reputation has begun to decline even among otherwise liberal American historians, not only because he got relatively little accomplished—that, in fact, was an unintentional virtue—but because behind the Kennedy mystique too much of his background and behavior was difficult to admire.

## Guess what?

★ FBI records reveal that mobster Sam Giancana bankrolled JFK's campaign in return for promising to help his mob out of federal investigations. Giancana's money went to bribe election officials into doing what they had to do to get out the vote for Kennedy.

★ LBJ was thought to have lost his Senate race until it was discovered that he received an additional 202 votes from a small precinct. Interestingly, they voted in alphabetical order!

## JFK, author?

It is an open secret that JFK's two major books, though passed off as the young politician's own work, were essentially ghostwritten by others. *Why England Slept* (1940) was a more polished version of JFK's senior thesis, which he had submitted to Harvard in March 1940, four months before it appeared in published form. His father's personal speechwriter, who was asked to attend to the manuscript, later recalled: "When I got it, it was a mishmash, ungrammatical. He had sentences without subjects and verbs. It was a very sloppy job, mostly magazine and newspaper clippings stuck together." JFK's father, Joseph, eager for his son's book to become a best-seller, purchased between 30,000 and 40,000 copies and stored them away.

Joe Kennedy, who had become fabulously wealthy partly from selling bootleg liquor, served as U.S. ambassador to Great Britain from 1937 to 1940. When he sent copies of his son's book to Prime Minister Winston Churchill and to British intellectual Harold Laski, the latter replied: "In a good university, half a hundred seniors do books like this as part of their normal work in their final year. But they don't publish them for the good reason that their importance lies solely in what they get out of doing them and not out of what they have to say." Laski concluded by expressing his doubts that "any publisher would have looked at that book of Jack's if he had not been your son, and if you had not been ambassador." Few people spoke to Joe like that.

Likewise, few today would deny that *Profiles in Courage*, the 1956 book that won Kennedy the Pulitzer Prize, was in effect written by others, particularly by speechwriter Ted Sorensen, with Kennedy playing more of a supervisory role than anything else. Still, he took full credit as the book's author when awarded the Pulitzer, and his father had the FBI look into a group of writers who disputed Kennedy's sole authorship.

Less well known is that the barrage of articles, both popular and scholarly, as well as shorter books, book reviews, and the like that came out under Kennedy's name toward the end of the 1950s were also largely Sorenson's work. The sheer variety of publications with material allegedly written by Kennedy is impressive: *Life*, *Look*, *McCalls*, *Georgetown Law Review*, and *General Electric Defense Quarterly*, among others. Biographer Thomas Reeves remarked that "no national figure had ever so consistently and unashamedly used others to manufacture a personal reputation as a great thinker and scholar."

## *Getting out the vote*

Few cracks in the edifice of Camelot were apparent to the general public during JFK's presidency; only much later did Americans discover the extent of Kennedy's infidelities, and even today most Americans are certainly unaware of the deception and manipulation that went into forging his public persona and bringing about his electoral success. Joseph Kennedy dipped into the family fortune over the course of the campaign in order to help his son along. His father's fortune was not the only money that went into buying the presidential election of 1960; FBI records reveal that in a secret meeting with mobster Sam Giancana, the notorious Chicago godfather agreed to bankroll the Kennedy campaign in return for promised assistance in federal investigations. Giancana's money went to bribe election officials into doing what they had to do to get out the vote for Kennedy.

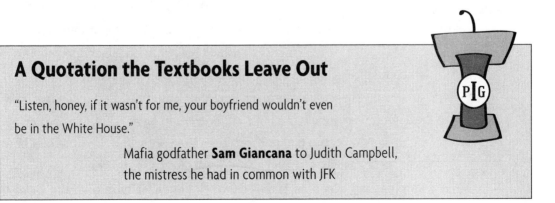

## A Quotation the Textbooks Leave Out

"Listen, honey, if it wasn't for me, your boyfriend wouldn't even be in the White House."

Mafia godfather **Sam Giancana** to Judith Campbell, the mistress he had in common with JFK

## ★ ★ ★ ★ ★ ★ ★ ★ ★ ★

# What's in a Nickname?

**L** yndon Johnson earned the ironic nickname "Landslide Lyndon" during his 1948 run for the U.S. Senate. In that election it looked as if LBJ had lost. But six days after Election Day, it was discovered in a precinct in the town of Alice that 203 people had voted at the last minute, 202 of whom voted for Johnson. These 203 people also happened to have voted in alphabetical order. Things looked suspicious to Johnson's opponent, Texas governor Coke Stevenson, but Supreme Court Justice Hugo Black upheld the result. Johnson was declared to have won the election by 87 votes. It was only in 1977, four years after Johnson's death, that the election judge in Alice admitted that he had helped to rig the election.

The election of 1960, in which Kennedy narrowly defeated Richard Nixon, was one of the closest in history, and was almost certainly stolen from Nixon. Irregularities in the returns in Illinois and Texas are impossible to explain other than as part of a deliberate campaign to commit vote fraud. Nixon was strongly advised by many friends, including President Eisenhower himself, to contest the election, but Nixon believed that such a challenge would have done too much damage to America's political fabric. JFK's victory stood.

Kennedy's presidency was more eventful in the foreign arena than the domestic, with much of JFK's legislative program languishing or suffering defeat in Congress. In foreign policy the situation was more dramatic but hardly more auspicious: An early summit meeting with Soviet premier Nikita Khruschev in 1961 left the Russian leader convinced that this upstart youngster was a mere novice who could be intimidated. West Berliners reacted with anger and frustration when Kennedy took no action as the Berlin Wall was constructed in 1961, staunching the flow of Germans from the Communist East to the free West, though it was not clear what Kennedy could have done. Western access rights to West Berlin had not been interfered with, and the situation, however tragic, hardly justified a world war. And a world war is nearly what Kennedy got when he stared down the Soviet Union over the issue of nuclear missiles in Cuba in 1962.

As every American knows, an assassin prematurely ended JFK's life in November 1963. His replacement was lifelong Texan politician Lyndon B. Johnson. It has taken historian Robert A. Caro three fat volumes to document Johnson's corruption.

## Lyndon Johnson: A legacy of failure

Johnson was very nearly the philanderer that Kennedy had been, and even boasted of illicit activities in the Oval Office. Politically, though, he was notably more adept at dealing with Congress than his predecessor. His ability to pressure, bully, and intimidate congressmen into adopting his position, combined with the boost his legislative agenda received from the nation's grief over the death of Kennedy, made him all but unstoppable.

Johnson's domestic political initiatives are often referred to as the Great Society programs, so named for a memorable reference in a Johnson address. Among other things, Johnson sought to eradicate poverty, a condition he and his supporters believed could be eliminated with the right government programs. It was a staggering and enormously expensive failure. From 1950 until 1968, the poverty rate had steadily declined by about one percentage point per year. In the years since the Great Society programs, the poverty rate has stagnated. This is no coincidence. These programs were fundamentally wrongheaded and in some cases they made problems even worse. Seven trillion dollars later, LBJ's programs have little to show for themselves other than as enormous drags on the American economy.

### The kids who were never educated

One of Johnson's programs, established by the Elementary and Secondary Education Act of 1965, provided federal dollars for the education of poor children. Those billions of federal dollars, however, yielded no results.

By 1977, a study by the National Institute of Education of the effects of Title I found that any gains achieved during one school year had dissipated by the next, and that Title I students entered new grades as far behind as they would have been in the absence of Title I. The same has been consistently true of Head Start, the well-known preschool program; any gains made one year have vanished by the next.

## A health care system that was already working

Medicaid and Medicare, which provide medical care to the poor and the elderly respectively, were also features of Johnson's Great Society. Despite what people have been led to believe, however, the poor had done relatively well in securing health care before Medicaid. The year prior to the introduction of Medicaid, for example, poor families had considerably higher hospital admission rates than did those in wealthier brackets. Moreover, while high-income individuals had an average of 5.1 doctor visits a year, low-income individuals had 4.3—hardly a dramatic difference.

What Medicaid did result in was a dramatic decline in the reduced-cost or pro bono services that doctors had once provided the poor. According to historian Allan Matusow, "Most of the government's medical payments on behalf of the poor compensated doctors and hospitals for services once rendered free of charge or at reduced prices. . . . Medicare-Medicaid, then, primarily transferred income from middle-class taxpayers to middle-class health-care professionals." Moreover, the hyperstimulation of demand created by Medicare and Medicaid played a substantial role in raising health care costs across the board. That, combined with the growth of third-party payers in health care (itself a trend stimulated by government

> ## What the Press Said
>
> "He's getting every-thing through Congress but the abolition of the Republican Party, and he hasn't tried that yet."
>
> **James Reston**

★★★★★★★★★★

# Reality Check: Poverty in America

**B**y any conceivable standard, the poor in America enjoy a standard of living that people in previous ages (and indeed elsewhere in the world today) could scarcely have imagined. Some 41 percent of our poor own their own homes, with another 75 percent owning automobiles and VCRs and two-thirds having air conditioning and microwave ovens. Virtually all own telephones, refrigerators, and television sets, all of which were once considered luxuries. The *average poor person* in America has more living space and is more likely to own a car and a dishwasher than the *average European*. What passes for poor in America today is doubtless an undesirable condition *by American standards*, but would have passed for fantastically wealthy in any other place or age.

intervention), undermined the natural market mechanisms that would inevitably have lowered the cost and even increased the consumption of medical services.

## The jobs that weren't created

The Great Society also proposed government-funded job training for the unskilled. The Job Corps, a vocational training program for the unemployed that began in 1965, aimed to take 100,000 unemployed young people and provide them with valuable job skills. It would train its recruits far from the slum environments in which they lived, bringing them instead to rural conservation camps or abandoned military bases.

The Job Corps did not have an auspicious first year. As Allen Matusow points out, recruits were charged with a variety of crimes, including burglary and window smashing; in Indiana, several were arrested for forcing a fellow corpsman to commit sodomy. Another trainee, in Texas, was stabbed in a fight while on leave. A food riot among corpsmen in Kentucky required the intervention of federal marshals.

What was the fate of those who managed to complete the course without being stabbed or sodomized? Early on, studies found that those who completed the program had no better success in the job market than so-called "no shows" (people who had been accepted into the Job Corps but who had never shown up), despite the fact that the program cost about the same as providing a Harvard education for every participant. Worse still, throughout the program's first decade, two-thirds of participants never even finished. Let that sink in: two-thirds *did not even bother to complete a free job-training program*—financed by hard-working Americans.

In the early 1990s, a private accounting firm performed an audit of the Job Corps. It discovered that a mere 12 percent of people leaving Job Corps programs found work in the field for which they had been trained. For that

★ ★ ★ ★ ★ ★ ★ ★ ★ ★

## Fast Forward: Stealing from the Young

**M**edicare spending spun out of control as the years passed, and the benefits it promised fast outpaced projected tax revenues. As of 2003, the program was underfunded to the tune of *$27 trillion*—nearly four times the entire national debt—in terms of future promises versus projected tax receipts. In addition, researchers Chris Edwards and Tad DeHaven found in 2003 that the average male reaching age sixty-five could expect to receive $71,000 more in benefits—mainly Social Security (established by FDR) and Medicare—from the federal government than he had put in. The average twenty-five-year-old male, on the other hand, could expect to pay $322,000 more in taxes than he would ever get back from federal transfer programs.

matter, only 44 percent found any job at all. The average hourly wage of that 44 percent was $5.09. That is what a program spending $21,333 per client has to show for itself.

### The truth about welfare: Did Johnson's programs make poverty worse?

The classic study of 1960s social policy, which practically defined the terms of welfare reform in the 1990s, was Charles Murray's *Losing Ground*. That book advanced the provocative thesis that the Great Society programs, as well as increased AFDC (Aid to Families with Dependent Children) availability, were themselves largely to blame for the stagnation of the poor. These programs, in short, were not only expensive, they were also counterproductive.

---

★ ★ ★ ★ ★ ★ ★ ★ ★ ★

## Fast Forward: The Job Corps Thirty Years Later

**n the late 1990s,** when President Bill Clinton said he intended to "end welfare as we know it," he proposed an *increase* in the Job Corps budget. So a program that had been a total failure for three decades, with very little to show for the billions it had squandered, was to be rewarded with a bigger budget.

---

## How '60s liberalism discouraged all the right things and encouraged all the wrong ones

*The Economist* reported in 1988 that less than 1 percent of America's poor was composed of couples who finished high school, got married and stayed married, and kept a job—even a minimum-wage job—for a year. The incentives introduced during the 1960s made it less and less likely that people would consider it worthwhile to follow these basic steps—namely, marriage and a steady job—that had meant escape from poverty for so many.

Interested readers should pay particular attention to chapter 12 of *Losing Ground*, where at great length Murray details the case of a typical couple in 1960 and in 1970. He shows how the incentives at work in 1960

★★★★★★★★★★

# Reality Check: The Many Faces of Welfare

**A**FDC accounted for only a small fraction of federal welfare spending. In 1994, in fact, just two years before President Bill Clinton transformed the program into Temporary Assistance for Needy Families (TANF), AFDC constituted a mere 6 percent of federal welfare spending. That puts into perspective the claims made by the hard Left that Clinton's welfare reform represented a sellout of liberalism or abolished the federal safety net. Still in force were feeding and nutrition programs, federal job training, food stamps, WIC (Special Supplemental Nutrition Program for Women, Infants, and Children), housing subsidies, educational programs for children of low-income families, day care programs, and still others. That's "ending welfare as we know it"?

would have led them to marry and led the husband to enter the job market, but that the incentives in 1970, in which countless types of welfare benefits were available in abundance, worked against marriage (AFDC benefits were taken away if the woman married) and encouraged the husband to enter the job market only intermittently, if at all. The resulting family instability, and the fact that modest economic security was, thanks to the government, now available outside of marriage, led to an explosion in out-of-wedlock births, and with it all the pathologies that social scientists have found among children born outside of two-parent households: poorer academic performance, much greater propensity to crime, drug addiction, and the like.

## Criminals went free

Sixties liberalism also sent the wrong incentives regarding crime and education. For a variety of reasons, in the 1960s a criminal's chance both of being caught *and* of going to prison if caught declined significantly. During the 1960s the absolute number of people in federal prisons dropped, despite a doubling of crime during those years. On top of that, increasingly liberal laws regarding juvenile crime made a life of crime practically costless for a young person. In Cook County, which includes Chicago, researchers found that by the mid-1970s, the average first-time reform school student had already been arrested an incredible 13.6 times. And since more and more states were making juvenile crime records practically inaccessible to employers and others—with some states actually destroying juvenile crime records when the delinquent turned eighteen—there seemed to be little practical reason for young people not to break the law.

Also during the 1960s, the federal courts sharply restricted schools' ability to discipline, suspend, or expel disruptive students. (More wonderful contributions to American life courtesy of the American Civil Liberties Union.) The result was increasingly unmanageable school populations, and more and more difficulty imparting education to those youngsters who wanted to learn. Teachers who insisted on standards of excellence found themselves threatened, assaulted, or otherwise made miserable. As time went on, the best teachers and the best students simply left, with the result that the school was now even less manageable than before. (At that point, the usual suspects in politics and the media would begin their drearily predictable demands for more money for the school in question, even though inner-city schools were already spending well over $12,000 annually per student by the 1990s.) Murray observes:

> All the changes in the incentives pointed in the same direction. It was easier to get along without a job. It was easier for a man to have a baby without being responsible for it, for a woman to have a baby without having a husband. It was easier to get away with crime. Because it was easier for others to get away with crime, it was easy to obtain drugs. Because it

was easier to get away with crime, it was easier to support a drug habit. Because it was easier to get along without a job, it was easier to ignore education. Because it was easier to get along without a job, it was easier to walk away from a job and thereby accumulate a record as an unreliable employee.

The dramatic expansion in welfare spending, along with the aggressive propagation of the "welfare rights" philosophy (more about this below), undermined what Murray calls "status rewards." The working poor family, which had once had the dignity of knowing that they were supporting themselves and not being a burden on their (usually poor) neighbors, now seemed simply foolish. According to Murray:

> Once these highly functional sources of status are removed, the vaunted "work ethic" becomes highly vulnerable. The notion that there is an intrinsic good in working even if one does not have to may have impressive philosophical credentials, but, on its face, it is not very plausible—at least not to a young person whose values are still being formed. To someone who is not yet persuaded of the satisfactions of making one's own way, there is something laughable about a person who doggedly keeps working at a lousy job for no tangible reason at all. And when working no longer provides either income or status, the last reason for working has truly vanished. The man who keeps working is, in fact, a chump.

## Lack of jobs doesn't explain large welfare rolls

Some have attempted to argue that the number of people on welfare, which exploded in the late 1960s, could be explained by a lack of jobs. But that explanation doesn't work. "Talk to intelligent urbanites in New York, Los Angeles, or Washington about welfare," writes Fred Siegel, "and almost the first thing they'll tell you is that people are on welfare because of an absence of jobs. When you point out that the welfare explosion in America not only began in New York but also coincided with the great economic and jobs boom of the 1960s, when black unemployment in the city was running at 4 percent, about half the national average for minorities, they look puzzled and tend to change the subject."

And no wonder they'd rather change the subject. Consider New York City, which was especially liberal in its welfare policy in the 1960s. The number of people on welfare in New York City grew by 47,000 between 1945 and 1960, but over the next five years, through 1965, it grew by more than 200,000.

> ### A Book You're Not Supposed to Read
>
> *Losing Ground: American Social Policy 1950–1980* by Charles Murray; 10th anniversary edition, New York: Basic Books, 1994.

It continued to get worse during one of the most prosperous periods in American history. By 1971 there were 1,165,000 people on welfare in New York City. Siegel points out that the number of people on welfare in New York City was larger than *the entire populations of fifteen states.*

Jobs were also abundant in the prosperous 1980s and 1990s, when the poverty rate nevertheless continued to stagnate. Myron Magnet points out that jobs requiring only basic secretarial skills were going unfilled for lack of qualified applicants. Other good-paying jobs required little more than that the applicant understand the concept of 75 percent and be able to divide one hundred by four. After twelve years of government-funded education, even the poorest person should probably be able to do these things, and there is no reason that a grown man or woman could not learn them independently if necessary.

## Welfare is a right!

The mid-1960s also saw a change in the way a good portion of the American intellectual class chose to view poverty and welfare. Contemptuously dismissed was any distinction between a "deserving" and a "non-deserving" poor; such thinking was said to be terribly judgmental. (Shame on you, in other words, if you see a difference between a widow with five young children and an irresponsible, self-centered couch potato who simply refuses to work.) At least as important was the additional idea that welfare payments were a *right* rather than a privilege. The *New York Times* spoke of "a new philosophy of social welfare" that "seeks to establish the status of welfare benefits as rights, based on the notion that everyone is entitled to a share of the common wealth."

Professors Richard Cloward and Frances Fox Piven encouraged this trend by co-founding the National Welfare Rights Organization (NWRO) in 1966. The federal Department of Health, Education, and Welfare added to the NWRO's influence by designating it as the official bargaining agent for the welfare poor. The Johnson administration even gave it federal money. It spent that money propagandizing and organizing the poor to *demand* what they were told was rightfully theirs. In so doing, they undermined the working poor's self-image: If there was nothing undesirable or shameful about receiving welfare, then conversely there was nothing particularly admirable about working and avoiding welfare.

### Gimme, gimme, gimme!

The federal government echoed this kind of rhetoric. The Office of Economic Opportunity funded some 1,000 "neighborhood service centers," dedicated to removing the stigma from government welfare payments and portraying them instead as rights to which recipients were entitled. Neighborhood legal attorneys belonging to the OEO counseled would-be welfare recipients to request more and more hearings if they were turned down. With each such hearing requiring anywhere from five to eight hours of work, it became clear even to the most reluctant figures in the welfare bureaucracy that the only feasible solution was simply to give in.

Sit-ins and sleep-ins at welfare departments began to take place, as putative welfare recipients, whether or not they were able-bodied or even minimally responsible, agitated for the right to a share of their fellow citizens' wealth. Scholars of the subject agree that the enormous growth in the acceptance rate for AFDC assistance is at least partially attributable to this kind of organized assault on welfare agencies. Bureaucrats, swamped with applicants and with constant disruption, simply gave in.

The result of this revolution in social values was to entrench millions of people in the trap of welfare dependency. Minimum-wage jobs that helped people enter the work force and taught responsibility, punctuality, and working together with others were looked upon with contempt. Thus jobs that had served as the first rung up the employment ladder seemed a waste of time to those who had been told that they were *entitled* to their fellow citizens' wealth. As Murray observes, people are not naturally hard-working and moral; only a nexus of economic incentives, moral exhortation, and social stigma encourages responsible, upright behavior. When those things are undermined, people's natural inclinations to choose leisure over work and immediate gratification over responsibility and good sense come to the surface.

## The Great Society and the Vietnam tragedy

The Great Society, argues historian Walter McDougall, had its foreign-policy analogue in the Vietnam War. In the attempt to protect South Vietnam's anti-Communist government from overthrow by a Communist insurgency tied to the North, the U.S. government sought to defeat the enemy not in the battlefield, but by establishing good liberal government in the South that would win the undisputed allegiance of the South Vietnamese.

President Kennedy's advisers were split as to what kind of changes they thought needed to be made in South Vietnam first. One group, whom historian Patrick Lloyd Hatcher has called the "Whigs," emphasized the importance of encouraging popular government in countries like South Vietnam. "Tories," on the other hand, emphasized the importance of *economic* progress, and "were prepared to tolerate authoritarian regimes so long as they were effective." McDougall describes how this divide among Kennedy's advisers applied to Vietnam:

> In the case of Vietnam, Whigs asked such questions as how many independent newspapers and radio stations there were, did religious minorities enjoy freedom of worship, how fair and frequent were elections, could citizens get justice in the courts, how humane were the police? But Tories thought it premature to expect a new state beset by a ruthless insurgency to pass an American civics test. They asked such questions as how many villages had sewage and clean drinking water, what was the ratio of doctors to citizens, how many telephones and motorbikes were there, how much fertilizer was needed, what was the rice yield and per capita income?

The Military Assistance Command Vietnam (MACV), assigned the task of gathering all this information, thus became "less like a comrade-in-arms to the Saigon regime than a nagging social worker."

This kind of approach to the war, as Henry Kissinger later argued, proved to be problematic. "[T]he central dilemma," he said, "became that America's *political* goal of introducing a stable democracy in South Vietnam could not be attained in time to head off a guerrilla victory, which was America's *strategic* goal. America would have to modify either its military or its political objectives" (emphasis added). The American government did neither. Instead, American officials turned on South Vietnamese leader Ngo Dinh Diem, whom they perceived both as authoritarian and as hostile to the kinds of political and economic reforms they wanted. The public self-immolation of Buddhists in protest of Diem's repressiveness was exactly the kind of thing that American officials believed a less autocratic figure might have been able to avoid. But after Vietnamese generals killed Diem (after getting word that the U.S. government would not look unfavorably upon Diem's ousting from power), the result was far greater political instability in South Vietnam than before, as a string of incompetents passed in and out of power. President Richard Nixon (and even LBJ) would later decry the decision to support Diem's overthrow. The chaos that resulted meant that the United States would itself have to take over the fighting, with tragic consequences.

★★★★★★★★★★

## Double Standard

Anticommunist South Vietnamese president **Ngo Dinh Diem** was pilloried when Buddhists protested his policies by burning themselves alive in 1963. Not long after the Communists took power in South Vietnam in 1975, more Buddhists immolated themselves, this time in protest of the Communist government's persecutions. Hardly anyone noticed or cared.

McDougall describes Vietnam as "the first war in which the United States dispatched its military forces overseas not for the purpose of winning but just to buy time for the war to be won by civilian social programs." Instead of taking the war to the North and thus attacking the insurgency at its source, American officials sought to export the welfare state to Vietnam. The end for South Vietnamese anti-Communists finally came in April 1975—just over two years after the peace accords of January 1973—when the North launched an overwhelming invasion of the South, ultimately merging North and South into the Republic of Vietnam.

The exodus from South Vietnam was immediate. Some 600,000 South Vietnamese, many of whom had endured French colonial rule, years of Japanese occupation, and the intense war conditions of the late 1960s and early 1970s, decided that the one thing they could *not* live through was a Communist Vietnam. Fleeing Ho Chi Minh's reign of terror, they took to the South China Sea in anything that would float, and became known as the Vietnamese "boat people." Other horrors occurred at the hands of the Communists in Laos and especially Cambodia, where the Communists' murder of one-third of the population gave us the phrase "the killing fields." People of goodwill may disagree about the methods and the political wisdom of the Vietnam intervention, but it is no longer possible—if it ever was—to claim, as the hard Left did, that a Communist Southeast Asia would usher in a reign of peace and "social justice." On that subject, history has spoken.

Chapter 17

# THE DECADE OF GREED?

ver since the New Deal, no successful American presidential candidate had run on an anti-government, pro-freedom platform; certainly none governed that way. This was true even of the Republicans of the postwar period: Eisenhower had been a moderate in domestic policy, and Nixon, who seriously considered establishing a minimum income for all Americans, bordered on liberal.

## How was Reagan different?

In this respect, Ronald Reagan, elected to the first of his two terms in 1980, was different. As he memorably observed, "Government is not the solution to our problems. Government is the problem." Reagan's popularity, coupled with his support for privatization, his confidence in the American entrepreneurial spirit, and his belief in the moral superiority of the free market went a long way toward making these positions, ridiculed and despised during the 1960s and 1970s, intellectually respectable once again.

Critics called it the "decade of greed." That's hardly a surprise; as Joe Sobran once said, "Today, wanting someone else's money is called 'need,' wanting to keep your own money is called 'greed,' and 'compassion' is when politicians arrange the transfer."

## Guess what?

★ In the "decade of greed," charitable giving grew at a 55 percent faster annual rate than the rate at which it had grown over the previous twenty-five years.

★ Reagan did not slash the budget. Spending on programs that include children and families increased by 18 percent.

## Charitable giving during the "Decade of Greed"

The fact is, the 1980s were no such thing. The most direct refutation of this phony claim is that charitable giving—which, after all, represents pretty much the opposite of greed—increased substantially during the 1980s, and at a much faster rate than it had been increasing in previous decades. In real terms, charitable giving increased from $77.5 billion in 1980 to $121 billion in 1989. And charitable giving grew at a 55 percent faster annual rate than the rate at which it had grown over the previous twenty-five years. This tremendous increase is evident both in individual and in corporate giving. And as Richard McKenzie points out, the increase in charitable giving was *vastly* greater than the increase that occurred in expenditures on a great many goods and services that might be thought of as extravagant, including jewelry and watches, alcoholic beverages, restaurant meals, and personal services (such as health clubs, beauty salons, and the like).

### The Quotable Reagan

Government's view of the economy could be summed up in a few short phrases: If it moves, tax it. If it keeps moving, regulate it. And if it stops moving, subsidize it.

The nine most terrifying words in the English language are, "I'm from the government and I'm here to help."

## The truth about Michael Milken, the man the media loved to hate

Some critics, when referring to the 1980s as the decade of greed, have in mind such high-profile men of wealth as Michael Milken. But Milken, who received a prison term and a $600 million fine for his activities, was not only *not* guilty of any crime, but in fact he performed a useful and salutary social function. Previously, it had been difficult for new and promising firms to gain access to the capital they needed, since banks and investors tended to confine themselves to investing in firms whose bonds had investment-grade credit rankings. That is, they invested only in firms that had established track records in meeting their obligations when it came to issuing and honoring corporate bonds. Milken's genius lay in realizing that new firms often outperformed established firms. He gave great impetus to the high yield or "junk bond" market—so named because the bonds were issued on behalf of firms without established credit histories. These bonds brought substantial returns to those willing to bear the risks.

**A Book You're Not Supposed to Read**

*What Went Right in the 1980s* by Richard B. McKenzie; San Francisco: Pacific Research Institute for Public Policy, 1994.

There can be no question that Milken's work was socially beneficial. According to Glenn Yago, junk bonds "gave many smaller businesses the access to capital, and hence to many of the privileges, once exclusively enjoyed by our nation's largest corporations. Junk bonds became an important agent of social and economic change." *Fortune* magazine conceded in 1996:

> The fact is, while you can disagree on whether Milken was a saint or a sinner during his 1980s heyday, you simply can't argue anymore about the singular importance of the junk-bond market he created. "We securitized business loans," Milken says, and he's right. And look, too, at the businesses he backed with his junk bonds! He was present at the creation of the cable industry and the cellular industry. Milken's junk bonds made it possible for MCI to compete with AT&T. He backed companies like Turner Broadcasting and McCaw Cellular because he saw something others didn't.

The same kind of financing was used to back corporate takeovers. The Williams Act of 1967 had made corporate takeovers very difficult, and had thereby (in the words of economist Murray Rothbard) "fastened the rule of inefficient, old-line corporate managers and financial interests upon the backs of the stockholders." But corporate takeovers, in which outside financial interests bid for stockholder support against entrenched, unresponsive managers, provide an indispensable check against managerial arbitrariness. Milken pioneered the use of high-yield bonds to finance corporate takeovers. That made it easier for entrepreneurs to acquire firms and toss out unresponsive managers who were more concerned with their own security and well-being than with the interests of stockholders.

Milken made enemies for himself for a number of reasons. First, big banks were not pleased with Milken's method of financing takeovers, since by floating high-yield bonds on the open market he bypassed the banks altogether. Second, his bonds competed against those of other firms, which of course referred contemptuously to Milken's as "junk" bonds. The envy-driven media, for its part, had a field day with Milken's extremely high income—he must have been a crook if he earned so much money so quickly. Even David Rockefeller, absurdly enough, was heard to complain, "Such an extraordinary income inevitably raises questions as to whether there isn't something unbalanced in the way our financial system is working." To which Rothbard answered that it did indeed raise questions, but not the ones Rockefeller probably had in mind.

> It raises grave questions about the imbalance of political power enjoyed by our existing financial and corporate elites, power that can persuade the coercive arm of the federal government to repress, cripple, and even jail people whose only "crime" is to make money by facilitating the transfer of capital from less to more efficient hands. When creative and productive businessmen are harassed and jailed while rapists, muggers, and murderers go free, there is something very wrong indeed.

Milken found himself brought up on ninety-eight charges of securities fraud and racketeering. He was eventually convicted on only six petty charges, and even those were technicalities that had never before carried jail time. That Milken received a ten-year prison sentence (later reduced to two years) to the cheers of the media and the political class even though he had broken no law goes to show that the 1980s were far more the decade of envy than they were the decade of greed.

## The myth of budget cuts

Still other critics claim that "budget cuts" during the 1980s were symptomatic of "greed." But budget cuts were, in fact, few and far between. As Democrats portray things, New Deal and Great Society programs are constantly in danger of repeal by right-wing zealots, and only constant vigilance (as well as hefty donations to the Democratic Party) keeps them alive. Republicans also have a vested interest in preserving this illusion, since the idea that they really are poised to abolish various government programs plays well during fund-raising campaigns. The Democrats always sound as if they are losing; Republicans always speak as if they are winning.

Statistics from the 1980s tell a rather different story. Hysterical yelps about Reagan-era "budget cuts" left the impression that Reagan slashed government spending. Although the annual *rate of increase* in government spending slowed considerably when compared with previous presidencies, it nevertheless continued upward. Federal spending increased dramatically during the 1980s, and not just because of the president's defense buildup. Nondefense spending had been at 10.1 percent of GNP in 1965, but by 1985 it was at 17.5 percent. In his memoir, counsellor to the president and later attorney general Ed Meese pointed out that "in the aggregate, there were neither tax nor budget cuts in the Reagan era. Both trend lines continued to grow, although the spending line grew faster than the taxing line." Economist Martin Anderson, a policy adviser to Reagan, admitted in his laudatory memoir, "On the whole, President Reagan set spending records right and left. Holding to his many pledges over the years to strengthen social security, the health care system, and welfare, and to build up our national defenses, he directed massive increases in social welfare and welfare spending and for national defense."

Agriculture spending, for example, skyrocketed during the 1980s. Legislation passed in 1983 paid dairy farmers to produce less milk—the first time that the principle of subsidized acreage reduction had been applied to dairy farmers. The federal cotton subsidy increased sevenfold throughout the decade, and by 1989 some nine million bales of cotton were left in warehouses.

Even welfare spending increased, though some individual programs experienced slight cuts. From 1981 to 1989, AFDC experienced a 1 percent cut, food stamps a 6 percent cut, and school lunch programs a 4 percent cut. But overall, spending on programs that included children and families increased by 18 percent between 1981 and 1989. Medicare funding was dramatically increased as well.

## The tax bite

Over the course of the decade, Reagan succeeded in bringing about significant income tax rate reductions across the board, including a reduction in the top marginal rate from 70 to 28 percent. On net, however, taxes actually increased throughout the 1980s, with later tax increases more than offsetting the reductions of 1981. Increases in Social Security taxes in the early 1980s were among the largest tax increases in U.S. history, and parts of the Tax Reform Act of 1986 effectively increased taxes by closing loopholes and eliminating certain tax credits. The federal tax bite averaged 18.9 percent of GNP during the 1980s, as compared to 18.3 for the 1970s and 18.2 for the 1960s.

The statistics reveal that hysteria about the 1980s is entirely misplaced. Yet the same sources that complained of "budget cuts" in that decade made the same dire statements in the 1990s as well. Liberal commentators gave the impression that Republican budget proposals would have dramatically slashed federal spending. Would that it were so. By and large, though, Americans believed the steady drumbeat they heard about alleged budget cuts. A Time/CNN poll in 1995 found that 47 percent of Americans agreed that "the cuts in federal spending proposed by the Republicans in Congress" have "gone too far." But the difference between President Bill Clinton's seven-year budget proposal and that of the Republicans was that Clinton called for a $500 billion increase in spending and the Republicans called for a $350 billion increase. Where are the cuts?

The debate over Medicare was more absurd still: people called House Speaker Newt Gingrich all kinds of names for his Medicare "cuts." In fact, Clinton proposed an annual rate of Medicare spending growth of 7.5 percent, while the Republicans favored growing the program at an annual rate of 6 percent. This is what dishonest reporters and political commentators mean by a cut—a reduction in how fast government grows!

The real problem with the 1980s, then, was neither "greed" nor tax cuts nor budget cuts. The problem was not that Reagan had done too much, but rather that he was unable to do *more* of what he had hoped to do. But one thing that history can't deny him: He challenged the Soviet Union to tear down the Berlin Wall and defeated Communism, while hardly firing a shot.

# Chapter 18

★ ★ ★ ★ ★ ★ ★ ★ ★ ★

# CLINTON

At the beginning of 1992, hardly anyone outside of Arkansas had ever heard of Bill Clinton. By November he was the president-elect of the United States.

He was only the second president in American history to be impeached. The charges against him revolved around false statements he made under oath, in a sexual harassment case in which he was the defendant, with regard to his amorous relationship with White House intern Monica Lewinsky. His carefully worded denials of wrongdoing were emblematic of his political style in general, such that figuring out what the president really meant became a matter of reading between the lines and identifying the loopholes that his choice of words had left available to him.

The Clinton years, especially after the tremendous Republican victories in the off-year elections of 1994, proved to be a great missed opportunity for the Republican Party. As despicable as the president's philandering was, the GOP leadership's decision to dwell upon various aspects of the president's *character* left the impression—even if unintended—that his *policies* were not so objectionable. With the occupant of the White House so reviled by so many people, the Republicans had a golden opportunity to make the case for limited government. By and large, they did not.

## Guess what?

★ Clinton was not a "centrist."

★ At the Pentagon, "special permission [was] required for the promotion of all white men without disabilities."

★ Clinton helped spread Islamic radicalism into Europe in his anti-Serb campaigns in the Balkans.

★ Clinton dispatched the military overseas forty-four times during his eight years. The U.S. military had been deployed outside of America only eight times in the previous forty-five years.

## Clinton, a "centrist"?

Government continued to expand under Clinton, though not to the extent seen under Johnson's Great Society or FDR's New Deal. On domestic policy, no better book has been written on the Clinton presidency than James Bovard's *"Feeling Your Pain": The Explosion and Abuse of Government Power in the Clinton-Gore Years* (2000). The book details damaging and counterproductive expansions of government power, particularly in agricultural, housing, and environmental policy; the massacre of innocents that occurred at the hands of federal law enforcement in Waco, Texas, in 1993; and boondoggles like AmeriCorps.

Clinton's claim to be a "New Democrat" was meant to suggest that he was no partisan of the liberalism of yesteryear. But hardly anything changed under Clinton. Consider his administration's posture on affirmative action. Clinton spoke the language of moderation so he wouldn't alienate the moderate middle-class whites who had supported him. At times he even criticized strict racial quotas in hiring. But nothing changed under the Clinton administration. Speaking of affirmative action, the president declared: "We should have a simple slogan: Mend it, but don't end it."

And when he said *don't end it*, he meant it. When in 1996 California voters successfully passed Proposition 209, which outlawed affirmative action quotas by state and local governments, the Clinton Justice Department filed a brief with a federal appeals court seeking to disallow the

## A Quotation the Textbooks Leave Out

"Because it's not their money."

> **Bill Clinton** on why local school boards should not have more say in deciding how federal education dollars should be used

measure—arguing, absurdly enough, that it violated the equal protection clause of the Fourteenth Amendment. That's right: The Fourteenth Amendment, which declared all Americans to be entitled to the *equal protection of the laws*, was being cited on behalf of the idea of *special treatment* for members of certain protected groups.

## "Only unqualified applicants may apply"

Bovard rightly suggests that the administration's feelings on affirmative action may be accurately gauged by a glance at federal hiring policies. Thus in 1995, the Pentagon let it be known that "special permission will be required for the promotion of all white men without disabilities." The Food and Drug Administration's "Equal Employment Opportunity Handbook" advised that such clerical and secretarial requirements as "knowledge of rules of grammar" and "ability to spell accurately" should be de-emphasized when seeking to fill such jobs, since those requirements may make it more difficult to attract "underrepresented groups or individuals with disabilities."

Most absurdly, perhaps, was the case of the U.S. Forest Service: Criticized for not having hired enough female firefighters, the Forest Service posted a job announcement that proclaimed, "Only unqualified applicants may apply." A later announcement read, "Only applicants who do not meet [job requirement] standards will be considered." We now know that as a result of this bizarre policy, critical firefighting positions were left vacant for lack of unqualified applicants.

## CNN foreign policy

The area in which Bill Clinton largely received a free pass, even from those who claimed to be his opponents, was foreign policy. Yet Clinton was at his most misleading and did by far his greatest damage in the foreign arena. Retired Air Force lieutenant colonel Buzz Patterson wrote in his book *Reckless Disregard* that Clinton carried out "CNN Diplomacy—foreign policy driven by television news coverage and political polling." Commander-in-chief Clinton dispatched the military overseas an amazing forty-four times during his eight years. The American military had been deployed outside of our borders only eight times in the previous forty-five years. "The [role of the] American soldier," Patterson wrote, "changed from homeland defender to nomadic peacekeeper."

### Mogadishu: "snatch and grab"

When Clinton took office, the American military was already in Somalia on a humanitarian mission to help feed the starving. President George H. W. Bush intended U.S. forces to deliver humanitarian supplies and then withdraw, but Clinton broadened that mission to include nation-building and the pursuit of warlords. Major General Thomas Montgomery, the commander of U.S. forces in Somalia, faced with the new nature of his mission, had requested additional tanks, armored fighting vehicles, and gunships, but was denied by Clinton's secretary of defense, Les Aspin.

A month later, on October 3, 1993, the president sent fourteen helicopters carrying Rangers and the elite Delta Force to seize members of the Somali National Alliance at the Olympic Hotel in Mogadishu. The operation was a disaster. American airmen and soldiers were trapped in a firefight for thirteen hours. For the rescue, the U.S. military therefore had to borrow four Pakistani tanks and twenty-four Malaysian armored personnel carriers. In all, eighteen Americans died; eighty were wounded.

## Balkan Misadventures: How Clinton abused power, abetted Islamists, lied, and wasted billions of taxpayer dollars for nothing

Of Clinton's many foreign interventions, his putting American troops into the Balkans—an area of no strategic interest to the United States—was one of the most egregious. When Yugoslavia began separating into ethnic republics, it did so at first peacefully (Slovenia) and then violently (Croatia, Bosnia, and Herzogovina, the city of Kosovo) with atrocities on all sides: Croatian, Serbian, Muslim.

Clinton orchestrated the 1995 Dayton peace accords that have created an uneasy, unstable, and unenforceable peace in the region, which has occasionally erupted again into civil war. It has also resulted in an apparently permanent American military presence in an area of no American national interest and a bill that had reached $15 billion even before Clinton left office. Moreover, the Clinton administration fanned Islamic extremism in the area, not only by siding with the Muslims against the Serbs, but even going so far as to help import *mujahedin* (radical Islamist jihadists) from the Middle East—something that even Clinton's chief peace negotiator, Richard Holbrooke, called "a pact with the devil."

Clinton, acting through NATO, also orchestrated a bombing campaign against Serbia from March until June 1999. He did so without the consent of Congress—the House of Representatives actually voted *against* authorizing Clinton's bombing war against the Serbs. No president in American history has ever waged war in the face of direct congressional opposition.

To support its unconstitutional war, the Clinton administration whipped up a propaganda campaign that was mendacious even by Clintonian standards. The U.S. Information Agency suggested that as many as 400,000 Albanian Muslims had been massacred by the Serbs. Other administration officials quoted numbers ranging from 225,000 to 100,000 Albanian Muslims missing or possibly murdered. In fact, the Spanish forensic surgeon Emilio Perez Pujol, who was dispatched to uncover evidence of Serbian atrocities, reported that "we did not find one—not one—mass grave." He added, "The final figure of dead in Kosovo will be 2,500 at most. This includes lots of strange deaths that can't be blamed on anyone in particular."

What did Clinton's intervention achieve? The Balkans remain seething with violence and hatred; radical Islam was given a boost in the area; American troops were deployed and billions of taxpayers dollars wasted in countries that most Americans couldn't find on a map; and where no lasting good has yet been—or perhaps can be—achieved through American efforts.

## Did Clinton bomb to distract attention from his scandals?

On August 20, 1998, Clinton personally ordered the bombing of the El Shifa Pharmaceutical Industries Company in Sudan, allegedly in response to the bombing of U.S. embassies in Kenya and Tanzania. It was believed that the plant did not produce medicines and veterinary products as it claimed, but manufactured chemicals used for nerve gas, and that it was funded by terrorist mastermind Osama bin Laden.

All of these claims were subsequently shown to be false. Secretary of Defense William Cohen admitted that the plant did in fact produce medicines and veterinary products. It was later conceded that no direct connection existed between the plant and bin Laden. As for the production of chemical weapons, the Clinton administration mysteriously refused to provide the soil sample collected outside the plant that allegedly contained traces of illicit chemicals. Clinton even opposed calls for an on-site inspection of the plant in the wake of the bombing.

Worse, as Christopher Hitchens points out, is that Tom Carnaffin, the British engineer who had served as technical manager of the plant's construction, explained that the plant had not been constructed with sufficient space for the kind of secret production that Clinton alleged. Other experts concurred. And although only one person died in the bombing, "many more have died, and will die, because an impoverished country has lost its chief source of medicines and pesticides," Hitchens said. The El Shifa plant had produced more than half of Sudan's human and veterinary medicine. Clinton's wild bombing played right into the hands of bin Laden, of course, who must have been delighted with the opportunity to paint the American regime as arbitrary and lawless in its treatment of Muslim peoples.

The bombing made so little sense that it inevitably provoked suspicion. Why had Clinton done it? None of the proposed explanations held water. Was it really just a coincidence that the bombing occurred the very day of Lewinsky's return to the grand jury and the same week that Clinton's televised apology (in which, in classic Clintonesque fashion, he did not actually apologize) for his lying and misbehavior had gone over so badly with the American people? That we feel the need to ask such questions speaks volumes about Clinton's character.

## "The era of big government is over"—say what?

Toward the end of his term, President Clinton said, apparently in all seriousness: "The era of big government is over." He said that while presiding over a government so enormous that the Framers of the Constitution would have fainted at the sight of it. The *Federal Register*, which lists all federal regulations in effect, continues to hover between 60,000 and 80,000 pages. Through the Medicare and Social Security programs, the federal government has made promises of benefits that over the next several decades will prove to be underfunded to the tune of *tens of trillions*. The level of taxation necessary to fund them would grind the economy to a complete standstill. The era of big government does not, in fact, seem to be over just yet—unless these unfunded liabilities should bankrupt the federal Leviathan once and for all.

Meanwhile, the federal courts routinely violate the self-government of the states. Throughout the 1990s, voters approved state ballot initiatives on questions ranging from immigration to affirmative action, only to have imperial federal judges strike them down. So much for self-government, the principle on which the War for Independence had been based. As we have seen, the Framers of the Constitution had expressly sought to avoid precisely this: a federal government whose own power went essentially uncontested, while it struck down perfectly constitutional state laws that it happened not to like. And Americans, by and large, do not know enough of their own history to be able to challenge any of it, or even to realize that a problem exists.

It was on that sobering note that the twentieth century, sometimes called the American Century, drew to a close.

# BIBLIOGRAPHY

This list of books and articles serves not only to acknowledge my intellectual debts, but also to supply readers with reliable sources they can consult to read more about some of the topics raised in this book.

Adler, David Gray and Michael A. Genovese. *The Presidency and the Law: The Clinton Legacy*. Lawrence, Kan.: University Press of Kansas, 2002.

Anderson, Martin. *Revolution*. San Diego: Harcourt Brace Jovanovich, 1988.

Anthony, Carl Sferrazza. "The Most Scandalous President." *American Heritage*, July/August 1998.

Armor, David J. *Forced Justice: School Desegregation and the Law*. New York: Oxford University Press, 1996.

Baird, Charles W. "Freedom and American Labor Relations Law: 1946–1996." *The Freeman*, May 1996, 299–309.

———. "Labor Law Reform: Lessons from History." *Cato Journal* 10 (Spring/Summer 1990): 175–209.

Barnes, Harry Elmer. *Perpetual War for Perpetual Peace*. Caldwell, Idaho: The Caxton Printers, 1953.

Barton, David. *Original Intent: The Courts, the Constitution, and Religion*. Aledo, Tex.: Wallbuilder Press, 1997.

Beale, Howard K. *The Critical Year*. New York: Harcourt, Brace, 1930.

———. *Theodore Roosevelt and the Rise of America to World Power.* Baltimore: Johns Hopkins Press, 1956.

Beisner, Robert L. *Twelve Against Empire: The Anti-Imperialists, 1898–1900.* Chicago: University of Chicago Press, 1968.

Bennett, James T. and Thomas J. DiLorenzo. *Official Lies: How Government Misleads Us.* Alexandria, Va.: Groom Books, 1992.

Berger, Raoul. *The Fourteenth Amendment and the Bill of Rights.* Norman, Okla.: University of Oklahoma Press, 1989.

———. *Government by Judiciary: The Transformation of the Fourteenth Amendment,* 2nd ed. Indianapolis, Ind.: Liberty Fund, 1997.

Best, Gary Dean. *Pride, Prejudice, and Politics: Roosevelt versus Recovery, 1933–1938.* New York: Praeger, 1991.

Boorstin, Daniel. *The Americans: The Colonial Experience.* New York: Vintage, 1964.

Bork, Robert H. *The Tempting of America: The Political Seduction of the Law.* New York: Touchstone, 1990.

Bovard, James. *The Farm Fiasco.* San Francisco: ICS Press, 1991.

———. *Feeling Your Pain: The Explosion and Abuse of Government Power in the Clinton-Gore Years.* New York: St. Martin's, 2000.

Brownson, Orestes A. *The American Republic,* ed. Thomas E. Woods, Jr. Washington, D.C.: Regnery, 2003 [1875].

Carson, Clarence B. *The Growth of America, 1878–1928.* Wadley, Ala.: American Textbook Committee, 1985.

Channing, Stephen A. *Crisis of Fear: Secession in South Carolina.* New York: W.W. Norton, 1974.

Choate, Rufus. *The Political Writings of Rufus Choate,* ed. Thomas E. Woods, Jr. Washington, D.C.: Regnery, 2002.

Conquest, Robert. *The Harvest of Sorrow: Soviet Collectivization and the Terror Famine.* New York: Oxford University Press, 1986.

Coogan, John W. *The End of Neutrality: The United States, Britain, and Maritime Rights, 1899–1915.* Ithaca, N.Y.: Cornell University Press, 1981.

Costello, John. *Days of Infamy: MacArthur, Roosevelt, Churchill—The Shocking Truth Revealed*. New York: Pocket Books, 1994.

Coulter, Ann. *Treason*. New York: Crown Forum, 2003.

Coulter, E. Merton. *The South During Reconstruction, 1865–1877*. Baton Rouge, La.: Louisiana State University Press, 1947.

Cowen, Tyler. "The Marshall Plan: Myths and Realities." In *U.S. Aid to the Developing World*, ed. Doug Bandow. Washington, D.C.: Heritage Foundation, 1985, 61–74.

Craven, Avery O. *The Coming of the Civil War*, 2nd rev. ed. Chicago: University of Chicago Press, 1957.

Denson, John V., ed. *The Costs of War*. New Brunswick, N.J.: Transaction, 1997.

———. *Reassessing the Presidency*. Auburn, Ala.: Ludwig von Mises Institute, 2001.

DiLorenzo, Thomas J. "Anti-trust, Anti-truth." Mises.org, June 1, 2000.

———. *How Capitalism Saved America: The Untold History of Our Country, from the Pilgrims to the Present*. New York: Crown Forum, 2004.

———. "The Origins of Antitrust: An Interest-Group Perspective." *International Review of Law and Economics* 5 (1985): 73–90.

———. *The Real Lincoln*. Roseville, Calif.: Prima, 2002.

Doenecke, Justus D. *Storm on the Horizon: The Challenge to American Intervention, 1939–1941*. Lanham, Md.: Rowan & Littlefield, 2000.

Dyson, Michael Eric. *I May Not Get There With You: The True Martin Luther King Jr*. New York: Free Press, 2000.

Ebeling, Richard M. and Jacob G. Hornberger, eds. *The Failure of America's Foreign Wars*. Fairfax, Va.: The Future of Freedom Foundation, 1996.

Edwards, Chris and Tad DeHaven. "War Between the Generations: Federal Spending on the Elderly Set to Explode." Cato Institute Policy Analysis No. 488, September 16, 2003.

Epstein, Julius. *Operation Keelhaul: The Story of Forced Repatriation from 1944 to the Present*. Old Greenwich, Conn.: Devin-Adair, 1973.

Epstein, Richard A. "A Common Law for Labor Relations: A Critique of the New Deal Labor Legislation." *Yale Law Journal* 92 (July 1983): 1357–1408.

Evans, M. Stanton. "The *Amerasia* Affair." *Human Events*, July 12, 1996.

———. "McCarthyism: Waging the Cold War in America." *Human Events*, May 30, 1997.

Feuer, Lewis S. "American Travelers to the Soviet Union 1917–32: The Formation of a Component of New Deal Ideology." *American Quarterly* (Summer 1962): 119–49.

Fischer, David Hackett. *Albion's Seed: Four British Folkways in America.* New York: Oxford University Press, 1989.

Fleming, Thomas. *The Illusion of Victory: America in World War I.* New York: Basic Books, 2003.

Flynn, John T. *The Roosevelt Myth*, 50th anniversary edition. San Francisco: Fox & Wilkes, 1998.

Folsom, Burton. "Herbert Dow and Predatory Pricing." *The Freeman*, May 1998.

Folsom, Burton W., Jr. *The Myth of the Robber Barons.* Herndon, Va.: Young America's Foundation, 1991.

Foner, Eric. *Free Soil, Free Labor, Free Men: The Ideology of the Republican Party Before the Civil War.* New York: Oxford University Press, 1970.

Freud, Sigmund and William C. Bullitt. *Thomas Woodrow Wilson: A Psychological Study.* New York: Avon, 1966.

Gallaway, Lowell E. and Richard K. Vedder. *Out of Work: Unemployment and Government in Twentieth-Century America.* New York: Holmes & Meier, 1993.

Gamble, Richard M. *The War for Righteousness: Progressive Christianity, the Great War, and the Rise of the Messianic Nation.* Wilmington, Del.: Intercollegiate Studies Institute, 2003.

Graham, John Remington. *A Constitutional History of Secession.* Gretna, La.: Pelican, 2002.

Greene, Jack. *Peripheries and Center: Constitutional Development in the Extended Polities of the British Empire and the United States, 1607-1788*. New York: W.W. Norton, 1990.

Gunderson, Gerald. *The Wealth Creators: An Entrepreneurial History of the United States*. New York: Penguin, 1990.

Gutzman, K. R. Constantine. "The Virginia and Kentucky Resolutions Reconsidered: 'An Appeal to the *Real Laws* of Our Country.'" *Journal of Southern History* 66 (August 2000): 473–96.

Gutzman, Kevin R. "A Troublesome Legacy: James Madison and 'the Principles of '98.'" *Journal of the Early Republic* 15 (Winter 1995): 569–589.

Halbrook, Stephen P. *That Every Man Be Armed: The Evolution of a Constitutional Right*. Oakland: Independent Institute, 1994.

Hazlitt, Henry. *The Conquest of Poverty*. New Rochelle, N.Y.: Arlington House, 1973.

Healy, Gene. "The 14th Amendment and the Perils of Libertarian Centralism." Mises Institute Working Paper, May 5, 2000. (Available at Mises.org.)

Henry, Robert Selph. *The Story of Reconstruction*. Indianapolis, Ind.: Bobbs-Merrill, 1938.

Higgs, Robert. "Regime Uncertainty: Why the Great Depression Lasted So Long and Why Prosperity Resumed after the War." *Independent Review* 1 (Spring 1997): 561–90.

———. "Wartime Prosperity? A Reassessment of the U.S. Economy in the 1940s." *Journal of Economic History* 52 (March 1992): 41–60.

Hitchens, Christopher. *No One Left to Lie To: The Triangulations of William Jefferson Clinton*. London: Verso, 1999.

Hollander, Paul. *Political Pilgrims: Western Intellectuals in Search of the Good Society*, 4th ed. New Brunswick, N.J.: Transaction, 1998.

Holt, Michael. *The Political Crisis of the 1850s*. New York: Norton, 1983.

Holt, W. Stull. *Treaties Defeated by the Senate: A Study of the Struggle Between President and Senate over the Conduct of Foreign Relations*. Baltimore: Johns Hopkins Press, 1933.

Hutt, W. H. *The Strike Threat System: The Economic Consequences of Collective Bargaining.* New Rochelle, N.Y.: Arlington House, 1973.

Iriye, Akira. *The Globalizing of America, 1913–1945.* Cambridge: Cambridge University Press, 1995.

Johnson, Ludwell H. *North Against South: The American Iliad, 1848–1877.* Columbia, S.C.: Foundation for American Education, 1995.

Johnson, Paul. *A History of the American People.* New York: HarperCollins, 1998.

———. *Modern Times: The World from the Twenties to the Nineties.* New York: HarperPerennial, 1992.

Kilpatrick, James J. *The Sovereign States: Notes of a Citizen of Virginia.* Chicago: Henry Regnery, 1957.

Kolko, Gabriel. *The Triumph of Conservatism: A Reinterpretation of American History, 1900–1916.* New York: Free Press, 1963.

LaFeber, Walter. *The American Search for Opportunity, 1865–1913.* Cambridge: Cambridge University Press, 1993.

Lawson, Robert A. "We're All Rawlsians Now!" *Ideas on Liberty,* June 2002, 49–50.

Leuchtenburg, William E. "Progressivism and Imperialism: The Progressive Movement and American Foreign Policy, 1898–1916." *Mississippi Valley Historical Review* 39 (December 1952): 483–504.

Livingston, Donald W. "A Moral Accounting of the Union and the Confederacy." *Journal of Libertarian Studies* 16 (Spring 2002): 57–101.

———. *Philosophical Melancholy and Delirium: Hume's Pathology of Philosophy.* Chicago: University of Chicago Press, 1998.

———. *Secession and the Modern State.* League of the South Papers Series, no. 1, 1997.

Lyons, Eugene. *The Red Decade.* New York: Bobbs-Merrill, 1941.

Magnet, Myron. *The Dream and the Nightmare: The Sixties' Legacy to the Underclass.* San Francisco: Encounter Books, 2000.

Malkin, Michelle. "The Deafening Silence about the Death of an Affirmative Action 'Hero.'" *Jewish World Review*, August 7, 2002.

Matusow, Allen J. *The Unraveling of America: A History of Liberalism in the 1960s*. New York: Harper & Row, 1984.

McDonald, Forrest. *The American Presidency: An Intellectual History*. Lawrence, Kan.: University Press of Kansas, 1994.

———. *A Constitutional History of the United States*. Malabar, Fla.: Robert E. Krieger, 1982.

———. "Was the Fourteenth Amendment Constitutionally Adopted?" *Georgia Journal of Southern Legal History* 1 (Spring/Summer 1991): 1–20.

McDougall, Walter A. *Promised Land, Crusader State: The American Encounter with the World Since 1776*. New York: Houghton Mifflin, 1997.

McGee, John W. "Predatory Price Cutting: The Standard Oil (N.J.) Case." *Journal of Law and Economics* 1 (1958): 137–69.

McKenzie, Richard B. *What Went Right in the 1980s*. San Francisco: Pacific Research Institute for Public Policy, 1994.

Meese, Edwin, III. *With Reagan: The Inside Story*. Washington, D.C.: Regnery Gateway, 1992.

Millis, Walter. *Road to War: America, 1914–1917*. Boston: Houghton Mifflin, 1935.

Morison, Samuel Eliot. *The Oxford History of the American People*. 2 vols. Vol. 1: *Prehistory to 1789*. New York: Meridian, 1994 [1965].

Morse, H. Newcomb. "The Foundations and Meaning of Secession." *Stetson Law Review* 15 (1986): 419–36.

Murray, Charles. *Losing Ground: American Social Policy 1950–1980*, 10th anniversary edition. New York: Basic Books, 1994 [1984].

Olasky, Marvin. *The Tragedy of American Compassion*. Washington, D.C.: Regnery Gateway, 1992.

Olson, William J. and Alan Woll. "Executive Orders and National Emergencies: How Presidents Have Come to 'Run the Country' by Usurping Legislative Power." Cato Institute Policy Analysis No. 358, October 28, 1999.

Payne, James L. *Overcoming Welfare*. New York: Basic Books, 1998.

Pipes, Richard. *A Concise History of the Russian Revolution*. New York: Knopf, 1995.

Powell, Jim. *FDR's Folly*. New York: Crown Forum, 2003.

Raico, Ralph. "The Politics of Hunger: A Review." *Review of Austrian Economics* 3 (1989): 253–59.

Rand, Ayn. *Capitalism: The Unknown Ideal*. New York: Signet, 1967.

Reed, Lawrence W. "A History Lesson for Free-Market Pessimists." *The Freeman*, March 1997.

———. "Ideas and Consequences: Of Meat and Myth." *The Freeman*, November 1994.

Reeves, Thomas C. *A Question of Character: A Life of John F. Kennedy*. New York: Free Press, 1991.

Reisman, George. *Capitalism*. Ottawa, Ill.: Jameson Books, 1996.

Reynolds, Morgan O. *Making America Poorer: The Cost of Labor Law*. Washington, D.C.: Cato, 1987.

Richer, Matthew. "Busing's Boston Massacre." *Policy Review*, November–December 1998.

Richman, Sheldon. "Reading the Second Amendment." *The Freeman*, February 1998.

Roberts, Paul Craig and Lawrence Stratton. *The New Color Line: How Quotas and Privilege Destroy Democracy*. Washington, D.C.: Regnery, 1995.

———. *The Tyranny of Good Intentions: How Prosecutors and Bureaucrats are Trampling the Constitution in the Name of Justice*. Roseveille, Calif.: Forum, 2000.

Rockwell, Llewellyn H., Jr., ed. *The Economics of Liberty*. Auburn, Ala.: Ludwig von Mises Institute, 1990.

———. *Speaking of Liberty*. Auburn, Ala.: Ludwig von Mises Institute, 2003.

Rothbard, Murray N. *America's Great Depression*, 4th ed. New York: Richardson & Snyder, 1983.

————. *Conceived in Liberty.* 4 vols. New Rochelle, N.Y.: Arlington House, 1975–1979.

————. *Making Economic Sense.* Auburn, Ala.: Ludwig von Mises Institute, 1995.

Schansberg, D. Eric. *Poor Policy: How Government Harms the Poor.* Boulder, Colo.: Westview Press, 1996.

Schwab, Larry M. *The Illusion of a Conservative Reagan Revolution.* New Brunswick, N.J.: Transaction, 1991.

Schweikart, Larry. *The Entrepreneurial Adventure: A History of Business in the United States.* Fort Worth, Tex.: Harcourt College Publishers, 2000.

Shogun, Robert. *Hard Bargain: How FDR Twisted Churchill's Arm, Evaded the Law, and Changed the Role of the American Presidency.* Boulder, Colo.: Westview Press, 1995.

Siegel, Fred. *The Future Once Happened Here: New York, D.C., L.A., and the Fate of America's Big Cities.* New York: Free Press, 1997.

Smiley, Gene. *The American Economy in the Twentieth Century.* Cincinnati, Ohio: South-Western Publishing, 1994.

Smith, Hedrick. *The New Russians.* New York: Random House, 1990.

Sowell, Thomas. *Civil Rights: Rhetoric or Reality?* New York: William Morrow, 1985.

————. *Inside American Education: The Decline, the Deception, the Dogmas.* New York: Free Press, 1993.

Springer, James Warren. "American Indians and the Law of Real Property in Colonial New England." *American Journal of Legal History* 30 (1986): 25–58.

Tanner, Michael. *The End of Welfare: Fighting Poverty in the Civil Society.* Washington, D.C.: Cato, 1996.

Taylor, Jared. *Paved with Good Intentions: The Failure of Race Relations in Contemporary America.* New York: Carroll & Graf, 1992.

Thernstrom, Stephan and Abigail Thernstrom. *America in Black and White: One Nation, Indivisible.* New York: Simon & Schuster, 1997.

Thornton, Mark and Robert B. Ekelund, Jr. *Tariffs, Blockades and Inflation: The Economics of the Civil War*. Wilmington, Del.: Scholarly Resources, 2004.

Tindall, George Brown and David Emory Shi. *America: A Narrative History*, vol. II, brief 5th ed. New York: W.W. Norton, 2000.

Trifkovic, Srdja. "Jihadist Hotbed in the Balkans: The Truth Is Out." http://www.chroniclesmagazine.org/News/Trifkovic04/NewsST011004.html

Vaughn, Alden T. *New England Frontier: Puritans and Indians, 1620–1675*. Norman, Okla.: University of Oklahoma Press, 1995.

Veale, F.J.P. *Advance to Barbarism: The Development of Total Warfare*. New York: Devin-Adair, 1968.

Watts, Dale E. "How Bloody Was Bleeding Kansas? Political Killings in Kansas Territory, 1854–1861." *Kansas History* 18 (Summer 1995): 116–29.

Woods, Thomas E., Jr. "Cobden on Freedom, Peace, and Trade." *Human Rights Review* 5 (October-December 2003): 77–90.

———. "Great Depression: Ending." In Robert Allison, ed., *History in Dispute*, vol. 3: *American Social and Political Movements, 1900–1945: Pursuit of Progress*. Detroit: St. James Press, 2000, pp. 65–9.

# INDEX